PROFESSIONAL ISSUES
FOR PROPERTY PEOPLE

by

A.F. MILLINGTON
BSc(Estate Management), FRICS, FCMI

One time: Professor of Land Economy, University of Western Sydney, New South Wales, Australia; Dean of the Faculty of Business & Land Economy, University of Western Sydney; Professor of Land Economics and Head of the Department of Land Economics, University of Paisley, Scotland; Lecturer in Land Management at the University of Reading; Lecturer in Valuation at the College of Estate Management. Fellow of the Australian Institute of Valuers and Land Economists, 1988–1996.

2003

A division of Reed Business Information
Estates Gazette, 151 Wardour Street, London W1F 8BN

ISBN 0 7282 0426 6

Typset by Amy Boyle, Rochester, Kent
Printed and bound in Finland by WS Bookwell, Juva

Contents

Foreword

Aims, objectives and professional behaviour; Journals, libraries, and information services; education; professional standards and disciplinary committees; continuing professional development; professional performance testing; compulsory professional indemnity insurance; compensation for clients; service to clients.

Current demands on professions; educational aims and objectives; part time or full time study; graduate entry; the content of courses; simulated practical studies; the students; academic staff and resources; entry levels and examinations; continuing education.

Background observations; the comparative method of valuation; the investment (or capitalisation) method of valuation and discounted cash flow approach; the contractors' method of valuation (or summation); the residual (or hypothetical development) method of valuation; the effect of new developments on existing markets; the profits (or accounts) method of valuation; knowledge of the market place; the significance of international investment; the problem of unusual leasing arrangements; the problem of contaminated sites and properties; the valuation of large properties; concluding observations.

General; market value and the property market; the theory of price determination and problems of price estimation; the circumstances of the buyer and the 'different faces' of a property investment; professional development and research; reporting to clients; the assessment of value to an individual; conclusions.

General; determining suitable valuation methods for specialist properties; specially constructed buildings; properties used for specialist trades; public buildings; properties which are used for non-profit making activities; properties where the use is dependent upon a licence; leisure and recreation facilities; properties used by the extractive industries; properties subject to monopolistic or oligopolistic market conditions; the estimation of trading profits; the valuation survey; the analysis of survey information; insider knowledge; large property investments; use of the comparative method of valuation; the contractors' method of valuation; the residual (or hypothetical development) method of valuation; summary of approach to specialist valuations.

Background observations; the value of property assets; problems experienced in the past; the valuation of property assets; the development of Valuation Standards; Valuation Standard for the market basis of valuation; some valuation bases other than Market Value; valuations for the purpose of financial reporting; valuations for bank security purposes; professional considerations; concluding observations.

Introduction; the conventional approach to retail property valuation; the determinants of property values; general factors affecting retail property values; valuation by comparison; the estimation of rental value; the profits method of valuation; variables which affect retail property values.

The current situation; traditional shopping streets; catalogue shopping; factory and warehouse outlets; television retailing; computer shopping; the implications of developments in retailing methods; the capital value of retail accommodation; the long term prospects for retail properties.

Foreword

In writing this book I have sought to cover a range of matters – many of which are outside the normal study areas in property orientated degrees and post graduate courses – which I believe ought to be of interest to those who study property markets and property valuation. It is hoped that some of the considerations and observations may also be of interest to those in other professions and to some lay persons. In starting on this task I was fully aware that many of these points generally get inadequate consideration, and it is to a large extent in the hope of encouraging greater consideration of these matters that the book has been written.

References to and extracts from the Valuation Standards of The European Group of Valuers Associations (TEGoVA) are reproduced with the permission of TEGoVA and Estates Gazette Limited who hold the copyright to these Standards.

I am particularly grateful to Estates Gazette for having supported this venture by agreeing to publish the book, and in particular to Mr Colin Greasby, Group Publications Manager with Estates Gazette, for his support and assistance with this and previous books.

Alan F Millington
June, 2003

Chapter 1

Interested in Property?

The objective of this book is to discuss a range of issues which are of importance to the property professions in particular, but some of which also impact upon society in general. The various topics discussed are not necessarily inter-connected, although some are, and for that reason there is some repetition in different parts of the book to enable each chapter to be read as a discrete item without the need to cross-refer to other parts of the book.

The contents could be described as a miscellany of considerations relevant in particular to those practising in the property professions, to those studying for careers in the property professions, or for others who are just 'interested in property'. Some items are included in the book because the author considers them to be important despite the fact that they generally receive limited or even no attention from those who might be expected to consider them, with little being written about them to assist consideration by a wide range of people.

Some matters covered are frequently the subject of discussion and consideration, being topics of general interest to a wide range of people, but others are more regularly considered only by specialists who encounter them in a professional capacity. Nevertheless, some matters which fall into this latter category have implications for the wider public in that developed property is required for virtually all the activities of modern society, whilst the large sums of capital invested in property and its relevance as a factor of production mean that considerations which relate to the efficient use of property are of considerable economic importance. As a result they may have significance for general members of the public without them necessarily being aware of that fact. With pension and superannuation funds as major investors in property, there are in modern societies few people who are untouched by the performance of property investments and factors which affect their value, yet it is apparent from the problems that some funds have experienced that many lay people would benefit from being better informed and more aware of many aspects of the property world. It is hoped that some of the discussion may assist in that process.

Some of the matters are of particular significance to members of the property professions, and to those who practice as valuers and property consultants in particular. As a property professional himself who specialised in valuation, the author considers that some of these issues are important for those entering the professions to be aware of and to consider, yet there is little written on some of these issues to facilitate these processes, hence their inclusion in this book, whilst many of the issues covered have little or no coverage in many educational courses.

Some of these issues, in the author's view, ought to be covered in educational courses, whilst they also often receive inadequate consideration by professional bodies. In particular these include consideration of the role of professional organizations – including consideration of what perhaps they ought to do rather than what they appear to do currently – and the questions of ethical standards and the qualities which ought to be exhibited by professional people. There was a time when the author considered such matters to be outside the ambit of educational courses, primarily because he believed it was axiomatic that a professional organization and its members would do what they ought properly to do, whilst he also believed appropriate ethical standards to be second nature to professional people, or those claiming to be professional people.

With the benefit of experience it is clear that none of these assumptions can justifiably be made, and this has been evidenced by such recent occurrences as the Enron scandal in the United States of America, and the subsequent demise of the long established, previously respected, world-wide accountancy group Arthur Andersen & Co. Other major company scandals in the USA (such as the WorldCom affair), the United Kingdom, and Australia have come to light in which the roles of professional consultants have been highlighted and their standards of performance and professional ethics have been called into question.

In the light of these events there is early discussion of the role of professional organizations and professional people, and the expectations which clients and the public in general have of them. A major objective of this discussion is to focus attention and thought onto what ought to be fundamental objectives for professional people and fundamental standards of behaviour of professional people, yet which it is clear have too often been ignored, perhaps because they have been considered unimportant. Alternatively, they may never even have been considered by many who would claim to be professional people.

The role of professional organizations and the standards of performance and ethics practised by their members are extremely important issues in a world in which consumers are becoming ever better educated and better informed. Indeed, professional people are now subject to such close scrutiny that there is the danger of increasing regulation of their activities by central governments if they do not put their own houses in order, yet it is likely that there is a considerable amount of complacency in many quarters where there may be a belief that, whilst others may default or under perform, the standards of their operations are always beyond question. There is nothing more likely to concentrate the minds of the general public upon the performance of professional advisers and consultants than something which hits their pockets, and the problems experienced by many insurance companies, pension funds, and superannuation funds in 2002 and 2003 in particular and their failure to be able to achieve forecasted levels of performance, will make many people whose pensions are not as high as anticipated question the role of the professionals involved in running and in advising under performing funds.

It is most important that members of the public should have complete trust in professional consultants whom they employ. However, it was reported in May 2003 that a market survey carried out across Australia revealed that out of 30 professional, administrative and service groups considered in the survey, only four groups were thought to be trustworthy by more than 50% of those surveyed. Real Estate Agents fared worst of all the groups with only 2% considering them trustworthy.

Following publication of the results it was particularly disappointing to hear a prominent estate agent, who was interviewed on the radio, protest that the results of the survey were obviously misleading, people's opinions of estate agents being adversely affected and therefore unreliable because property was the most expensive item they ever purchased, often involving sacrifice and financial strain on the part of the purchaser. He appeared unprepared to accept that the results just might be a reliable indication of the public's perception of the trustworthiness of real estate agents. His refusal to see a need for close consideration of the survey findings was, at the very best, disappointing.

It was more encouraging later to read an article in the Australian *Sunday Telegraph* of 1 June 2003 in which another prominent estate agent described the result of the survey as 'atrocious'. He lamented the fact

> ... that the actions of a few tarnish the image of the majority of professional, competent operators who act with honesty and integrity.

He was at least prepared to acknowledge that there were estate agents who let down their profession.

The article continued:

> However, the level of complaints to the NSW Office of Fair Trading reveals real estate agents were the worst offenders when it came to breaches of consumer legislation, rivalled only by pawnbrokers.

The article later reported:

> These problems have been tackled in the review of the Property, Stock and Business Agents Act, the biggest overhaul of the Act in more than 50 years. It was passed by State Parliament last year, coming into effect this August. Its chief purpose is to introduce transparency and with this may come increased trust.

It is to the disadvantage of NSW estate agents that legislation has been considered necessary to control their actions, for this need itself is likely to influence the public into considering them untrustworthy. The concept of 'no smoke without a fire' is likely to be encouraged by the imposition of legislation. It would be far better for a professional group themselves to ensure the observance of high standards of performance, trust, and integrity on the part of those within their profession, as the need for legislation to solve problems is likely to create the impression that those problems are widespread, irrespective of whether this is the case or not.

In the *Weekly Telegraph* (published by The Telegraph Group of London) issue number 603, 12 February 2003, Christopher Fildes reported as follows:

> Paul Volcker, former chairman of the US Federal Reserve, has called for a concerted effort to reform financial accounting and corporate governance, singling out the big accounting firms for shelving their principles.
>
> The fate of Arthur Andersen, Enron's auditors, was an object lesson in what had gone wrong, he told the annual banquet of the Guild of International Bankers in London.
>
> Mr. Volcker, chairman of the trustees of the International Accounting Standards Committee and a respected figure in banking and finance said of Andersen: 'The basic responsibility of the firm was corrupted by a business model that emphasised revenue and consulting services to clients over faithful allegiance to the interests of

the investing public in full and fair financial reports. That model has not been unique to Andersen.

'Professional standards have been eroded. Peer review and self-administered oversight have failed.'

Whilst Mr Volcker's observations were directed at financial and accounting professionals, it would be foolish of those in other professions to assume that such shortcomings do not apply to their own professions. Human nature being what it is, there must inevitably be some in all professions who fail to observe the high levels of ethics and high standards of operation which ought to be practised by all professional people, and the question whether 'peer review and self-administered oversight' is an adequate way of controlling standards in professional organizations has probably never been more in need of great consideration by all professional organizations than at the present time, a time when the savings of so many people are entrusted to the management of others whose professional performance will determine the future standards of living of those savers.

Accordingly the first few chapters of this book are devoted to considerations of the roles of professional organizations and professional people in the hope that whatever readers may think of the author's views, beneficial consideration of such matters will result.

Chapter 2

The Property Professions

Many of the following observations are applicable to professions in general, but as the author's own experience has been in the property professions the general emphasis of observations will relate to those professions.

The expression 'Property Professions' is regularly used, but what exactly does it mean? It is a generic expression which refers to more than one group of professional people, each of which has one thing in common, that is it is involved with property in a professional capacity.

The valuation, financing, purchase, development, marketing, disposal, leasing, management, maintenance of and investment in property all involve a wide range of considerations and actions and the use of a variety of skills, and in developed countries this has resulted in the evolution of a large range of specialised skills and professional expertize all relating to some aspect of property development, ownership, management, or investment. As a further development, people practising similar activities or possessing similar skills and expertise have in many cases gathered together to form what are generally recognised as 'professional organisations' each comprised of professional people practising in a specific area of the property world.

What exactly is meant when we talk of a 'profession'? A profession is not easy to define, although we can have recourse to a dictionary definition. *The Concise Oxford Dictionary*, seventh edition, defined a profession as:

> vocation, calling, especially one that involves some branch of learning or science,
> the body of persons involved in this.

These definitions contain a number of particularly significant words. 'Vocation, calling' suggests involvement in an activity which is of particular interest to one, and a situation in which there is dedication to the activity. 'Learning or science' suggests that education and knowledge, perhaps even knowledge of a technical or complex type, are required. 'Body of persons' suggests a group

7

of people pursuing the activity in an atmosphere of co-operation, assisting each other in the pursuit of and the development of the activity, and in the acquisition of and development of the requisite knowledge and skills.

As an alternative to a dictionary definition, one could seek to define a profession by contrasting it with a trade. A tradesman generally provides a service in respect of a relatively repetitive type of work, for example fitting electrical power points, fitting plumbing and sanitary items, tiling and other similar activities. Despite its somewhat repetitive nature, the work may require a high level of knowledge and good technical skills, and it may require a considerable amount of training in terms of both the range of skills required and the time required to obtain them.

A professional person generally also requires a high level of knowledge and technical skills, and will invariably, if not always, have to undertake considerable training. However, the practice of a profession generally involves a smaller proportion of routine repetitive work than does the practice of a trade, whilst a great amount of a professional person's work will entail the application of knowledge and technical skills in a wide range of differing situations. The consideration of problems and the formulation of solutions to them are likely to be major activities with professional people, such problems in general being very much more exacting than those generally faced by tradesmen.

Professions, therefore, generally deal with more complex situations than tradesmen; the electrician fits all the electrical fitments in an office block, but the professional consultant designs the appropriate electrical installations to satisfy the features of the building and the likely needs of its users, and also specifies the appropriate types of materials and fitments for the system he or she has designed. In doing this quite a number of complex calculations may have to be undertaken, important decisions may have to be made where alternative solutions exist, and quite a number of well-informed recommendations may have to be made to the client, which recommendations may often have substantial financial implications.

In this respect a professional person is much more of a problem solver than is a tradesperson who will regularly pass the more demanding problems on to the professional person. Because of their high level of knowledge and skills professionals are also regularly employed as consultants in a specialist capacity.

Ethics

A major feature of a profession is that ethical considerations should always be of prime consideration to a professional person, whereas, without in any way suggesting that tradesmen are lacking in ethics, commercial considerations are generally the prime considerations which influence the way tradesmen operate. Therefore, whilst ethics may be very important to tradesmen, one would not generally regard the existence of a specific code of ethics as being an important defining feature of a trade. It is also highly likely that in general ethical considerations will arise more regularly in the day-to-day work of a professional than would be the case with a tradesman.

What do we mean by ethics? The dictionary defines 'ethics' as 'the science of morals, moral principles, code of conduct'. Ethics determine the way in which we behave and operate, and many would say that the most important requirement of a professional person is that he or she should have extremely high ethical standards in addition to the appropriate specialist knowledge and skills.

What sort of ethical standards do we expect from professional people? Lay people employ professionals to give specialist advice or services in respect of matters on which they themselves normally have only limited knowledge and skills, or even no knowledge and skills. They therefore expect that they will receive a good level of skills, service, and advice from a professional person in return for the payment of fees. Over and above those basic provisions, the lay person also places his or her trust in the professional to act in their clients' best interests at all times.

Lay people take professional advisers into their confidence and they expect professionals always to respect that confidence. Additionally, in many instances lay people appoint professional advisers to act as their agents, that is to act on their behalf. In such circumstances professional advisers will have the power to act exactly as if they were the client as long as they observe any limitations contained in their clients' instructions, having the power to act for the client in making decisions and entering into commitments, which may frequently involve them spending the client's funds.

Clearly people employing professional advisers will expect them to act at all times in their best interests, and in a way which will enable the client to place complete trust and confidence in the professional adviser. If professional advisers at any time fail to act in the best interests of their clients they will in fact be acting unprofessionally and will not be observing the high ethical standards expected of them.

Professional negligence

Moreover, if they do not always act in the best interests of their clients and their clients suffer financial loss as a result, professional advisers may find themselves guilty in law of professional negligence, in which case they may be liable for the payment of compensation for any damage suffered by their clients. Sums awarded by the courts in respect of damages can, in the modern world, be very substantial indeed, in some circumstances amounting to many millions of pounds or dollars.

Over and above the normal expectation that professional people will observe high ethical standards, in financial terms it may also be in a professional adviser's best interests always to act to such high standards of skill and ethics that he or she could never be found guilty of professional negligence. That indeed is the level of service that clients expect to get when they hire a professional, and performance of such a level should in turn be highly beneficial to a professional as it should enhance their reputation and consequently their fee earning capabilities.

The implications of ethical requirements

The implications of the requirement that professional advisers should always act in the best interests of their clients are such that sometimes it may result in the professional person not even being able to act in his or her own best interests in terms of financial reward, if to do so would result in the professional not acting to the highest ethical standards and in the client's best interests. The professional person should therefore not do anything in pursuit of his or her own best interests if by so doing their client would not be as well off as would otherwise have been the case.

Professional organizations and codes of ethics

Human nature being what it is, people being different, and different cultures accepting or rejecting different standards of behaviour, there are different perceptions of what is ethical and what is unethical. Partly for this reason most professional organizations try to codify their ethical expectations by establishing (and regularly reviewing) rules and regulations which indicate to their members and the public the standards of performance and behaviour expected of their members. Taking out membership of a professional organization should in reality automatically result in a member accepting and always observing the rules, regulations and ethical standards of the organization. This should, as a result, influence and govern the way in which the member's future business activities are undertaken. Sadly, recent events in many large international companies and organizations indicate that this is not always the case or that the rules, regulations and ethical expectations of some professional organizations are either inadequate or inadequately enforced.

Chapter 3

Professions and Professional People

This leads naturally to a consideration of the features of a profession. Clearly different professions will possess different features dependent upon the objectives of each profession, the culture and the state of development of the country and the society in which they operate, and the state of development of a particular profession. However, there are certain features and qualities which one would hope to see in any professional group, and it is perhaps easiest to determine these features by asking what we ourselves would expect to see in such organisations.

It is arguable that a profession should exhibit the following features, although some of them may only be achievable after a profession or professional organization has acquired a substantial number of members and has reached a reasonable stage of maturity. Features that could be considered essential in a profession are:

1. It should comprise a group of people each of whom is specialising in a similar type of activity or closely related activities, the majority of them doing so for a livelihood. The latter requirement should ensure that there are sufficient members actively engaged in professional activities on a regular basis to ensure that overall the membership is aware of recent developments and current needs.
2. There should be a desire amongst the members to act in a co-operative and collaborative way to develop the skills, techniques, knowledge and overall standards of performance desirable for the profession and its members, in order that those members may always achieve high standards of performance in their professional activities.
3. The profession should have a stated code of ethics which stipulates the way in which its members are expected to operate and to behave. Such a code should be evidenced by the existence of policy statements, bye-laws, rules, and regulations to inform both its members and the general public of those expected standards. These standards should be determined

not just in the interests of the members, but also in the interests of the clients of members and of society in general. In particular, the standards of ethics and rules and regulations should be developed to serve and protect those members of society most likely to employ the services of members of the profession.

4. There should be in place systems and procedures to ensure that the members observe the required standards of conduct, with sanctions provided against those members who fail to observe them. There should also be a structure within the professional organization to oversee the professional conduct of members and to discipline those members who fail to observe the required standards.

5. A profession should recognize the need for specific standards of education and training among its members to ensure that they can perform to the required levels of knowledge and skill, and it should also recognize the need for its members to continually update skills and knowledge to keep up with the changing environment in which members operate.

6. Such recognition should be evidenced by the existence of a stated education and training policy with minimum acceptable educational standards being clearly defined, membership of the organizations being dependent upon the achievement of those educational standards.

The need for appropriate education often persuades a profession to provide its own systems of examination and assessment designed specifically to suit its own needs, although in many professions these duties may be delegated to approved specialist educational institutions. Where delegation to others occurs a profession should carefully monitor the educational offerings on a regular basis to ensure that courses and those being educated on them do not at any time fall below the requirements of the profession. Should the educational offerings fail to be of an acceptable standard the profession should be prepared to withdraw recognition from the proferring organization in order to ensure that its own standards do not fall below the minimum acceptable level.

A professional organization should not overlook the fact that the quality of education offered is always dependent upon the quality of academics who provide that education. The quality of education may deteriorate quite dramatically simply as the result of a change of course leader or a change in a key member or key members of staff. A diligent professional organization will consequently regularly monitor the quality of staff offering courses and students graduating from courses which are recognized by the organization.

7. In all its operations a profession should recognize that apart from acting in the interests of its members, the profession also has obligations to society in general, and particularly to those members of society who directly purchase the services of its members. It should be a major objective to ensure that those who employ members of the organization always receive high quality service, and this is even more important if a professional organization advertises on behalf of its members indicating that they provide a high level of expertize and service.

8. A professional organization should provide a range of back up services to its members to enable them to perform and develop more efficiently and effectively, and such services could include:

   (a) A regular programme of forums to enable members to compare ideas, knowledge and experiences;

   (b) A regular programme of meetings designed to provide continuing education opportunities for members subsequent to initial qualification;

   (c) The provision of library services specifically directed to the professional needs of members and to the continued maintenance of high levels of knowledge and skills. These services should provide members with essential reading and reference services, and, where appropriate, the provision of computerised data banks or information banks. Such data banks are particularly valuable in the property professions, but also in other professions such as the law which requires regular and easy reference to case law and to statutes, and medicine, where easy reference to new developments in practice is highly desirable;

   (d) A regular publication to inform members of developments and to provide the opportunity for their ideas and experiences to be recorded in the published form for the benefit of other members in particular, and to provide a forum for the exchange of ideas and experiences;

   (e) The publication of information pamphlets and brochures on items of specific or new interest for the benefit of both members and the public;

   (f) The provision of insurance services for members. The availability of insurance cover at an affordable price is particularly important for professional people in the modern world in which there is an ever growing tendency for aggrieved clients to sue their professional advisers, and for courts to award large sums in compensation in cases where professionals are adjudged to have been negligent;

(g)   The provision of public relations services for the profession as a whole and also possibly for specific areas of activity of a profession where such activities are little known of by the general public, or imperfectly understood by it, or where improved or new services are offered.

The above are some features the author would hope to see in a profession. Others might add other features or omit some or change emphases which might currently exist in a profession, whilst some professions – particularly where there is a small number of members and consequently limited funds – might find it completely impossible to implement some of the suggestions. In addition to the above, it is arguable that in the case of larger professional organizations there ought also to be a 'compensation fund' established to accumulate funds specifically dedicated to compensate clients of members who have been financially disadvantaged as a result of negligent or incompetent performance by members. Such a compensation fund might be particularly appropriate for circumstances in which it would be too costly or too time-consuming for a client to mount court action for damages, or in circumstances in which the disadvantaged client has limited financial resources which restricts their ability to take legal action, or in which the sums claimed do not justify the costs of legal action.

Overall, it is suspected that any thinking and informed person whom one might interrogate on the topic would stress that, above all other features, the need for a high standard of ethics in a profession and a professional person is of paramount importance. It is probable they would also emphasize the need to operate not just in the interests of the members of the profession, but also in the interests of society in general if a profession is to be generally well respected by society.

The attributes of a professional person

The above considerations can be further developed to determine the attributes one would expect to see in a professional person, and the best way of identifying those attributes is probably to ask oneself the question 'Were I to employ a professional person what qualities would I expect in them?'

It is suggested that desirable attributes include the following:

1. Scrupulous honesty, such that feelings of trust and confidence are inspired in those employing the professional;
2. The general observance of high moral standards and of high levels of integrity, such that the client can be confident the professional will always act in an honest and responsible way and will always act in the best interests of the client;
3. The possession of a high level of appropriate education and of appropriate skills and knowledge in the relevant specialist professional area;
4. Evidence of a diligent approach to the regular updating of levels of skills and knowledge, in order to keep pace with the rapidly changing environment of the modern world;
5. Evidence of the ability to utilise the skills and knowledge possessed in an efficient and effective way in practical situations;
6. The ability to think and reason coupled with the ability to consider problems, to compare a range of possible solutions, courses of action, or recommendations, and having done so to make reasoned and rational decisions;
7. The possession of very good skills of communication in the written word as well as in the spoken word, with the standard of formal reports being of high quality and in a format which fulfils the clients needs, that is they should be able to respond to the client's brief as a minimum level of reporting;
8. The ability to organise and administer work in an efficient and effective way, so ensuring that the client will get the required service without unnecessary cost or delay;
9. A thorough and diligent approach to carrying out a client's brief and to responding to a client's needs to ensure that the required service is in fact delivered;
10. The willingness not only to respond to the client's brief, but also to indicate to the client if further advice or action is considered necessary over and above that asked for by the client and described in the brief;
11. A conscientious attitude to work with timely attention to instructions and a high standard of punctuality in all professional activities;

12. On the personal side, a high standard of dress and presentation with a personable approach to people and the ability to communicate easily and effectively with a wide range of people;
13. The ability to exercise self-control to the extent that the professional can confidently be expected always to remain in control of any situation;
14. A courteous manner and an understanding of protocol which enables the professional to act with politeness, diplomacy and dignity at all times;
15. The ability to operate effectively within the wide scope allowed by professional freedom at the same time as always acting in the best interests of the client and in a manner which is both justified and justifiable. This amounts to the ability to use power and authority responsibly.
16. The ability and willingness to know his or her limitations and to advise a client or a prospective client when work is outside his or her capabilities, or when more expert advice is required;
17. The desire always to perform to the highest possible levels, and the desire to continually improve the level of professional performance.

With respect to points 1 and 2 the honesty and integrity of a professional should be such that a client should be informed immediately of any situations in which the professional might have a conflict of interests, or might be perceived by others to have a possible conflict of interests. The client can then decide whether they wish the professional to continue to act for them.

Conflicts of interests could arise when a professional is acting for a client in a matter in which another client of the professional or the professional's firm or organization has or may have an interest; in which the professional himself or herself has or may have an interest; or in which a relative, friend or associate of the professional has or may have an interest. The client should immediately be informed of such situations even when there is only a possibility of problems arising or even when the professional has such high integrity that the client's best interests would at all times be protected.

It is really irrelevant whether any of these parties actually acts in a way which jeopardizes the interests of the client, as, whatever may happen, the perception that a client's interests may have been adversely affected by a business or social relationship of the professional has to be avoided at all costs. A professional person should always ensure that no situation exists in which his or her honesty and integrity could be placed under suspicion. It is critical that the professional person should always disclose the possibility of conflicts of interest to the client, as it should always be the client rather than the professional who decides whether the circumstances are such that the professional cannot continue to act for them, or vice versa.

As all people are different, and because we all have different strengths and weaknesses, the acquisition to a high level of all of the above qualities by all professional people is likely to be impossible in the real world. However, the recognition of the importance of the above qualities for and by practising professionals is what is important, and the endeavour to achieve a high level of performance in these areas and to continually seek to improve performance is what can reasonably be expected of practising professional people.

Chapter 4

Licensing, Registration and Self-Regulation of Professions

In some countries there is provision for the control of professional organizations, and hopefully thereby professional standards, by central government or other government approved bodies, whilst in other circumstances these responsibilities are often left to professional groups operating through what is referred to as self-regulation.

As an example of state regulation of the property professions, in Australia there is provision for the control of real estate agency and the valuation profession through statutory systems. As a result, in order to sell real estate in New South Wales (NSW) one must be licensed by a NSW government agency, whilst in order to operate as a valuer one must be registered with a similar body. The systems of control vary slightly between the Australian states, but in general terms there is a requirement that, in order to satisfy the statutory requirements, a satisfactory standard of approved education must have been achieved, adequate and appropriate practical experience must have been obtained, and an applicant for either a licence or registration must be a person who is honourable and of good character. Statutory bodies have been established to implement the licensing and registration schemes, their duties including the supervision of appropriate operational standards and the disciplining of those who do not observe the appropriate standards of operation and professional behaviour.

It is interesting to reflect that if all professionals possessed the attributes referred to in earlier chapters there would be no need for such systems, as in essence licensing and registration systems exist to protect the public from incompetent or unscrupulous professional people or organisations. The rules and regulations are intended to ensure that such people cannot practise in a professional capacity, and if real estate agents or valuers do act in a manner which is either incompetent or unscrupulous to the extent of being dishonest or illegal, there is provision for their disciplining, which may entail withdrawal of permission to practise.

There is therefore an implication that where systems of licensing and registration are in force, there exists, or there would be likely to exist without those systems, some dishonest and unscrupulous people in the professions regulated by the systems. Human nature being what it is, that is not an unreasonable suggestion. Moreover, there is also an implication that the public could only be protected from such bad elements in a profession by a government organization exercising statutory powers.

The latter may not necessarily be the case, and in some situations professional organizations themselves are responsible for ensuring that membership can only be enjoyed by people of approved educational, professional and ethical standards (conditions which should in any event apply to all professions), whilst the professional organization may also be responsible for establishing and supervising the type of control systems currently enforced in New South Wales by the government in respect of real estate agents and valuers.

Where a profession is itself responsible for the control of its standards and those of its members it is commonly referred to as being self-regulating. Such a situation is not uncommon, and it exists in a number of countries in professions such as the legal profession and the medical profession, whilst in the United Kingdom it also exists in the valuation and real estate profession, with regulation and control of many branches of the property professions being primarily in the hands of the Royal Institution of Chartered Surveyors (RICS). In such situations aggrieved members of the public can make complaints against members to the professional body rather than to a government appointed regulator or organization, and they can also, of course, take action in the courts if it is thought a good case can be made against an incompetent, negligent or dishonest professional person.

It is arguable that self-regulation is a very good system of regulation as a professional group should best know its own needs and the needs of the public it serves, whilst it is also the best informed body of people to assess what are both desirable and possible within their professional group in terms of performance and behaviour. It should also best know the strengths and weaknesses of a range of possible control measures which may exist, and should therefore be able to devise the most desirable and most appropriate systems and rules of control. In devising such systems and rules it will be aware how easily and quickly they can be introduced and applied, and how effective they are likely to be in practice. It should also be aware of any problems which might be involved in maintaining the system, it should be aware of the likely costs of establishing and running such systems, and it should be the best informed on the relative qualities and likely effectiveness of a range of possible control measures.

However, there is always the danger that where regulation and control are the responsibility of a professional group, that group may exercise its powers more in the interests of its members than in the interests of its clients, the interests of clients and society in general possibly receiving scant consideration.

On the other hand, where such duties are placed in the hands of politicians and civil servants there may be just as great a danger of vested interests being cared for in the control system (although they may be a different group of vested interests to those of the profession). In addition, the design and operation of the control systems may be entrusted to people who are less well-informed and therefore less competent in their ability to design appropriate regulations and regulatory structures, and in their ability to apply them in practice.

Moreover, even where systems of regulation are statutory systems there is nevertheless the danger that those systems may impose a restraint of trade to the extent that they actually become systems which protect the professional group more than they protect the public. Restrictions on entry to a profession may in fact be utilised, either consciously or unconsciously, in a way that limits competition which, in consequence, may also limit the desirable development of a profession, and also the ability of the public to exercise desirable freedom of choice. However, it should be acknowledged that such undesirable results could also arise with a self-regulatory system of professional control, indeed, they may be more likely to occur where self-regulation applies.

It should not be inferred from the above observations that statutory control systems are never desirable. In situations in which there are a number of professional organisations and none of them is sufficiently large or powerful to control the overall operations of a profession in a desirable way; in situations in which the activities and operations of professional organisations are not clearly defined or not clearly definable; and in situations in which there is evidence of low ethical standards or past activity of an undesirable nature or a high probability of such activity in the future, then statutory regulation may be the only appropriate form of control over a profession.

However, there is much to support the argument that self-regulation is the most desirable form of regulation:

(a) where there is only one professional organization, or a small number which co-operate together and which have the same ideals and standards which in themselves are sufficiently high;
(b) where there are clearly defined areas of activity for the profession concerned;
(c) where the professions themselves can ensure that the appropriate types and levels of education and examination are available for members and prospective members;
(d) where there is no past evidence that statutory regulation is needed, or alternatively where evidence exists that any past deficiencies have been remedied; and
(e) where there is evidence that members of the profession individually and collectively operate in a responsible manner and to high ethical standards.

It is interesting to note that, although statutory regulation currently exists in New South Wales and Australia, largely as a result of government initiatives in recent years the systems of control in New South Wales were relaxed, and it was even suggested at one stage that government regulation might be replaced by self-regulation. It is also interesting to note that some of the loudest voices against such a move in respect of valuation came from within the profession. This is disturbing as it raises the fear that members of the profession may lack confidence in its ability to control itself and its members to ensure sufficiently high levels of practice and behaviour, or, alternatively, that it may fear that the abolition of government regulation might result in greater competition within the profession to the detriment of those already in it.

Concluding observations

Whether a group of people constitutes a profession or not depends upon the way the members of the group collectively conduct themselves as practitioners and people. Only if all members, or all but a very small minority, operate in an appropriate manner will a true profession or professional group exist.

At the end of the day, whether a person is a true professional person or not depends very much upon their general behaviour and beliefs. Apart from the possession of a high level of general professional knowledge and competence, it is the strength of character, the personality, the behavioural standards, and the ethical standards of a person which determine whether they are truly professional. Without high standards in all these areas it is impossible to be truly professional. Being truly professional is in reality a way of life, a way of thinking and acting, and it necessitates having a philosophy which extends beyond one's professional activities and which is in effect a philosophy of life.

Chapter 5

The Performance of Professional Bodies

Aims, objectives and professional behaviour

Having considered the features which might be considered desirable in professional organizations and in professional people, it is appropriate to consider whether such qualities are in fact generally exhibited by such bodies and their members. Most professional organizations clearly state their aims and objectives, whilst it is common for them also to have fairly comprehensive bye-laws, rules, and regulations designed to govern the behaviour both of the organization itself and its members individually in their professional activities. It is also common for them to have a disciplinary committee, or a professional practices committee, established to oversee the professional behaviour of their members, and where necessary to take action to reprimand or punish any member who fails correctly to observe the rules and regulations.

Journals, libraries, and information services

Most professional organizations of an adequate size – which probably is a minimum of several thousand members if sufficient funding is to be forthcoming to the organization – provide information to their members through a regular newsletter or journal, and in this way members are informed of the most important news and developments particularly relevant to their own professions. The quality and relevance of information so supplied is likely to vary considerably dependent upon the knowledge and skill of those entrusted with providing the service, and it is arguable that the supervision of such a service should be in the hands of someone qualified and experienced in the profession itself to ensure the relevance of information supplied, and to ensure that important information is not omitted.

Indeed, it is also arguable that the ultimate administration of a professional organization ought to be in the hands of a similar person, for intimate knowledge of a profession must be an invaluable quality in its chief administrator or senior administrators. Despite this there are professional organizations in which there are very few members of the profession actually employed in the day to day management and administration of the organization, this being likely to result in situations in which a lack of intimate knowledge of the day to day professional activities of members may result in administrative and managerial inefficiencies and shortcomings.

Professional organizations of any substantial size also provide good, and often excellent, library services for their members, which is particularly useful support for small professional practices which could only afford to establish a limited internal library themselves because of financial constraints. A wider range of texts can thereby be made available to even the sole practitioner, and nowadays library services are also supplemented by an extensive amount of information available from professional organizations via the Internet, many of them having developed excellent web pages for the support of their members. The Royal Institution of Chartered Surveyors (RICS) has in recent years put considerable resources towards an internet service which gives members almost instantaneous access to many of the services of the Institution.

Education

The development of educational policies and the establishment of recognized qualifications is recognized as an important matter by most professional organizations, and this is evidenced by the existence of stated educational objectives and requirements, education committees, education officers as established members of the administration, and examination boards. In the surveying and valuation world the RICS at an early stage of its formation paid great attention to these needs, and in 1919, in co-operation with other property professional organizations, The College of Estate Management was established specifically to provide for the education of all branches of the surveying professions. For many years it provided correspondence courses for a range of surveying specialisms – as it still does – full time courses for the property professions' own examinations, and approved diploma courses. In the early 1920s it began to offer courses for the newly established degree in Estate Management of the University of London, whilst a degree in Estate Management was also established at the University of Cambridge.

The property professions in the United Kingdom have therefore put much emphasis upon the possession of good academic qualifications for a great many years, and in the 1960s the need for high standards of education was further emphasized by the recognition of new degree courses specifically designed to educate students for the property professions. From a situation in the early 1960s in which there were only two estate management degrees in the United Kingdom and less than 10% of new entrants to the professions were graduates, in the period subsequent to 1965 the situation changed rapidly to the extent that by the early 1980s there were about 20 recognized estate management or similar degree courses, and also a large number of recognized degree courses for other branches of the surveying professions. By then a very large percentage of new entrants were graduates, and in due course the decision was made by the RICS that there should be graduate entry only. This resulted in the abandonment by the RICS of its own long established examinations and the delegation of responsibility for the examination of entrants to the profession to full time educational establishments – universities, polytechnics, and colleges – offering courses approved by the RICS.

There are obviously benefits from leaving full time education in the hands of institutions whose primary objectives include such provision and which have full time appropriately qualified staff teams to provide courses, but there are also problems which result from the delegation of responsibilities to other organizations, and in particular when the delegation is to a large number of other organizations. The question of the provision of appropriate education is so important to a profession, that this matter will be further discussed in a later chapter.

Professional standards and disciplinary committees

Such committees frequently take action against members, and it is not unusual to read that surveyors, valuers, accountants or doctors have been disciplined by their profession's disciplinary committee, such disciplinary action sometimes resulting in a member being expelled from an organization. In the case of doctors and lawyers such expulsion will, depending upon the country and the system of professional regulation applicable therein, generally result in the expelled member being unable to practise in a professional capacity, membership of the organization regularly being an essential qualification for practising professionals. In the case of surveyors and valuers in the United Kingdom this is not the case, and a member expelled, for example, from the RICS could in fact continue to practice professionally, although that member would not be allowed to call himself, or herself, a Chartered Surveyor.

This can be considered a weakness of the situation in which the RICS is the major professional organization in a self-regulating profession. However, such a situation could be overcome by the Government giving a professional organization the power and the duty to issue practising certificates to its members, the possession of which certificates would be an essential practising requirement with the withdrawal or expulsion of a member from the professional organization being accompanied by the withdrawal of a practising certificate.

An argument against giving such powers to a professional organization is that members of the organization delegated to oversee standards and disciplinary matters might be loathe to act against members of their own profession except in the most extreme circumstances, possibly often taking the view when judging a complaint against a fellow member 'there but for the grace of God go I!' In any event, it can be argued that in such circumstances there would be a tendency to issue a lighter punishment than might be merited, for example giving a reprimand in situations in which the general public might anticipate expulsion being appropriate. There is little doubt that with many members of the public, and probably also with some members of professional organizations, there is the perception that professional organizations entrusted with the task of disciplining their own members sometimes take an extremely benevolent view of the misdemeanours of their fellow members, to the extent that they are often suspected of 'whitewashing' situations in which members of society anticipate strong disciplinary action being taken.

Whether that is the case or not is open to debate, but it is undoubtedly a fact that the perception of many outsiders is that when organizations are responsible for the disciplining of their own members, appropriate justice frequently will not be administered and sufficiently severe actions will not be taken against defaulting members. One even sees such views expressed with relation to church disciplinary groups and the clergy, to police disciplinary committees and members of the police, and to Courts Martial and the military. When the public perception is that a profession does not exercise a sufficiently tight control over the professional behaviour and performance of its members, it has to be to the detriment of that particular profession.

In recent years the RICS has modified its disciplinary committees somewhat in that there is now representation from people who are not professional members of the organization, and that has to be a move for the better. How strong an influence such external members can have on the operation of a professional group is uncertain, and much depends upon the general abilities and strength of character of those appointed to such posts in determining how effectively they can operate as members of a committee in which they may be outnumbered by practising professionals. The latter are likely to have far greater knowledge of the practices of their profession than the outsiders can possibly have, to the extent that the outside members may be reluctant to assert their views in some situations or, when they do, those views may quickly be dissipated or dismissed by other committee members. The method of appointment of such members is also important, for if they are chosen by the profession itself there is the danger that they may be apologists for the profession appointed as much for appearances as for any other reason. It is also desirable that they should be representatives of the public in general rather than representatives of extremist groups or extremist views.

Professional organizations are likely to resist the establishment of external disciplinary bodies to oversee their professions, to a large extent simply because of objection to outside intervention in the running of their organization and the loss of power which is likely to result from a situation in which they would no longer be completely in control of all the affairs of the organization. This is a reason why many professionals are opposed to state intervention in the form of government licensing or registration schemes, although it appears that where the latter exist there seems to be greater transparency and a perception amongst the public that professional people are being properly overseen in their professional activities. Whether this is always so is debatable, for it may often be rather like a situation in which speed limits are in force but no police are available to implement those limits; in just the same way, setting up statutory regulatory systems will not ensure a higher standard of performance and higher ethics on the part of professional people unless there is an accompanying structure which ensures regular and thorough inspection of performances and the appropriate disciplining of defaulters.

It is arguable that many professional organizations have

themselves not been diligent enough in this respect. For many years in some professions the only requirement to enable one to practise was the need for an initial approved qualification, such as passing professional examinations or possessing an approved diploma or degree, generally coupled with the completion of a satisfactory period in professional practice as a trainee gaining appropriate experience. In such circumstances approval of the period of professional experience was sometimes little more than a mere formality, with nothing done to ensure that the experience gained really did equip an applicant to be a fully-fledged member of the profession. Clearly, such a state of affairs is unsatisfactory, and it is to its credit that, about 30 years ago, the RICS introduced more demanding requirements for the period of professional experience, requiring probationary members to obtain experience in specific areas of work, to record their activities during this period, and to satisfy an examining group that they were properly equipped to become recognized as fully qualified members of the Institution.

Notwithstanding that move, it is still a fact that in the RICS, as in many other professional groups, one can still continue as a fully recognized member without ever being re-examined after first passing approved examinations. There is therefore no process in place to ensure that all members remain competent professionals once they have satisfied the initial entry requirements, apart that is from the hope that members will observe the rules and regulations and ethical expectations of the Institution, the discipline which may be exerted by the possibility that a dissatisfied client may complain to the Institution about a member's performance, and the requirement that members should undertake a certain amount of 'professional development' each year.

Continuing Professional Development (CPD)

The levels of knowledge and ability of its members must be an important consideration for any true profession, a fact recognized by the RICS when it established CPD requirements in 1981. The bye-law introducing CPD was as follows:

> Every person elected a Professional Associate on or after the 1 January, 1981 shall for so long as he remains a Member undergo in each year such courses of continuing professional development and shall from time to time provide to the Institution such evidence that he has done so as the Regulations shall provide.

Subsequent to the introduction of the bye-law members were expected to comply with it, to keep records as evidence of their compliance, and to be prepared to produce those records to prove compliance if so required. The requirements could be satisfied by attendance at approved conferences or courses run by approved organizations, or by a range of other activities which included studying for approved courses or even private study of an appropriate type, although haphazard reading, even though it might have related to professional matters, was not acceptable. The basic requirement was that each member had to complete 60 hours of CPD activities in any three-year period, or double the time if CPD compliance was based on structured and approved private reading and correspondence courses, that is 120 hours over three years if all CPD activities were of that nature.

The introduction of the concept of continuing professional development was commendable. However, many would argue that the very concept of a professional person should have made the requirement irrelevant, as, in any event, true professionals would, and did, ensure that they kept abreast of developments in their professions and took positive steps to maintain a high level of professional performance. It was therefore arguable that the bye-law was superfluous except in the case of the less professional type of member. Indeed, prior to the bye-law most good professional surveyors and valuers would have averaged far more than 20 hours per annum in beneficial professional development activities.

Since the introduction of the original scheme there have been some changes in the requirements particularly relating to monitoring provisions. Members were originally required to provide proof of compliance if required, but there is now a system of random checking by the Institution's administration which is accompanied by the requirement for members to keep a compliance log on an annual basis providing clear details of the activities on which their compliance has been based. Members who are found to have fallen short of the requirements are subject to disciplinary action administered by the Institution.

Subsequent to the introduction of the bye-law requirement, the most popular form of compliance has probably been to attend short courses and conferences, and the one thing that can be certain about CPD requirements is that they have resulted in a boom in short course and conference provision, many of these being expensive, whilst the quality and relevance of some events is not always clear. For some members compliance may entail a substantial financial outlay relevant to their annual income, that outlay including conference fees, travel costs, perhaps the cost of overnight accommodation, and loss of earning time when attendance is during work hours. Despite this there are many CPD approved events which have limited substance and which do little to help maintain high standards of competence among members. Additionally, there will probably be some members who satisfy CPD requirements by doing little more than paying a conference fee, booking in, eating the lunch, and drinking the wine at lunch, whilst their ability to perform professionally to a high level and to enhance the reputation of their professional organization may receive scant assistance.

The concept has much to commend it but, sadly, the CPD system may guarantee little more than profits for those supplying CPD approved conferences and other approved activities; whether it has really helped significantly to enhance the standing of the Institution in the eyes of the general public and professional clients is probably not known. In reality it would be desirable for there to be a measure to indicate whether the standards of performance of members has improved since the introduction of CPD requirements, and whether they continue to improve, but in the absence of more positive oversight of CPD requirements, such as periodic performance testing, this is likely to remain unknown.

Having said that, the scheme of CPD operated by the RICS is not dissimilar to schemes applicable to other professions and other professional organizations, the general concept adopted by most being that there should be an obligation on members to take positive steps to maintain, and preferably improve, their level of professional performance after initial qualification. The major criticism which could be levelled at many of these schemes is that probably too much trust is placed on members, this creating no problem when members are good professionals with high ethical standards and a conscientious approach to their professional activities. However, by virtue of the system of random sampling of CPD returns, it is in fact only chance which will result in the administrators detecting those members who are negligent both in respect of CPD requirements and also with respect to the service they provide to clients. Indeed, the present system allows members who are poor representatives of a profession to continue as normal if they are found, on being chosen for a random check-up, to have satisfactory CPD evidence. A major flaw which the system does not therefore remedy is that there is no positive check to ensure that members who bring a profession into general disregard by virtue of their consistently inferior performance are not allowed to continue as members.

Professional performance testing

The maintenance of adequate professional standards would be more likely to be ensured by replacing the Institution's CPD organization with a random testing unit which could call upon individual members to submit themselves, as and when required, for assessment in their area of practice. Failure to satisfy the unit that a member's performance is adequate as indicated through the assessment (which could preferably include consideration of evidence of past performance in their day to day work and reference to past clients) would result in membership status being withdrawn. It would not require a large organization, indeed the numbers required for such a scheme need be no larger than those required for the present random sampling of CPD requirements. The fear of being as it were 'breathalysed' when driving could result in those who are under performing improving their performance for fear of losing membership status, which could only be good for the overall credibility of the Institution. By indicating minimum acceptable levels of performance it could also weed out those who do not deserve membership, thereby ensuring an acceptable level of quality among members. This should enhance the reputation of the Institution and its entire membership, which would in turn make membership more desirable to members and potential members. It should in addition enhance the standing of the profession in the eyes of the general public and its customers in particular, for it only requires a relatively few poorly performing members of a profession to lower its prestige and that of all its other members.

Compulsory professional indemnity insurance

Many if not most professional organizations now require their members to have professional indemnity insurance at a level adjudged to be sufficient to cover possible claims which might be brought against them for professional negligence. The RICS introduced such requirements about a quarter of a century ago, and during the time the requirements have been in force the price of purchasing cover has increased dramatically. The increases have resulted partly from price inflation in general, but a major reason has probably been the frequency of claims brought against members coupled with the high levels of compensation often awarded by the courts or agreed by insurers.

It is suggested that the best way of reducing the level of premiums would be for property advisers in general to improve their level of performance and service to the extent that there would be extremely few occasions on which claims for professional negligence could be founded. Coupled with that would be the refusal of institutional membership to those who perform inadequately as professionals, or whose likely performance would be inadequate. No matter how competent and diligent a professional is there is always the danger of circumstances arising in which they may be subject to a claim for professional negligence, but, as with motoring accidents and speeding fines, a competent level of performance and appropriate attitude can greatly reduce the risk of mishap. It may well be that some professional organizations, in the quest for strength through numbers, have overlooked the fact that ultimately their group will be judged primarily by the quality of its members and their quality of performance rather than by the size of its membership, and that in assessing performance the general public probably notices the poor performers more than the others. As restaurants are frequently judged by the bad meals they serve, so is a profession often likely to be judged by society in general by the standards of performance of its poorer members.

If a professional organization decided to insist upon membership standards such that a high level of professional service was the norm and inferior service rare, it could quite possibly run its own insurance scheme relatively economically with there being only limited risk of claims against the fund. Indeed, the overview of an internal insurance scheme of this nature could also be tied to the overview of general performance by members, thus serving two purposes and also acting as a controlling influence on the incompetent, reckless, or indifferent minority of members who might cause problems. Such a suggestion would probably be dismissed by many as being impractical. However, the present situation, in which many professional people in different professions are finding the cost of professional indemnity insurance to be exceedingly high to the point where some can hardly afford it, certainly is not desirable, and may be such that existing indemnity schemes may be unsustainable in the longer term.

There is another problem with professional indemnity insurance in that in practice it probably protects the professional more than the client. Additionally, in much the same way as having comprehensive insurance and safety devices in a car may lull a driver into a false sense of security encouraging him or her to take risks which would not be taken were there no safety devices coupled with the danger of having to pay compensation for damage to others out of his or her own pocket, the professional with indemnity insurance may become less diligent than one without it. Certainly the fear of loss is likely to make most people more careful, and it may be that some of the insurance claims which do arise have resulted partly from a certain element of abandonment encouraged by the perceived protection of insurance cover.

To enlarge upon the statement that insurance probably protects the professional more than the client, a dissatisfied client who wishes to make a claim against a professional person based on the accusation of negligence in the provision of a service does not simply have to take issue with the professional person concerned, but with the might of an insurance company backed by extremely large financial resources which is possibly willing to resist payment to the extreme. In such a case the very process of stalling, which a large insurance company might be able to indulge in indefinitely, could so increase the costs of making a claim that most would-be claimants would have to give in the battle at an early stage. In consequence, it may be that the holding of professional indemnity cover actually protects many professional people who in fact have provided unsatisfactory services to the financial detriment of their clients in circumstances in which the latter in reality have clear cases for compensation. Whilst this might protect and benefit the individual professional concerned, such a state of affairs would do nothing to enhance the reputation and standing of the profession in general.

Compensation for clients

Such circumstances as those referred to above can create situations in which clients who have received poor service from professional advisers actually have far less protection than shoppers who have purchased defective goods from retailers. If an article is bought from Marks & Spencer or Boots and there proves to be something wrong with it, customers will get instant attention, and almost certainly instant satisfaction, by drawing the problem to the notice of Marks & Spencer or Boots. The same applies to many retailers and to many other firms, whilst there are business and trade organizations which have indemnity or compensation funds to provide for the misdeeds of 'sinners' amongst them.

The RICS is probably typical of most professional organizations in that, although recently it has taken steps to improve the complaints procedure for dissatisfied clients of members, the situation is still such that there is nothing to persuade a potential client to use a member on the basis that they will be guaranteed satisfaction in the event of the service proving to be less than could reasonably be expected. If one gets inferior service from a Chartered Surveyor (as with many other professionals) one can sue for damages, but in most cases such a course of action is completely impracticable for all but organizations with substantial financial backing, and even then substantial sums of money generally need to be in dispute to justify the resultant trouble and expense. Suing for damages is out of the question for most people or organizations because of the high cost of instigating legal action and the time and disruption involved in pursuing it. As discussed earlier, the existence of compulsory insurance requirements is also of limited value to the customer, who is likely to be confronted by the opposition of the insurer with the finances to hire 'big-guns' to oppose the claim, and the experience to make life as difficult as possible for the claimant.

Complaining to the Institution about inadequate service provision is also of little or no benefit to many dissatisfied clients, as while it will involve them in additional work it will not result in them obtaining compensation to adequately cover losses and costs which may have resulted from a member's poor performance. In such circumstances a client who receives inadequate or negligent service from a professional person is in fact not as well protected as most shoppers for retail goods, and the existence of a professional body does little to protect the consumer. This, it is suggested, remains a deficiency with many professional organizations, and there is little doubt that many members of society perceive them as being established primarily for the benefit and protection of their members, rather than for the benefit of society in general and the protection of those utilising the services provided by members.

Service to clients

It is most important for any professional group to strive to better serve the needs of society, in the case of the property professions particularly those people or organizations likely to need the provision of high quality property advice and other property related services. It is in the interests of any professional group to recognize this fact, for if it does not act responsibly as far as society is concerned it will be more likely to suffer from future government interference and control in various forms.

The major *raison d'être* of most professions is to provide specialist services to clients, and the ultimate test of whether a professional group has succeeded in doing so satisfactorily must be the assessment by clients of the services provided. The author is unaware of any professional group which actually and systematically seeks feedback from the clients of its members to monitor their assessments of professional services purchased, although there are individual firms which do this. It could probably be argued that such a system would be superfluous as the best indication is the proportion, be it small or large, of dissatisfied clients who complain to a professional organization such as the RICS. However, the latter does not accurately measure the number of dissatisfied customers, for many who fall into that category may decide simply to learn from experience and not use a specialist adviser again, others may decide that although they are dissatisfied they cannot afford the time or money to pursue their grievance, whilst others may decide that complaining will not be worthwhile as the profession will simply close ranks and protect their colleague member rather than pursue the complaints of an aggrieved customer. Whether the latter would be a correct perception is irrelevant, for even if such a perception is unfounded it nevertheless colours peoples' attitudes regarding a profession, and is a fundamental problem for a self-regulating profession.

A further shortcoming of the present state of affairs with the RICS – and probably also with other professional organizations – is that currently there is also no means by which the percentage of clients who are truly, or even reasonably, satisfied with the performance of members can be assessed accurately. With modern communications systems constant monitoring of the assessment of service by clients of members could be initiated relatively easily, which would probably result in cost savings in other areas of administration, particularly CPD monitoring. With respect to this suggestion it is interesting to note that the Carsberg Report of 2002 (see Appendix A) has recently suggested the introduction of the monitoring of some valuation work by the RICS, this being evidence of the perceived need for greater transparency.

Summary

In seeking a good standing in the eyes of the public, it is advisable for any professional organization to concentrate on the quality of membership rather than the size of membership, for if an organization has a body of high quality members it is likely to be well thought of by society in general.

Concentration on ensuring quality among the members of a professional organization is critical, which in turn necessitates the weeding out and rejection of poor performers. Customers ought also to be given confidence through the knowledge that the organization makes positive efforts to guarantee standards, and if this is the case complaints ought to be rare. When justified complaint does exist, knowledge that a client may be compensated by the professional body would be a real incentive to customers to use a member of that organization. Such would necessitate the establishment of a compensation fund, but if poor performers are not allowed to be members, poor performance should be rare and payments from the fund few, whilst professional indemnity insurance premiums should be lower if overall standards are higher. As far as the costs of implementing the suggestions made above are concerned, there is no reason whatsoever why, with good management, they could not be implemented within acceptable cost limits in well run organizations, whilst they should also result in cost savings in other areas of activity.

Chapter 6

Education for Professions

It is essential for the well-being of any country that those who wish to enter its professions should receive relevant and high quality education. Industrial and commercial activities need the backing of competent professionals in areas such as law, banking and the property professions, whilst competent professional people also have much to contribute to society in respect of social and ideological issues. It is therefore important that courses designed for the various professions should produce the right sort of professionals for conditions in the modern world, which are very different from those of only the relatively recent past.

Initially it is apt to consider what the objectives of such education should be. *The Concise Oxford Dictionary*, seventh edition, defines 'to educate' as 'give intellectual and moral training to; provide schooling for; train'. All these definitions are acceptable, but in designing courses for the professions it is essential to do something more than just provide a course of instruction and training. It is desirable to produce students who have acquired not only knowledge and skills, but also the ability to think and reason, to rationalize and to make sensible decisions where necessary, and to have the flexibility to adapt to changing circumstances in order to better serve the changing needs of society.

Clearly the professional body concerned is the critical element in decisions as to what studies should be included in a suitable course. It is also appropriate to consider what are, or what ought to be, the particular objectives of a specific profession. It is probably the objectives of a group of people pursuing a particular interest or means of earning a livelihood which determine whether that group in fact comprises a profession or merely a trade or occupation. As considered earlier, it is the desire to do something more than merely provide a technical service which should be a distinctive aim of a profession. There should be an inherent wish among true professionals to continually improve their knowledge and understanding of their own specialisms in pursuit of these objectives, and educational courses should be designed to develop such attitudes.

During a lunchtime conversation in which the objectives of clubs were discussed, one of those present said, 'the only reason for having a club is to keep people out'. An immediate reaction was that this was a somewhat drastic statement, but reflection persuades one that there is a lot of sound sense in it. In some cases such a policy could result in people being de-barred from membership of a group for reasons which most would find unacceptable such as one's origins or background, but in the case of a profession the quest for high standards should dictate that those who do not have an adequate level of technical knowledge, the right philosophy in the way they perform their services, and the correct ideals, should be kept out. Those who are not and who are unlikely to become a credit to a profession should not be accepted into membership.

The objectives in providing education for a profession should therefore be determined by the need to set standards, defining a minimum acceptable standard but also seeking to achieve higher standards than the minimum. The cynic might say that such a decision is dictated by ulterior motives, in that it helps to restrict competition and to protect the livelihoods of those in the club (or profession), but hopefully the success of a good educational policy should ensure that outsiders see the benefits of the imposition of minimum educational standards rather than seeing them as being an exercise of restrictive practices. Indeed, at no time should admission requirements relating to educational standards be used merely to restrict competition; to use them for such a purpose would bring discredit to a profession.

Current demands on professions

Today, both ever higher standards of performance and an increasing breadth of skills are being demanded of professions. It is more than a little saddening to have to suggest that many of the higher standards of performance which are required of professional people nowadays, may have been imposed on them as a result of outside forces rather than as a result of the inherent desire of the profession itself to improve its standards of performance. We live in an age in which the man in the street is better informed than he has ever been before, this resulting from better educational standards and the incredible amount of information which is now readily available to all via the printed word, radio, television and the internet.

Many of those employed in the media have in recent years realised the power they possess, and they have used this power quite unashamedly to expose what they regard as shortcomings in goods and services offered to the public. Often such criticism is justified, but sometimes these activities have reached the level of almost becoming vendettas against particular individuals or groups to an extent which is unacceptable to many. However, such campaigns are publicised to wide and credible audiences, and they do considerable harm to those under attack. In the case of companies targeted by critics of this type share prices and profits are often adversely affected. Whether we believe such campaigns to be acceptable, we have to recognize that they are a fact of modern life.

A profession should therefore realise, in determining its educational policies that high standards must be required of its members as they are likely to be dictated from outside if the profession fails to impose them itself. There are already examples in some countries of minimum professional educational requirements being dictated by statute. The problem with allowing this to happen is that those who determine the contents of such statutes do not always recognise shortcomings in their own legislation or the problems that may result from the knock-on effect of some of the provisions. For such reasons as these it is best that a profession should always seek to be at least one step ahead of pressure groups, politicians, and the legislature by imposing educational requirements which help to ensure a high level of competency amongst its members.

Educational aims and objectives

It is arguably axiomatic of a profession that it should by its very nature seek to demand high standards of its members, and that it should continually and continuously require them to seek to improve their standards, the overall objective being that the profession as a whole should offer an ever improving standard of service to its clientele. Some professional groups already require such high standards, which both does them credit and augers well for their futures. The quest for high educational standards can only be to the benefit of a profession, but in saying that it needs to be remembered that such education should be appropriate to the needs of the particular profession.

Part time or full time study?

The dictionary definitions refer to the need for a high degree of specialist knowledge and for training. In the past both knowledge and training were provided simultaneously by entrants to professions working during the day and studying in their spare time either at evening class or by correspondence course. This method of study still exists and it has many admirable features; the novices in a profession can get practical experience during the day which may well help them to better understand theory encountered in their evening studies. They may even be able to put such theory to the test in their daily routines, although a disadvantage of such education is that students will not necessarily gain practical experience of a type which is relevant to the studies they are currently undertaking. It must also be accepted that in some organisations the practical experience obtained may be of a kind which will not necessarily assist the student. There is in general the difficulty that work experience cannot be sufficiently controlled to ensure that it is always relevant to studies being undertaken at a particular time.

In spite of this problem there are many benefits from being able to undertake practical activities and studies simultaneously, but a great problem with part time study in today's world is that life seems to become ever more complex with each passing day, with the result that with the passage of time professional people need to know more and more about greater areas of knowledge. Technology develops at a breath-taking pace in most areas of modern life, whilst at times politicians seem hell-bent on passing legislation at a pace with which it is impossible to keep up. The sheer quantity of knowledge a professional person needs to acquire today makes it difficult to design suitable studies for some professions which can be properly pursued to a sufficient depth on a part time basis.

Anyone who achieves high educational standards by part time study is to be admired, such is the dedication and hard work normally required of them. Even when one is successful through such study methods there is a definite limit to the depth to which one can study because of the range of demands on available time, and it is largely for this reason that in recent years full time education has become more and more popular as a method of qualifying for professions.

Whilst in most areas of professional education full time study is most appropriate in the modern world, for a variety of reasons there is likely to be a need for and a strong demand for part time study for many years to come. First, it is unlikely that governments will provide sufficient funds in the foreseeable future to expand full time places to satisfy total demand at prices which would-be students can afford. Second, the geographical distribution of populations in some countries is such that some potential students can only be properly served by making education available to them in their home localities, such local provision frequently only being feasible on a part time basis. Third, for personal reasons there will always be some students who cannot take advantage of full time courses for a variety of good reasons. It is therefore important that great emphasis should be placed on the design of suitable courses for study in an external mode if possible both by evening class and distance learning. It is only right that competent and dedicated part time and external students should have the opportunity of getting high level qualifications – their reward for study – and external degrees and post graduate qualifications as well as diplomas should be available to them.

Graduate entry

Although there have been degree courses designed for the professions in the United Kingdom for very many years, in many professions the majority of entrants have until relatively recently been part time educated, whilst this is even more so in some other countries. In the past, so few in number were graduates in some professions that there was a considerable problem bridging the credibility gap with long-standing members of some professions who viewed graduate entrants with a certain amount of suspicion which sometimes amounted almost to distrust of their capabilities. The situation in many countries and professions is very different today, and there has been a very substantial increase in education for professions via full time courses, particularly degree courses.

In the United Kingdom the now defunct Council for National Academic Awards (CNAA) was a major stimulus for such expansion, having the power to accredit courses including those of degree and post graduate level. Using this power it in turn delegated powers to individual teaching institutions to run approved courses, and in doing so it required staff development in areas such as research and consultancy in order to ensure that staff were capable of providing high quality and relevant education. The CNAA was from 1965 the catalyst for a great expansion of degree level and post graduate education designed for the professions in public sector educational institutions, and the realisation by the university sector that this was an important educational market resulted in an expansion in that sector also. One of the effects of this expansion is that whereas in 1975 only about 10% of new entrants to most property professions in the United Kingdom were graduates, the current entry is almost entirely university educated.

The question of how graduates have been received by professions is important. There is no doubt that in the United Kingdom in the 1960s, and even in the 1970s, in the property professions there was still considerable opposition to graduate entrants, and many diehard professionals firmly maintained that graduates could not possibly become proper professionals as they had not had the right initial grounding in the practical environment. Many of those same diehards as recently as the 1970s were also saying that pocket calculators should not be allowed as they dulled the brain, and that advanced financial forecasting techniques were neither appropriate nor necessary.

However the professions in the United Kingdom have themselves been largely responsible for the trend towards graduate entry, not only because of the realisation by their governing bodies that higher educational standards must be good for a profession if in turn they result in more competent professionals, but also because of the failure of individual members to give part time student employees the correct working conditions to facilitate part time study. Many employers failed to appreciate that students cannot be worked extremely hard throughout a long day and then work effectively at part time studies during the evening. The result was that many part time students found it difficult to qualify, and there was much voting with their feet by would be entrants to professions who chose to take full time courses, recognising them as a more effective way of studying for what are often very demanding syllabuses. Organisations such as the Royal Institution of Chartered Surveyors (RICS) recognised that educational standards are important and positively encouraged the development of higher educational standards and of degree courses in particular. This resulted in educational institutions being able to concentrate on satisfying the educational needs of the profession knowing that they had its support, which, although not expressed in financial terms, was often strongly expressed in the corridors of power when educational matters were discussed.

There is much to commend full time education as it allows one to study seriously in a supportive environment and in the company of others with similar objectives, assisted by educators to whom one can turn when in trouble and with access to well equipped libraries and laboratories. When life was simpler it was perhaps practicable to acquire all one's technical knowledge on a part time basis, picking some of it up whilst engaged in professional activities. The quantum of knowledge required today is so great that full time study must have advantages, whilst pressure in the work place regularly seems to result in employers neglecting to give part time students the opportunity to pick up technical knowledge which could in reality be best acquired in the work place. There is now a very widely held feeling amongst many professionals in the United Kingdom that, although a part time qualified employee may perform better in the work place for the first 12 months or so after qualification, subsequently the majority of such people are likely to be left behind by graduates.

The content of courses

This leads to consideration of the content of courses and the specific objectives of full time courses. It is impossible, even in a full time course, to cover all the areas of study which might be considered relevant to people wishing to enter professions. This is a measure of the complexity of modern professional life, and with most professions there are long lists of study areas which could be considered relevant to subsequent professional life and therefore worthy of inclusion in a curriculum. Probably first in any list will be what might be called 'main stream' subjects, those in which considerable technical knowledge is absolutely essential.

It is necessary to ensure those areas receive considerable attention in order that students can acquire sufficient essential knowledge, and for general property consultants and valuers these studies should probably include economics, valuation, town and country planning, relevant areas of law, and building construction. Determination of the actual syllabuses for subjects included in a specific course will depend upon the particular emphasis of that course, which in turn will be dependent to a large extent upon the actual skills and experiences of the staff team offering it. The emphasis of a course may in turn be influenced by where most of its graduates are expected to eventually work, so in land economics courses it might be particularly important for a course in a developing country to include substantial inputs of land surveying, building technology, and perhaps rural based studies, although such inputs might be considered relatively unimportant in a course designed to produce graduates for employment primarily in financial and investment organizations. However, there is a danger in making course design too employment orientated, for demands from potential employers may vary considerably with changing economic circumstances and with the passage of time, which could result in graduates from highly specialised degree courses finding it difficult to satisfy the changed demands of employers. There is also the danger that too much concentration on a limited range of specialist subjects in an undergraduate course may result in students not benefiting from the breadth of education that a broad range of subject studies can give, whilst it may also restrict the ability of graduates to change their career direction at a later date should they wish to do so or should employment circumstances change.

It is also essential to ensure that there are inputs in appropriate stages of the curriculum of other studies which will be invaluable in professional life, and which are necessary back-up for the mainstream subjects. In property courses, for example, these could include subjects such as finance, management and administration, and information technology, which merit sufficient coverage to give students good basic groundings in them, thus enabling them to be used when appropriate. With limited time and limited teaching resources perhaps the best way to do this is to give essential basic instruction in these areas and then to encourage their use and development in such things as project work and assignments.

In the light of recent corporate disasters in a number of countries some of which have resulted substantially as a result of unprofessional behaviour by senior executives and professional advisers and consultants, it would appear highly desirable that all professionally orientated courses should in addition contain a study unit covering such matters as ethics, required and expected standards of corporate behaviour, the responsibilities of agents and trustees, and the moral and legal responsibilities of professional advisers.

Simulated practical studies

It is important in full time courses to try to compensate for the lack of practical experience of many, if not most, students. In recent years in many courses the emphasis on 'chalk and talk' has decreased considerably – although some academics appear to find it difficult to get away from this approach – and a greater emphasis has been placed upon self education by students. This approach requires careful supervision by staff to ensure that the less independent, less motivated, or less confident students do not fall by the wayside. There also remains a need for a considerable amount of formal teaching in the form of lectures and tutorials, particularly in the early stages of courses, to ensure that students have enough fundamental knowledge and an adequate understanding of the essential areas of study to equip them to operate in a practical situation. Having acquired these basic essentials, students can be set project work which simulates real world situations. Such a situation obviously lacks the final test of accountability, but this differs little from the market place situation of trainees or junior staff who are not finally accountable for the reports they draft, that responsibility resting with the partner or director who actually signs them and pays the insurance premium for the professional indemnity policy. Indeed, in well designed project work students are likely to have more independence and to be given more scope to use initiative than some employees are ever given in their employment.

The great benefits of well thought out project work include the need to think practically, but they go further than that. In today's world the only certainty is uncertainty. The task of forecasting the future, is extremely difficult and if we look back just five years, more so if we look back 10 years or longer, we will realise just how rapid the pace of change is. Because of this it is arguable that, although a certain amount of basic knowledge must be acquired by students, it is more important that they should develop the ability to learn, the ability to adapt to changing situations, the ability to reason, to compare alternative situations, to make judgments and to make decisions. It is essential that these qualities are cultivated in educational processes, although there is no way to ensure that students can ultimately make decisions, as, although one can cultivate all the other abilities, the ability to finally make a decision is something very personal and appears either to be born into somebody or lacking in them.

Why are these qualities important? In developing a course, the development period will probably take a minimum of one year and it is likely to be four or five years at the very least before students from that course enter the market place. The world may be very different by then, and some technical knowledge acquired in the first year of a course, or even in the final year, may be out of date by the time the student occupies his or her first job. For this reason, although it is essential that students acquire a considerable amount of technical knowledge, it is absolutely critical that educators ensure they produce graduates who can adapt to the changing needs of society because they are thinking, reasoning people. Those who complete courses should appreciate professional ethics and ideals to the extent that they wish to remain front runners and to continually improve their own level of performance because they wish to provide a high level of service to their employers, their clients, and society. Competent and progressive professionals will be of great value to society, and society is likely to value them highly. This is also important as a large part of the funds in education generally comes from government, or more correctly from tax payers, and it is most important that tax payers are given value for money.

The students

The needs of the professions and the responsibility of educators to society in general have been considered. In designing courses there is also a responsibility to students who join those courses; they may either suffer or enjoy a course, and it should be the duty of educators to try to ensure that it will be the latter. Most students select a particular course to achieve a variety of objectives which may include the wish to become better educated, the wish to enter a particular vocation, and hopefully they also choose a course because they think it will be enjoyable. The professions offer interesting and challenging study areas, and if educators do not make courses exciting, interesting and challenging they have failed dismally.

Students who enter courses are generally at a critical stage of their lives; having left school they are at an age where life offers so much and the prospect of the future is exciting. Educators should ensure that courses educate in ways in which the education provided is more than just the acquisition of knowledge or training. By seeking to monitor the needs of professions it should also be possible to ensure that courses lead to good job opportunities, and by the use of project work, that is by the application of knowledge as it is acquired, the level of excitement in courses should be greatly increased. The response of students to the simulated work place environment has in the author's experience been excellent, and the quality of the work they produce has accordingly been higher than that resulting from more traditional approaches.

With the rapid expansion of degree courses in the United Kingdom, and in other countries also, since about the late 1980s, there are substantial doubts as to whether the necessary quality of education has been achieved in all courses. Some course documents and descriptions emphasize the teaching and learning aspects of courses to the extent that one fears those are the sole emphases of the course, with the wider aspects of education receiving little or no attention. This is worrying, for at the extreme one can teach animals and they can learn, and if the course processes do not extend beyond teaching and learning the students produced may be lacking the abilities to think, reason, compare and decide, which have to be critical abilities for professional people. If these wider and critical areas of graduate education are not given adequate emphasis in a course, it is not going too far to say that students completing such a course are in fact being cheated in that they are being offered a sub-standard course rather than a true degree course.

Academic staff and resources

There is a fourth group involved in the consideration of education and that is the staff who man the courses offered. The educational process ought to be satisfying to them also if they are to perform properly. Just as in other activities in life, the participants are only likely to perform to their maximum ability if the activity is both challenging and enjoyable. Educational managers should pay considerable attention to ensuring that staff are able to work in a challenging and satisfying environment which will encourage them to contribute to the maximum of their abilities and to make the educational offering challenging and exciting for their students. For example, course design should take such considerations into account, and where project work has become an important part of a course, many teachers who were previously finding their job rather unexciting and boring have often become new individuals with a fresh interest in their job resulting from the challenge that project work gives to them as well as to students.

However there are often problems in recruiting suitable staff for professional courses, for those who might make the best teachers are frequently also those who have abilities which are in high demand in practice, and who can often command far higher salaries there than can be obtained in education. An additional problem has arisen in many countries since the large expansion of professional education in universities, in that there are undoubtedly cases in which the consequent large increase in demand for academic staff has resulted in a dilution in the quality of some of those eventually employed, with the consequence that the quality of education offered has suffered.

The two most valuable possessions any country has are first, its people, followed by its land and natural resources. It seems completely logical that in order to ensure the maximum returns to each of these it is necessary to ensure that there is an appropriately educated and more competent work-force. Unfortunately, although it is often difficult to see returns to educational expenditure within five years, it is all too easy to see the saving from cuts almost immediately. It has therefore often been the practice in the past for governments throughout the world to cut back expenditure on education when experiencing economic downturns. Countries do this at their peril, and even though there is sometimes inefficient use of money in educational circles, cut backs in expenditure do not solve that problem. There is waste in many other areas including the private sector, and cut backs are not necessarily solutions.

The solution to inefficient expenditure is better management, particularly better personnel and financial management. The problem with financial cut backs in education is that educational standards may be jeopardised by them, and whilst it is in any event frequently difficult to tempt competent staff of an adequate standard and philosophy into education, it is all too easy to lose better staff who see greater returns outside education. A great long term threat to educational standards is that if salary and working conditions deteriorate in relative terms, there may be a situation in which the majority of those remaining in education are the less competent educators. That possibility must pose a very great threat to educational standards, to the future standards of professions, and to future economic prospects.

Because of the substantial expansion of professionally orientated degree courses in some countries and the recruitment of staff who might not previously have been considered appropriate for lecturing appointments, it may be that a government can argue that relatively low academic salaries are adequate remuneration in view of the diluted average level of ability of an academic community. However, whilst there may be some truth in such an argument, policies which result in poor remuneration for academics are ill designed to entice the more talented members of professions to devote their skills to careers in education rather than to professional practice with its higher earning power.

In the past in some countries there has been a perception that business and professional courses can be run cheaply with high student numbers per staff member, but this is a belief which needs to be resisted. Insistence on unreasonably low production costs will usually result in inferior products, and modern business concepts and techniques cannot be properly taught at the high student staff ratios often considered appropriate in the past. Modern professional people need to have command of a wide range of skills which were not required in the past, and the necessary education for the modern world cannot be provided 'on the cheap'.

Entry levels and assessment

In the recent past there has been considerable discussion, including disagreement, on the required qualifications for those entering degree courses designed for various sectors of the RICS. Whilst it is important that would-be students should already have sufficient education to give them good prospects of satisfactorily completing a course upon which they wish to embark, the likelihood of success is not always best indicated by existing qualifications on admission to a course. In addition, the level of motivation and dedication to a chosen study programme and career are extremely important, and often highly motivated students with mediocre entry qualifications end up achieving extremely good degrees. Ultimately the quality of a student at the end of a degree programme is what matters most, and too rigid an admissions policy may deny a profession what might in fact have been extremely well qualified graduates.

The quality of students at the end of a programme will be to a large extent a function of the structure of the educational programme, the quality of the teaching, the abilities and attitudes of the students, and the methods of education and assessment employed in the programme.

The value of project based education has been emphasized, but its main value is as an educational method, there being, in the author's mind at least, grave dangers in its use as a method of assessment. So great has been the emphasis in some degree courses on continuous assessment using project work and other course work for such purposes, that in some courses end of year and end of programme written examinations are only of limited significance. It may even be possible in some courses to perform poorly in them and still to achieve a degree pass by virtue of marks accumulated through continuous assessment during the programme.

A major problem with the assessment of course work is that in many cases it is completely impossible to know for certain whose work is being assessed, the insistence of many institutions that submitted work must be produced by word processors even eliminating the possibility of identifying the true producer of work by identification of handwriting. With an abundance of information being available on the internet, the downloading and reproduction of the work of others is an easy task for dishonest students, whilst it is impossible for the academic marking such work to have such comprehensive knowledge as to be able to identify all plagiarized work.

A further problem exists with the assessment of work produced by students working in teams, as in such cases the efforts of under performing students may often be handsomely rewarded by virtue of them being a member of a high performing team, whilst the converse may apply to an excellent student who is unfortunate enough to be a member of an otherwise poor or below average group of students. It is arguable that group assessment is in fact likely to lead to mediocrity in mark levels rather than clearly indicating the relative merits of students from the worst to the best.

Just as ultimate success in sporting events is determined at the end of a game or race, so it is the quality at the end of a degree programme which is really critical and which should finally determine the quality of degree awarded to a student. For these reasons the author is still a great believer in the importance of end of year written examinations as the true indicator of quality, with course work and project work being essential educational tools designed to bring students to an appropriate level to ensure ultimate examination success. For students on professional courses the challenge of the end of year examinations is not very different from the need of the professional person to prepare reports for their clients, and in this respect the ability to perform adequately in this type of examination is probably directly relevant to the student's career needs.

Continuing education

The need for professionals to continually wish to improve their performance has been referred to earlier, and in order to do this professional people should accept the need for post qualification education. In the modern world there tend to be regular changes in legislation which affect the professions, such as the introduction of new taxes and variations in existing taxes. Often the processes which lead to change involve complex legislation, and there need to be sufficient facilities and opportunities with respect to such developments to enable professionals to continue their education throughout their professional careers. This again is an area where there is generally a shortage of funds in education, and it is probably correct that governments should not finance such activities as the provision of conferences and short courses, but should expect the necessary finance to be generated from within the relevant professions.

The result is that conferences need to be cost effective as a result of which they are often expensive; indeed, if they are manned by professionally qualified people it is only appropriate that they should earn professional returns. Members of higher earning groups should be prepared to spend some of their salaries to maintain and strengthen the abilities which enable them to command those earnings in the first instance. Governments should, of course, recognise the need for and benefits produced by such expenditure by making it tax deductible. There is also an element of self defence in such expenditure, as unless professionals acquire expertise in new and developing areas they will soon find that others move into their markets. There have been great developments in North America and the United Kingdom in this area of education for professions, and it is of increasing importance in other countries also.

In summary, it is essential that professions place the provision of a high standard of service and technical performance very high in their priorities. Appropriately high educational standards for members can help to ensure this and also that the products of the educational system are, both initially and throughout their careers, thinking, reasoning people, capable of making sound judgments and decisions to the extent that they will be of service to and appreciated by society in general.

There will be great benefits to a professional group from placing a proper emphasis on a high standard of relevant education, including increased efficiency, increased profits, increased public credibility, and increased respectability. It is essential that those in education remember that they are producers of a product and that continuous market research is necessary to ensure that the product remains acceptable to potential students, the professions, and society in general. Continued and regular liaison between educators and professional groups must be an important part of that market research, whilst continuing research into the needs of society in general is also most important.

Chapter 7

Valuers – Thinkers or Creatures of Habit?

In the light of the earlier consideration of the rôle of the professions it is appropriate to consider the author's own branch of the property professions in assessing how professional the average practitioner really is. The above title suggests the question: 'are valuers thinking people, or do they simply pursue their activities as creatures of habit, acting in a repetitive manner with little consideration given to whether the habits they follow, perhaps acquired over many years and possibly acquired from an earlier generation of valuers, are in fact appropriate procedures for the valuation problems faced in the modern world?' As the answer almost inevitably is that there are indeed some thinkers in the valuation profession, it is pertinent to consider whether there are enough thinkers, and whether there is in general enough independence of thought. Independence of thought may be critical in the judgemental process, but in circumstances in which statutes or professional rules and regulations dictate how professionals must operate, real independence of thought may be dangerous or impossible to incorporate in a valuation process, even though in some circumstances it might be highly desirable because it would result in a more realistic valuation.

It may be difficult or impossible to reach definite conclusions on the matter, and it may be that, even if it is believed that there are shortcomings within the valuation profession, it may nevertheless be concluded that it may be no worse than other professions in this respect. Even if valuers are creatures of habit this may not necessarily be bad if the habits practised are good, based on sound principles, and modified and adapted as and when found necessary based on experience gained over the years. Good habits are quite acceptable, but even they should not be used on a continuing basis without regular and searching scrutiny to determine whether they are still appropriate, whether they need modification, or whether they should be abandoned in some situations, or even completely abandoned in all situations.

It is not clear that this latter process has always been carried out in the valuation profession, but it is encouraging that in many countries in the past 25 years or so the growth of education provision for the profession, together with the commercial and financial pressures of the modern world, have resulted in a growing and healthy introspection within the profession. As observed in chapter six, traditionally in many countries education provision was principally by means of correspondence courses, part time courses, and a few full time courses leading to the examinations of professional organisations. In time such methods of study were supplemented by full time diploma and degree courses at colleges and universities, but the production of graduates was such that they formed only a very small proportion of the total of professional valuers. In the more recent past the development in many countries of a substantial number of new universities has in turn led to the growth in the number of degree courses and post graduate courses also. This has resulted in a transformation in the profession in some countries in that most new valuers now enter their chosen profession via a degree course in which they should have been encouraged not merely to learn, but to consider, analyse, question and reason. At the same time a substantial body of career academics has grown up in the profession; valuers who have chosen to concentrate on the development of relevant academic thought as their life's work, in much the same way as is the case with other longer established academic disciplines.

This is a healthy development which can only be good for the profession, as it should produce well educated professionals equipped to deal with the type of problems likely to be encountered in a rapidly changing, ever more technological and seemingly more complex world. In the past education was often acquired in a world which changed much more slowly than currently, and in which there was no involvement on a large scale in the property market of multi-million pound property companies and big spending financial institutions. Methods of valuation and practices recounted in correspondence notes and textbooks tended to be regarded as sacrosanct, and it is probable that in the markets of bygone years they were in fact adequate for most valuation situations, producing results within a tolerable margin of error.

However, one suspects that many valuers used the various methods of valuation without knowing or understanding what they were really doing, particularly with respect to the mathematical concepts involved. Valuation methods and valuation tables were often, if not regularly, used primarily because the valuer had learnt to use them as a student; habits had been cast in a die to be followed by a lifetime of hardening. Indeed, at a London conference in the early 1970s a senior partner of a leading national firm ridiculed the idea that discounted cash flow techniques had anything to do with valuation despite the fact that Present Value of £1 tables and Years' Purchase tables – regularly used by valuers for many generations – are in reality discount tables.

Again, in 1972 there was extensive correspondence in the United Kingdom published *Estates Gazette* on Discounted Cash Flow Analysis in which the view was expressed that 'nowhere has its practical application to valuation practice (in the widest possible sense) been demonstrated by reference to market transactions. Until it is so demonstrated it is right to question it'. It was also suggested that the topics covered in education for the profession should involve concentration on 'those subjects with which the surveyor is most directly concerned in his practice'. On the face of it this may be acceptable, but only if the treatment of such subjects encourages a thoughtful and enquiring approach from students and those who practice in the profession. The first statement might also be acceptable if the surveyor in question was a thinking person, ever desirous of developing his or her professional expertise.

It is difficult to believe these views were expressed so recently, particularly when one realises that valuers have been discounting cash flows as their basic valuation approach for a very long time, albeit using a somewhat simple version of the approach frequently used today. The fact that modern discounted cash flow calculations, which are in fact usually a more elaborate version of the tried and trusted investment valuation, were recently considered revolutionary and unacceptable is a reflection both on the valuation profession and property education in the past. One suspects that in the past some education concentrated on passing on to students a traditional body of knowledge, without encouraging them to think and reason, or even sometimes to question convention. It is arguable that in the past much education has been so fundamental as to be inadequate for a true profession, although possibly adequate enough to permit survival in the market place in periods of market calm.

It is to be hoped that property education today, whilst still passing on appropriate knowledge, also develops those other qualities, and regularly reviews the relevance of the knowledge it passes on. If it does not those in education are failing their profession and, more importantly, their students.

It is interesting to consider whether in the recent past the valuation profession has been a thinking profession, and if so what the result has been. There have certainly been substantial changes in attitudes in recent years, and Discounted Cash Flow Analysis is now generally accepted and regularly used. What can have brought about such a change?

The property boom and subsequent crash of the 1970s, and other subsequent booms and crashes, definitely made the property professions aware of the need for high levels of education and expertise if practising professionals were both to survive in financial terms and to avoid situations in which their professional competence would be questioned. The advent to the investment market in a very significant way of the large financial institutions has been another important factor in the valuation scene, and has emphasised the need for valuers to develop high standards of valuation practice and analytical skills.

The main feature of the early 1970s was the apparently large fortunes made, often by relatively new investors and firms. Many of them appeared to pay unjustifiably large figures for property interests, such prices apparently being vindicated by means of discounted cash flow analyses which revealed large internal rates of return. Interest liabilities were often 'rolled up' – that is payment was deferred – for a number of years, this practice being justified by the eventual fortunes that would be made as a result of predicted large future rental growth. In the event, for many investors, and for a variety of reasons such as high international interest rates, the crash came before rental growth eventuated, and many of these new investors with their supposed new valuation methods went to the wall. Most of those who had stuck to the tried and trusted conventional approaches survived the crisis, and it was easy to blame the failures on the use of 'new techniques' and to imagine that those who survived did so because they rejected them.

A closer inspection of the facts would probably have revealed that it was not so much the 'new techniques' which caused the difficulties to their users, but a lack of expertise – or even carefree abandon in a number of instances – in the way these approaches were used. Those who survived the troubled times probably did so because they only purchased after careful analysis and consideration of past transactions, and because they gave full consideration to all aspects of their valuations. Such consideration would have included assessment of the validity of the various inputs and of the results, so emphasising the need for and benefit of careful thought. Some, of course, may have survived simply because they were operating within their own limitations, which may in itself be evidence of commendable thought and sensible policies. Similarly, those who failed may have done so not because of the valuation methods they used, but because of a failure to apply them sensibly. There is little doubt, however, that the thoughtful professional stands a very good chance of being successful, irrespective of the appraisal methods used, for he or she will carefully consider every stage of every valuation they undertake.

It is possible that some encountered problems in the 1970s because there had been too much change in approaches in too short a period of time. That may have been the case, although it is difficult to consider the changes of that period as having been substantial. However, the problems of that period would only emphasize the need for a thoughtful approach, whilst in any case change should only take place after thought, which change should also be accompanied by thoughtful implementation.

Discounted Cash Flow formats for valuation are certainly very much in vogue today, and it is appropriate that they should be. However, one suspects that their adoption by many in the valuation profession results largely from force of circumstances and the fear that remunerative investment valuation work might otherwise be monopolised by the accountancy and other professions. This development has been welcome, although it is not always apparent that those using such approaches fully understand them, or that they necessarily appreciate the considerations relevant to their use. In short, it is not clear that their application is always by thinking persons; in reality the more complex the techniques, the more need there is for thinking people to apply them. It is also a little disappointing that their adoption over recent years probably results more from commercial pressures and the desire to survive in the market place than from the natural development of a thinking profession.

Another feature of the past 30 years or so has been the significant number of cases in which valuers have been successfully sued for professional negligence. In some cases very large sums of money have been awarded in damages, and it is therefore even more expedient for every valuer to examine his or her habits and to adopt a particularly attentive approach to any valuation task. Negligence frequently results from nothing more than a lack of thought or from carelessness, and the rising incidence of claims against professional people in general is perhaps evidence that the public may in some cases be more thoughtful than some professional advisers.

The valuation profession may not necessarily be to blame for what some may see as its imperfections. It may be that the public does not in general want sophisticated and progressive techniques and is not prepared to pay for them, and perhaps the ultimate test is the market place. Perhaps in the majority of transactions the average valuer using simple, traditional techniques can get as near to an acceptable answer, and an appropriate answer, as anyone. Valuers in the residential property market in particular generally appear to operate with an acceptable degree of accuracy for most clients, and this may be a situation in which good habits usually result in an acceptable level of service being provided.

But is that enough? Is it sufficient for the professional person simply to try to satisfy the consumer? Perhaps he or she should do more, even to the extent of trying to educate the consumer, where necessary, even at the expense of his or her own commercial objectives.

Mr Richard Luff, the then President of the Royal Institution of Chartered Surveyors, said in his Presidential Address as long ago as November, 1982

> 'I believe that the real test of a profession is the maintenance of an outward-looking view, with its first priority a strong commitment to the ethics of confidentiality, integrity and a high sense of public responsibility.'

There is little doubt that professional integrity and a high sense of public responsibility demand that we should not simply operate through habit. Mr Luff continued

> 'what is required is not blind opposition to progress, but opposition to blind progress.' 'As an Institution we have sometimes been slow to gear ourselves up to new challenges.'

Mr Luff was well aware of the professional pressures and needs at that time, and there is no doubt that since then there have been great challenges for all professional people in a rapidly developing world.

Professional people should always seek standards of excellence, and this must involve a constant quest for improved methods. It is certainly not always evident that this has happened in the past as Mr Luff seemed to imply in 1982.

There are many who were convinced that but for the high rate of inflation in the period 1965–1980 in particular, there would have been many more successful claims of professional negligence against valuers. Had inflation indices (or property value indices) been applied to many valuations done in the period 1960–1980 the results might well have revealed quite reckless approaches by some valuers, and valuations which would have been very difficult to justify at the time they were made. Certainly, there were probably many valuers who, but for inflation, might have had many restless nights. The only basis for many valuations was probably little more than the opinions of the valuer, frequently unsubstantiated by any rational and systematic analysis of market transactions or of underlying market and economic conditions.

The attitude of some valuers to research has in the past suggested that some did not even appreciate the need for it or its usefulness to the valuer, although it is hoped that such attitudes are no longer widely held. Much research is highly desirable in that it should enable valuations to be based on better informed opinions. Well directed research of past transactions and markets should be regarded as essential because it should enable a professional valuer to determine current levels of value and variations in value, the factors which have affected value, and trends in value. The thoughtful application of the results of well directed valuation research must assist the competent professional to perform better.

Most larger valuation firms now have research departments, hopefully because they appreciate that good research can easily be justified by commercial organisations in that, by enabling them to perform better, their reputations are likely to be enhanced thereby giving them the edge in the market place together with improved financial returns. However, it ought to be obvious to valuers that their performance should benefit from the existence of data which has been systematically analysed – always assuming there is evidence to analyse – whilst it should result in a reduction in the number of items on which arbitrary decisions have to be made. Accordingly, sound research should provide a basis for better informed judgements. Despite this, the author has encountered situations in which this has not been perceived as a benefit of research, the firm undertaking the research merely seeing the objective of their research efforts as being to produce attractive, glossy brochures with which to market their name to potential clients.

Many smaller firms may find it difficult, both in practical terms and financial terms, to devote resources to research, but that does not mean that the benefits of research must be lost to them. There is scope for a professional organization to arrange 'pooled research' without infringing any confidentialities, and each contributing firm could become involved for a relatively small cost. Such arrangements could be set up on a national or regional basis, or locally through the co-operative efforts of a number of firms.

Over the past 25 years or so there has been a lot of thought given to the compilation of valuation standards by various professional organisations in a considerable number of countries, the standards agreed being the result of long and careful thought by many practising professionals, particularly valuers and accountants. They are bringing about a greater standardisation of practices within the profession, greater conformity with the practices of other professions such as the accountancy profession, and greater standardisation between the practices used in different countries. Such developments are highly commendable, but there is the fear that the existence of standards and guidelines might be used as an excuse by some valuers for blindly following them at all times, so excluding the application of careful thought.

It is pertinent to ask the question 'are valuers any worse than other professions?'. Many developments have taken a long time to happen, but in the early years of the 20th century valuers adopted dual rate years' purchase valuation tables, whilst after the Second World War the preachings of such people as the late Jack Rose resulted in the adoption and use by valuers of valuation tables adjusted to allow for the effects of income tax on rental income and sinking funds. More recently modern discounted cash flow approaches have been adopted. Things have happened, albeit slowly, but perhaps that is true of other professions also. The introduction of current cost accounting methods was not a particularly easy process in the accountancy world, but this approach is now in common use.

However, the fact that valuers may be no worse than other professional men should not deter them from wanting to improve. The general quality of service and advice from valuers must be very much dependent upon the quality of thought in the profession, and professional men and women should constantly seek to improve their standards and the quality of service provided by them. The constant search for improvement and the quest for ever higher standards of excellence should be the hallmark of the professional person. Although old habits die hard, if they are inappropriate to the modern situation then die they must. To encourage greater thought within the profession should be, and is, an important role for the academic sector. The very imprecision of the valuation of interests in property and the subjective nature of many of the judgements which have to be made, make it all the more important for the profession to be a thoughtful, enquiring and reasoning profession.

Should some of the above observations appear unduly critical, it should be remembered that criticism itself is a marvellous stimulus to improvement. It should also be remembered, that with only slight amendment many of the above observations could be applied to a number of professional groups.

Chapter 8

The Operation of Property Markets

Consideration of what actually happens in property markets should give an indication of the way in which property professionals operate in the real world and of the situations and problems they are likely to encounter. In earlier chapters reference was made to a number of property market considerations in the 1960s and 1970s, and it may be enlightening to consider some of the events of the period from 1980 through to 1992. This was a time of considerable activity in property markets world-wide, and in a number of major markets there were periods of depressed demand and limited development and investment activity, interspersed with upswings in property markets. A significant boom period in the late 1980s was followed by the almost inevitable 'bust' at the end of the decade through into the 1990s. So big was the 'bust' in some property markets that it has taken them to the present day to return to their previous levels of stability, whilst in some sectors the levels of rent achieved in the late 1980s have not yet been bettered, despite the passage of time.

The level of demand for property is extremely dependent upon the general state of an economy, be it local or national, whilst the value of an individual property is very much a function of the overall level of demand and the utility of the particular property to would-be users. The level of economic activity, and more particularly the trends in an economy, are therefore critical determinants of the level of activity and values (and trends in values) in property markets. Events in the 1980s might suggest these factors were not generally given enough consideration in the past by many valuers. Macro-economic conditions and trends at both international and national levels can have a significant effect on local property market activity and consequently on local property values, a fact which events of the late 1980s and the early 1990s should have brought home to many who previously might not have accepted such a proposition.

If, as a result of events in the property markets of the 1980s, the valuation profession in general learnt that property markets do not operate in isolation from the general economy but are part of that economy and are affected by events in it, then some benefits will have resulted from the traumatic happenings in the property markets of that period.

A case study of events in the Sydney property market reveals many similarities with property markets in other major cities both in Australia and in other developed countries, there being considerable similarity in events in markets world-wide during that period. Property transactions do not take place in a centralised market place, there being a series of local property markets, each local market in turn operating as a number of sub-markets dealing with specific classes of property, such as offices, retail properties or residential properties. Despite the existence of these different markets, events in the Sydney Central Business District (CBD) Office Market during the period under consideration provide a picture of events which was mirrored in most other Australian property markets over the same period, with only minor variations in emphasis occurring from market to market.

The similarity in events within the different property markets emphasises the dependency of property market activity and property values on general national and international economic factors. Whilst the property markets of large cities are generally, by virtue of the distances between them, quite separate markets, they are subject to the same external influences and are dependent upon financial institutions many of which operate on a world-wide scale. It is not surprising, therefore, that there was a marked similarity in the general course of events in property markets throughout Australia during the 1980s, whilst events in city markets in other countries, particularly the United Kingdom and the USA, were remarkably similar.

Consideration of the Australian economy in the 1980s reveals that growth in the Gross Domestic Product varied considerably from year to year, with growth of about 5% in 1980 being followed by 2% growth in 1981 and a figure of –1% in 1984. At no time after 1980 did the rate of growth in Gross Domestic Product reach 3%, whilst for much of the time it was at or below 1%. Similarly, consideration of the Gross National Product per capita figures for Australia reveals that whilst in 1950 Australia was fourth in the world behind the USA, Canada and Switzerland, by 1987 it was only the ninth richest economy in the world in per capita terms, whilst by 1992 it had slipped to thirteenth.

In the period 1970 to 1980 the seasonally adjusted figures for unemployment had for much of the time been below 5% and had at the worst only risen to about 6%. However, in the 1980s the picture was quite different with the rate consistently remaining above 5% and exceeding 10% in the early 1980s and likewise at the end of the decade. Although the high level of unemployment resulted in part from the fact that the population was increasing throughout this period, it was a disturbing fact that the level was consistently above 5% which should perhaps have counselled caution to such as property developers, particularly when considered in conjunction with the national productivity statistics.

During the 1980s there were also uncomfortably high levels of inflation and for most of the time very high annual balance of payments deficits, so high in fact that Australia subsequently had to devote much of its earnings to funding the accumulated overseas debt.

During this period there were therefore indications of problems in the economy with, if anything, a generally adverse trend in a number of important economic indicators. Overall there appeared to be a lack of a sufficiently positive trend in any of the main indicators to support many of the ambitious property development decisions which were made in the 1980s.

There was during the second half of the decade a very active development market in Sydney, so active that when the recession and eventual depression of the period 1990 to 1992 occurred, an extremely large stock of new office developments (and other types of property) existed in various stages of development from the drawing board to completed and ready to let. The advent of the recession resulted in many planned or partially completed schemes being suspended, whilst many of those which were already completed became either unlettable or lettable only at very much lower rents than were originally anticipated. As a result there were numerous bankruptcies of developers, investors, and speculators, whilst banks and other lending institutions were left holding property loans which often exceeded the values of the properties on which the loans were secured.

In retrospect it appears difficult to understand how such a situation could have occurred. It is probable that in part at least it was attributable to the limited availability in most property markets of reliable market information. This state of affairs was exacerbated by the practice of inserting confidentiality clauses in many contracts to ensure that details of the contract arrangements did not become widely known. Additionally, the long time required to conceive and complete new property developments was probably also a contributory factor.

It would also appear that many developments are planned without the developer being fully aware of other planned developments which will compete with his or her own scheme, although it is suspected that well directed research would in fact reveal a reasonably helpful level of information on such matters. It is possible that, rather than lacking information of this nature, many developers do not pay sufficient regard to its significance, relying rather on an almost blind faith in the quality of their own proposed development and its ability to succeed in the market however strong the competition might be.

This optimism was probably built into many of the appraisals which were done for prospective developments, the use of discounted cash flow layouts and computer technology enabling complex valuations to be produced which incorporated estimations of such things as rental growth for many years into the future, as many as 20 years in some cases. There is little doubt that in some cases many of the growth predictions used by developers and their advisers were extremely optimistic, and it is suspected that some of the inputs to such valuations were used to support the optimism of the developer rather than to test the soundness of the proposed scheme. It is also likely that many projections included annual rental growth much in excess of that which could be supported by any economic indicators. Moreover, it is also probable that a review of the past performance of similar properties would have cast doubt on the likelihood of predicted rental growth being achieved.

A very significant factor in the development boom which occurred in the late 1980s was the lead time needed to plan and develop a modern scheme. A time period of five to six years is quite common, whilst the apparently ever increasing size of modern developments has tended to exacerbate this problem. Similarly, the great size of many developments has created a situation in which the costs incurred in the planning stages are so great and the development period so long, that once construction is started it is often not practicable to suspend work even though market conditions may change dramatically during the development period. It is also extremely difficult, if not impossible, to accurately predict the condition of the economy and property markets at the time a completed development is likely actually to be placed on the market.

The depressed years of the 1970s resulted in there being only limited development activity during that period and through into the first half of the 1980s, and the eventual result was that by the early 1980s the vacancy rate (that is the percentage of unoccupied accommodation) in the Sydney CBD was down to about 2.5% of the total CBD office stock. This is generally considered to be a low vacancy rate and is such that prospective developers are likely to be persuaded that there is in reality an unsatisfied demand for accommodation, to the extent that they are likely to commence new developments. In the event, from the relatively low level of building commencements from 1976 through to 1983, there was a marked increase in the annual number of building commencements from 1984 to the end of the decade. With a construction period which would quite often be about three years and sometimes even longer, buildings commenced in the mid 1980s did not in fact reach the market until the late 1980s, whilst those commenced in the late 1980s had in some cases not been completed by 1992.

The relative inactivity in the development sector in the period 1976 to 1983 had helped to create these low vacancy rates, which in turn led to increasing rental levels by the mid 1980s and increased confidence among and increased competition between property investors. With a relatively static supply of properties, market values increased and provided the stimulus to developers to increase the supply of developments.

Development activity was in fact further stimulated by the overnight stock market collapse of 19 October 1987, the reaction of many investors to that collapse being to transfer their investment activity to property markets, there appearing to be an almost blind faith amongst many that it is impossible to lose in property investment. Activity in the property investment and development markets was assisted by an apparently similar belief amongst lending institutions which lent generously for such activities, often to the extent that developers and investors had to put very little of their own funds into their schemes and investments. In situations in which lenders had accepted optimistic development valuations and had lent a high percentage of such valuations, developers might in fact have had none of their own funds at risk, whilst in some cases the funds lent exceeded the true values of developments even before the slump came. With only limited amounts of their own funds at stake developers were, it is suspected, tempted to venture into projects which they may well have considered too risky had more of their own funds been at stake, and many lenders were to rue their actions in lending so generously when 'the bottom dropped out' of the property market at the end of the decade.

A factor which caused many lending institutions to lend so generously to many developers and over generously to some was undoubtedly the deregulation of the financial sector by the Australian Government in 1985. Increased competition resulted between lenders, and it is almost certain that the desire of lenders to both retain and increase their market share was a factor in at least some of their lending decisions. Their desire at that time to make their mark in the competitive market must subsequently have been regretted by many. It is interesting that in 2003 there again appears to be a cult amongst financial institutions of generous lending for property development. Time alone will tell whether with the passage of time current generosities will prove to have been ill advised.

As observed earlier, it appears that developers and investors did not pay sufficient heed to the lack of any really positive economic indicators in the Australian economy, whilst few forecasters in Australia or elsewhere foresaw the very significant and almost world-wide recession (which in some countries was of depression proportions) which was to occur from about 1989. A combination of the perhaps over optimistic attitudes of investors and developers, their failure to adequately consider the significance of general economic factors, the trend towards very large development schemes, the apparent ease with which finance could be obtained from lending institutions, the reliance of many schemes upon highly geared financial arrangements (that is a high percentage of borrowed funds), and the excusable inability to foresee the impending and significant world economic slump, were significant elements in the collapse of Australian property markets which occurred at the end of the decade.

The results of that collapse were:

(i)   a surplus of available property with few potential occupiers and resultant greatly reduced rental levels and high vacancy rates in most types of property;

(ii) drastically reduced capital values which resulted from a number of factors including lower rents, higher capitalisation rates caused by reduced investor confidence, and reduced competition amongst investors;

(iii) the bankruptcy of numerous entrepreneurs and companies caused by the collapse of property values;

(iv) the recall by banks and other lending institutions of loans against property investments and developments where recall was practicable, and their not unnatural reluctance to be further involved in property funding; and

(v) the abandonment or suspension of many planned or partially completed developments.

All of these factors created property market scenarios which were a far cry from the heady days of the boom period of 1988 in particular. Some of the leading lending institutions actually became major property owners, a rôle they never envisaged for themselves but one which circumstances forced upon them when they were forced to take possession of properties against which bad loans had been secured.

Faced with situations in which mortgagors were often not only unable to make periodic repayments of capital but also unable to pay interest charges when due, the sale of mortgaged properties was in many cases impractical because of the absence of potential buyers, or at least buyers at what were considered acceptable prices. In fact the absence of buyers in part resulted from a change of attitudes on the part of the lending institutions which, having burnt their fingers very badly with much of their previous over generous property lending, became so opposed to making further loans for property investment that they themselves played a part in restricting the number of potential purchasers in the market, so exacerbating the market situation.

From having been almost everyone's favourite investment medium, property (possibly with the exception of the family home) became a dirty word in many quarters. The poor world economic conditions resulted in poor industrial and commercial prospects which restricted the number of potential tenants, the restricted demand coupled with the glut of property on the market in turn creating a very depressed scene with low capital values. Indeed, so great was the fall in capital values that the market values of some modern buildings were only about half the equivalent cost of developing a suitable replacement.

The outcome of such a situation is inevitably the virtual cessation of development activity which, with the passage of time and revived economies, almost inevitably leads at a later date to a shortage of property once the existing surplus of the slump has been disposed of or leased. Amongst the difficulties facing the valuer and the property consultant in such circumstances are those of predicting exactly when market conditions will improve, to what levels values will in due course rise, and how rapidly they will rise. At the time many commentators predicted that it would take as long as 10 years for the 1992 surpluses of commercial accommodation in

Sydney to be let, whilst few were predicting less than five years for this to occur. This difference of opinion amongst specialists of about five years is itself of major significance, as with a minimum development period of about five years needed for most modern developments, a five year error in the commencement of future new developments could in due course help to contribute to a future shortage of accommodation or another surplus in supply.

Another result of the market collapse was that there were in 1992 and subsequently many very inefficient property investments. Many developments which were commenced at a time of rising rents and rising capital values, actually came to the market when rental values had collapsed. Potential tenants were scarce and were only prepared to pay very much lower rents than originally anticipated by the developers and investors. Indeed, not only did many investors have to accept low rents to obtain tenants, in many cases they also had to make other concessions to those tenants. Such 'market inducements' included giving periods of rent free occupation often of several years duration, generous fitting out allowances for the new accommodation, and even the purchase of tenants' interests in their old accommodation, following which the landlord of the newly let property was left with the problem of disposing of the premises to which their new tenants were previously committed. This was a far cry from the market scenario in which most of the new developments had been planned.

Inevitably such happenings left some developers with reduced or even no income from developments, whilst capital values were regularly far lower than anticipated both because of the low income flow and the absence of potential investment purchasers. Indeed, there were so many unknowns in the market that it was often quite impossible for valuers to determine whether there were any potential purchasers at all for properties, let alone to make realistic estimates of what the market value for a particular property interest might be.

Events in many other major property markets in other countries during the same time period were very similar to those in Sydney, this emphasizing the importance of international economic financial considerations.

Subsequent to the market problems outlined above, it was in fact approaching 10 years before the Sydney CBD market returned to a situation in which supply and demand for office accommodation was approximately in balance, albeit with vacancy rates in the region of 5%. In the intervening period there was for some time a depressed market with rental levels achieved being substantially lower than those of the boom. Some earlier development proposals were abandoned altogether, others were modified and commenced at a later date, whilst some developers sought to counter the surfeit of office accommodation by converting office blocks to residential apartments, a process which was also applied to some surplus hotel accommodation. The sequel to this is that at the time of writing (January, 2003) some analysts predict that there is likely to be pressure on the prices of an already oversupplied CBD apartment market, with a further 4,000 residential apartments to be completed in the next financial year in the Sydney CBD!

The problems for the valuation profession

One of the unfortunate outcomes of the problems described above was that valuers were frequently accused of being incompetent, and in many cases they were often blamed for having over valued development properties, thus causing developments and property investments to occur which later proved to have been unwise and to have produced losses. Many commentators with the benefit of hindsight expected valuers to have predicted the recession which others failed to foresee, whilst some even held them to be major contributory factors to the recession. Whilst it is unreasonable to place all the blame for some of the financially disastrous developments which took place on valuers, it is strongly suspected that there were valuers who were too ready to be influenced by the desires of their developer clients to the extent that over optimistic valuations were produced to facilitate the acquisition of loan funds.

The valuation of development properties is an extremely complex activity, and a wide range of apparently acceptable valuations can be produced for any one development project dependent upon the choice of variables made by the valuer. This matter is fully discussed in *Property Development* by AF Millington (Estates Gazette, London 2000). In retrospect, in many cases it will probably be impossible to reliably assess whether valuers actually over valued many of the development schemes of this period, or whether developers chose to operate on the basis that the most optimistic market scenario would indeed eventuate.

Whatever else may have happened, the property market collapse focussed attention on the role of the valuer and identified a number of major problems for valuers and the valuation profession to consider in the future. Amongst these factors and problems are:

1.   The difficulties caused when there is only limited availability of reliable market information, particularly at times when there is either limited market activity or when major changes have occurred in the market;

2.   The determination of the appropriate method of valuation for specific valuation situations and the correct application of each method;

3.   The need for consistency in the application of valuation principles and methods, particularly when valuations are to be made for asset valuation purposes, and also when valuations are made using evidence obtained from the analysis of market transactions;

4.   The implications of modern computing techniques and the application of discounted cash flow approaches to valuation;

5.   The growth of international property investment and the implications of the same;

6   The problems of valuing properties subject to unusual leasing arrangements, for example where inducements have been given to tenants or where there are turnover rents;

7   The problems of valuing very large property developments for which there is likely to be only a very limited number of possible purchasers, and possibly none at any specific point in time;

8.   The problems caused by the development of new 'vehicles' for property ownership and property investment;

9.   The valuation problems caused by the increased environmental awareness of society and by such specific problems as contaminated (or poisoned) sites;

10.   The need for valuers to take macro-economic considerations into account in addition to local considerations.

Each of the above factors needs careful consideration by the valuation profession if useful lessons are to be learned from past problems in the market and if valuers are to avoid in the future some of the criticism (often unjustified) which has been levelled at them in the past. These matters are considered further in *An Introduction to Property Valuation* by AF Millington (Estates Gazette, London, 2000).

The world changes constantly and many changes occur very rapidly, so it is also necessary for valuers to consider the relevance of past practices which may have only a limited role to play in the future, even though their wider use may have been quite acceptable in the past. It may also be the case that a number of fundamental valuation principles may need to be more keenly observed in the future if some of the problems experienced in the 1980s and 1990s are not to recur.

Chapter 9

Conventional Valuation Methods and Modern Valuation Problems

Background observations

Conventional valuation methods are regularly criticized as being inappropriate for current needs, and, as earlier observed, critics often blame their use as being responsible for valuations which have proved with the passage of time to have been inaccurate or misleading. Each time there is a slump in property values, which inevitably results in some property owners losing money, at least in paper terms and often in real terms if they actually sell property, there are those who seem ready to blame the use of conventional valuation methods for many of the problems that have arisen.

Accordingly it is pertinent to briefly consider those methods and to try to relate them and the conventional underlying principles of valuation to modern day circumstances and requirements. It is also appropriate to consider the specific problems which modern day valuers have to address when using conventional methods. Some of these considerations are necessary because of relatively recent developments, as a result of which there is limited experience in dealing with them in the valuation process, the valuer therefore having to work from basic principles and to use good judgement.

As observed in the previous chapter, in recessionary periods in particular there has frequently been considerable criticism levelled at valuers and valuation methods, with many seeking to blame valuers for some of the disastrous investment and development decisions made in many of the major centres of the world. It is suspected that much of the criticism has been made by those seeking to find scapegoats for their own mistakes, but it is only realistic to accept that almost certainly there have been some valuers who have been far from blameless, and who have operated in a way which has brought the entire real estate valuation profession into disrepute.

Valuation methods also have not escaped criticism and there is in many quarters a continuing debate on the relevance of the investment (or capitalisation) method of valuation, it being strongly argued by many that it should be replaced by use of discounted cash flow approaches. However, any shortcomings in the quality of results obtained by valuers may not be so much a function of the inadequacy of the methods used by them, but more a function of inadequacies in the way those methods are understood – or not understood – and in the way they have been implemented by some valuers.

It should not be forgotten that most of the conventional methods have stood the test of time in the valuation tasks for which they are appropriate, but it should also be acknowledged that great care is needed in the selection of the appropriate method, in the background research for each valuation situation, and in the analytical and judgemental processes involved in undertaking each valuation.

The investigative stages of a valuation are the critical stages of the whole valuation process, and the quality of information obtained in those stages will to a large extent determine the quality of the results obtained, whatever the valuation method that may be adopted. The quality of the valuer's judgement is also critical, whilst the need for thorough and exhaustive research before a valuation is made cannot be over-emphasized, neither can the need for thorough analysis of the information found, and for well-informed and careful judgement by the valuer in the use of all available information.

Whilst discussion here will be restricted to a consideration of market value only, which can be defined as 'the sum obtainable from a willing purchaser when a property interest is offered for sale by a willing vendor', it should be stressed that a valuer should always determine exactly what the purpose of a valuation is and on what basis an interest has to be valued when undertaking a specific task, as it is not always market value as defined above which has to be determined.

It is appropriate to briefly consider each of the conventional methods of valuation and to highlight some of the problems likely to be encountered in their use. For fuller consideration of these methods reference can be made to *An Introduction to Property Valuation* by AF Millington (Estates Gazette, London, 2000).

The comparative method of valuation

There are valuers who argue that there is really only one method of valuation in that all methods entail, at some stage, comparison with previous market transactions, the entire basis of valuation therefore being comparison, whatever the method the valuer actually adopts in any given situation. It is almost certainly the most commonly used method of valuation and is based on the use of any available evidence of sales of similar property interests to that being valued, the underlying concept being that if one person (or a number of people) have paid a certain figure for a property interest, then a similar figure is likely to be obtained on the subsequent sale of another similar property interest. In theory the method is simple to use, but in practice it is often far from simple as the assumption is not so readily applicable to interests in property as it is to products such as boxes of matches, or blocks of cheese or butter.

The valuer has to adjust available evidence to allow for differences between the properties previously sold and the property to be valued in respect of such things as quality of location, the size of the accommodation, the quality of the accommodation, the state of repair, and, more particularly, allowances have to be made for changes that have occurred in the market with the passage of time. The method can therefore be most easily used when there are frequent sales of similar interests in similar properties, when there are no significant differences in locational quality, when values and economic conditions are stable over the period in which transactions occur, and when the circumstances of the vendors and purchasers do not lead to distortions in any of the transactions. Whereas in past periods of time these conditions may often have applied, in more recent years it has frequently been rare for them to apply for anything other than a relatively short period of time, as a result of which each apparently comparable transaction has to be very carefully investigated to determine if it is indeed comparable enough to be used as evidence for the current valuation task.

It was suggested in Chapter 8 that in the past many valuers paid little (or even no) attention to macro economic factors as determinants of value, and it is probable that some development and property investment catastrophes have resulted from inadequate attention to such considerations by either valuers or investors, or both. In using the comparative method (and other valuation methods also), the valuer has to be fully aware of such things as the level of and trends in interest rates, gross national product details, levels of employment and unemployment, savings and investment levels and patterns, and the balance of payments situation. All of these are critical economic indicators from which an opinion of future likely market conditions can be formed, and it should never be forgotten that a valuer's task is to assess present and future value, not past value.

This is possibly the biggest difficulty in applying the comparative method of valuation as all the evidence indicates what happened in the past, which is not necessarily an indication of what will happen today or tomorrow, so rapidly does the modern world change. The valuer must therefore resist developing a blind faith in the power of comparable evidence, and must carefully assess which evidence, if any, is in fact a reliable indication of what is likely to be paid in the market today or tomorrow. A whole range of developments including the introduction of new laws, variations in interest rates, occurrences of international significance in other countries, can all significantly affect even the values of quite humble local properties if they affect the ability of individuals and organizations to raise money or their willingness to commit money. Consequently, although property changes hands to a large extent in a series of local markets and sub-markets, a thorough understanding of the implications of national and international factors on those markets is an essential part of the valuer's armoury.

Evidence of comparative sales remains one of the most useful sources of background information available to the valuer when it exists, and the above observations should not be taken as criticism of its relevance or of the comparative method of valuation. However, the need for intensive research, careful inspection and analysis of available evidence, thorough and up to date knowledge of local, national and international economic factors, and a very careful process of decision making in the use of the method, cannot be over-emphasized. The modern world is so complex that it is no longer possible to assume that evidence of past transactions indicates that similar transactions are likely to recur in the market place. The valuer should only decide that this is likely to happen after close and careful consideration of all the circumstances, including the factors referred to above.

Clearly, the collection and storage of available evidence is an important part of a valuer's activities, and modern computer facilities assist both the storage and recall of market data. Wherever data may be obtained from, it is important to verify its accuracy and to add as much reliable additional information as can be obtained if a data bank is to be as full and reliable a source of information as can possibly be accumulated. Because much available evidence is frequently limited in detail, the search for further reliable details is often an important process before comparable evidence can be used with justified confidence.

The Investment (or Capitalisation) Method of Valuation and the Discounted Cash Flow Approach

The Investment Method is based on the concept that the capital value of an interest in property is related to its income producing capacity, the valuation procedure entailing the estimation of future net income flows which are then capitalised to produce the present day capital value of the interest.

In brief, the approach to the valuation is:

	Gross annual rental income
Less	Outgoings necessary to maintain that rental
	Net annual rental income
	Appropriate Multiplier
Equals	*Capital Value of the Interest*

It has been traditional in the past for the appropriate multiplier (or capitalisation factor) to be obtained by comparison with multipliers used (or thought to have been used) by investors who have previously purchased other similar property interests, the multipliers being directly related to the yield (or rate of return) required from specific types of property by investors.

The method entails discounting predicted future income flows to present values, and in this respect the method is a discounted cash flow technique. The Discounted Cash Flow (DCF) approach consequently is not a new valuation approach, as valuers have been utilising the technique for many years, but what is relatively new is the ability to easily incorporate a wide number of variables and a large number of different time periods in the calculations. This has been made possible by the incredible calculation facilities provided by modern computers which now enable calculations which would previously have taken several hours to be completed in a matter of minutes. A DCF approach is, however, based on exactly the same basic principle as the investment or capitalisation approach, being merely a development of that method.

Each approach has its place, and in circumstances in which limited information is available and the valuation situation is uncomplicated the investment approach may still be the most appropriate method to use and may produce very reliable results. It is a case of the valuer needing to use good judgement to decide the most appropriate approach and then to use that approach with skill.

A DCF format is more appropriate where there is good evidence of a number of variables which are likely to affect future net income flows and where they can be incorporated in the valuation in a way which improves the quality and reliability of the result in comparison to that which could be obtained by use of the investment approach (capitalisation). The quality of the result obtained will only be as good as the quality of the variables incorporated in the calculations, and so the very careful investigation of all inputs is essential.

There is no doubt that many properties are now so large, possibly with a large number of different lessees each with different lease terms (for example a large shopping centre), that the valuation of such interests is ideally suited to use of a discounted cash flow format. In such a case the investment valuation format would be far less versatile, more difficult to use, and probably less likely to produce the most reliable result. In a similar way, the valuation of a development site for a large development project may also lend itself to use of a DCF format.

Both with the investment valuation (or capitalisation) approach and the DCF approach the results obtained will only be reliable if the method is used in appropriate circumstances and if the user is skilful. There are occasions when the use of a DCF approach is positively dangerous, particularly if use of the approach encourages the valuer to incorporate variables for which reasonably reliable estimates cannot be made. Just as a 1,000 cc Grand Prix motorcycle would be positively dangerous when used in rush hour by a novice and unskilled rider, so there are circumstances in which use of complex DCF approaches may be equally as dangerous.

In both the capitalisation and DCF approaches the quality of the inputs will determine the quality of the answer, and it is again critical that exacting research is done by the valuer. This is made doubly important by the fact that in recent years certain developments and changes have made the task of the valuer in estimating the value of investment properties very much more difficult than was the case in earlier years. Modern day complications include the very large size of many modern property developments in both physical and monetary terms; the varying needs of a number of large and important property investors; the wide range of lease terms now used in the leasing market; the considerable activity of international investors in some markets; and the 'knock-on' effect of the large over-supply of many types of accommodation which has frequently existed in some markets.

The Contractors' Method of Valuation (or Summation)

This approach to valuation is based on the concept that the capital value of a property should be related to the likely cost of providing a new and suitable alternative property, the underlying logic being that no-one would pay more for an existing property than the figure for which they could develop a similar property. It is arguable that it should be used as a check in every valuation situation as it should, at least in theory, represent the top figure of value applicable to any property.

The valuation equation for this method is:

	Cost of a suitable site
Plus	Cost of construction of a suitable building.
Equals	Total Cost of providing an alternative building.
Less	Allowance for depreciation and obsolescence.
Equals	*Present Capital Value of the Property.*

The most difficult aspect of applying this method is invariably the problem of estimating the deduction to be made for depreciation and obsolescence. The depreciation deduction is in recognition of the fact that what is being valued is in fact a used, and therefore partly worn, building whereas the first two stages of the valuation equation provide the cost of a brand-new building. The obsolescence deduction would be relevant in cases where a building is no longer ideally suited for the use for which it is intended, which may result from extensive physical deterioration, the fact that it is no longer ideally suitable in economic terms, the fact that it may no longer satisfy statutory requirements, or the fact that it does not measure up to modern design requirements. Whatever the cause of obsolescence, the figure deducted should represent the expenditure which would be necessary to make the building functionally suitable again, if in fact this is a realistic possibility.

In the past this was the only method of valuation which was thought to necessitate the calculation of obsolescence allowances, but it is suggested that this is a matter which will have to be considered much more frequently in future. The rate of development of modern technology is such that installations like elevators and air conditioning systems may well need replacing after a relatively short period of years, not necessarily because they are worn out or no longer function efficiently, but because replacement is necessary to provide up to date facilities in a building to enable it to compete effectively in the market place and to enable rental values to be maintained against the competition of newer buildings fitted out with the latest and best fixtures and fittings.

Accordingly, it is suggested that the allowance at appropriate intervals for extensive and possibly expensive refitting of many buildings is likely to be an important part of the valuation process in the future, and will need to be incorporated when other methods such as the investment, DCF, or comparative approaches are used. In order to do this valuers will need to have access to reliably calculated and realistic cost estimates which will either require them being knowledgeable in such matters or utilising a specialist consultant. The assumption that in the majority of cases property values will be maintained without any expenditure on modernisation is certainly not always appropriate in today's highly competitive world.

Likewise, as the complexity of modern buildings increases, as their size gets greater, and as the degree of specialisation in their design increases either because of statutory requirements or user requirements, so the relevance of valuation using the contractors' method is likely to increase, as unless buildings are directly suitable for other potential users, considerable expenditure on adaptation works may be forced upon any purchaser. If this is the case, clearly any sensible potential purchaser would compare the available property and the trouble and cost of modernising it or adapting it, with the alternative of constructing a brand-new building, built to modern design standards and equipped with state of the art technology.

The Residual (or Hypothetical Development) Method of Valuation

This method is used for the valuation of properties in which it is thought there may be latent development value, and the objective of its use is to determine whether the value for development purposes exceeds the current use value of a property. Development or redevelopment is a likelihood if this proves to be the case. The valuation equation in this case is:

	Value of completed development
Less	Total costs of creating the development including the required development profit.

Present value of the property for development purposes.

The fundamental problems in the use of this method result from the fact that the valuer has first to estimate the value when completed of a development which at the time of valuation is nothing more than a figment of the imagination, in addition having to estimate all the research and consultancy costs, construction costs, financing costs, and marketing costs which would be involved in its creation. The difficulties of this exercise have resulted in much criticism of the method and the suggestion by some that the comparative method of valuation is a more reliable method for the valuation of development potential.

However, the use of the comparative method in such circumstances is fraught with danger. The qualities of different development sites may vary so greatly, even when they are located close to each other, that the value appropriate to one site may be a completely inappropriate guide to the value of another site. A small difference in location can create a great difference in value if one site is ideal for a particular purpose whilst another is only marginally useful for that purpose. Suitability for a purpose can also be very much affected by differences in the size, shape, and physical characteristics of sites (including geological factors), quality of access, availability of services, and the details of planning control requirements. Consequently, when differences in such matters are taken into account, market evidence of the sale of one site may in fact not be dependable evidence of value for another nearby site, even if planning control would permit a similar type of development.

Changes in the underlying economic and market factors with the passage of time can also result in otherwise comparable evidence being out of date and inappropriate, whilst the simple possibility that the purchaser of a similar site at an earlier date may have made a serious error and paid too much should not be overlooked. There have been many examples of this type of situation.

Despite all its uncertainties and problems, the only truly effective way to estimate the market value of a possible development site is by use of the Residual Method, but, as if the problem of accuracy in valuation was not great enough already, the vast scale of many modern development projects makes the problem even greater. It is a fact that property markets tend to move in cycles, with periods of great activity and high market prices followed by periods of depression and low prices, and the fact that many development projects are now so large that they take five years or more from conception to completion means that many which are conceived at a time of relatively strong market conditions actually reach the market during recessions.

The problem is generally not so great with small projects, but it is a fact that with large developments an extremely difficult part of the valuation exercise is predicting the state of the market at the likely date of completion of the scheme. In doing this in the past, as suggested earlier, it is probable that many valuers and developers paid far too little heed in their valuations to macroeconomic indicators which should give an indication of trends in an economy, whilst in addition not enough developers appear to have paid sufficient attention to the effect on market value of competing schemes. No matter how good a project may be, if there are a number of competing schemes likely to come to the market at roughly the same time, each is likely to adversely affect the success of the others. If the total market demand at the time they reach the market is less than the total new supply of accommodation the problem is likely to be even greater, and there have been many examples of this problem in many major centres in the world. It is suspected that in some centres the collapse of commercial property values in the past has sometimes been as much a function of the oversupply willingly created by a number of developers acting independently, as it has been of recessions in many economies. In undertaking a development valuation it is essential for the valuer not to look at the project in isolation, but to take into account the effect of competing schemes (even the collective effect of a number of smaller schemes) on the ultimate value of the proposed development.

The effect of new developments on existing markets

The effect on the market of new developments is not restricted to those new developments alone as they may have a ripple effect throughout the whole sub market, adversely affecting the values of what had previously appeared to be sound property investments. The oversupply of new and high quality office accommodation in some centres and the anxiety of their developers to let space has often resulted in extremely good quality accommodation becoming available on extremely favourable terms, often better than those to which lessees are already committed on older (but nevertheless good) accommodation. The result in such circumstances can be, and has been, the rush, on the first possible opportunity, of tenants from their existing accommodation to new accommodation, the developer of the new building salvaging some value at the expense of previously well established property investments.

The assumption, which has probably not unreasonably been held by some valuers in the past, that once a property investment is let to good quality tenants it is extremely likely to remain a good investment for a considerable number of years, may therefore have to be rejected by a valuer. Economic conditions can change rapidly, new developments can have a great effect on the market, and user requirements tend to change rapidly such is the speed of change in the modern world, to the extent that predicting the capital security of a property investment more than a few years ahead is extremely difficult and possibly dangerous.

It is interesting to note how low have been the yields on some prime investments in the past and to wonder whether such low yields will be acceptable to investors in the future. When 'state of the art' shopping centres and office buildings can become out of date in the period of 15 or 20 years it is suggested that the low yields which were often common in the past can only be acceptable in the future if accompanied by generous allowances in the valuation process for substantial refurbishment at regular intervals. Just as today's model of car is likely to rapidly date and become less valuable as a result of use and the introduction of more sophisticated models, so the valuer has to remember that the same is happening in the property market where the adverse effect of the new model on the existing property stock can be just as great.

The Profits (or Accounts) Method of Valuation

This method of valuation is not used frequently, normally being restricted to the valuation of properties that are used for trade and which enjoy some sort of monopoly situation which is considered to make valuation by comparison inappropriate. The method is based on the concept that the rent a would-be user would pay for the use of a property would be related to the profit earning capacity of the property for trading purposes, the valuation equation being:

	Gross Takings from Business
Less	Cost of Stock
Equals	Gross Profits
Less	Trading Expenses
Equals	Net Profits
Less	Allowances for Interest on Capital Employed, Salary of Trader, and Allowance for Risk.
Equals	*Balance available for the costs of property occupation.*

Although this method is used only infrequently by most valuers, it is a very important concept as it indicates the position of property rent in a trader's calculations, and indeed stresses the fact that to a trader rent is a residual sum. Even in the relatively recent past many valuers paid no regard to the trading potential of different businesses, and it was regularly assumed that because a shop let for a certain rent to an audio business, a similar shop would be equally suitable to and would command the same rent from a butcher or a greengrocer. The advent of large, purpose-built shopping centres has brought with it an awareness amongst property practitioners that the locational and accommodation needs of different types of trade are different, whilst it has also been recognized by some that the ability of different trades to pay specified levels of rent varies greatly because of differing levels of trade profits. However, there is still a need for valuers in general to pay more attention to the ability of would-be property users to pay rent or capital sums, and this will entail valuers becoming more familiar with the needs of those seeking property, their business and user requirements, and their financial capabilities. These matters will be considered more fully in Chapter 13.

In this respect the profits method of valuation could well become more widely used, with valuers making serious estimates of who is likely to want to occupy a property and what is likely to be paid in rent, rather than assuming that the last market transaction indicates what is likely to happen in the next transaction. This emphasises earlier observations about the relevance of comparable evidence, and the fact that the valuer's task is to seek to estimate what will happen today in the light of future expectations, rather than to place undue emphasis on past events.

Knowledge of the market place

Many of the observations to date have emphasised the need for the valuer to have knowledge of those in the market place as it is only by knowing who is in the market for a property, what finance they have available, what their user requirements are, and what the level of competition is, that the valuer can really operate effectively. Although this raises the problem of possible conflict of interests, it is arguable that the most effective valuer is likely to be the valuer who is also close to the marketing of real estate, that is a valuer who operates out of an establishment which is also a real estate agency. Such a valuer should have direct access to recent market evidence kept in the organization's data bank and should consequently be well informed on current market activity. Where such a situation does not exist then it is essential that valuers work hard to ensure that they 'know the market'.

This is particularly important in the investment market where there is a wide range of investors each with different resources and different investment requirements, which are likely to vary with the passage of time and with each transaction they make. Investment properties may have widely different values to different investors, and it is the task of the valuer to try to identify the most probable purchaser and the price they are likely to be prepared to pay.

However, when valuers operate out of firms which are also real estate agencies there is always likely to be the danger that conflict of interests situations may arise, with for example a valuer who is valuing for sale possibly being aware of a potential purchaser and also of their purchasing capability. There may be a temptation in such circumstances to provide a valuation which might facilitate the completion of both transactions, and it is therefore essential to ensure in such circumstances that a strictly impartial and completely objective approach is taken in all valuation work.

If the circumstances are ever such that a conflict of interests might be likely to arise, or such that others might perceive the possibility of a conflict of interests existing, the valuer should immediately inform his or her client of the circumstances, the latter then being in a position to determine whether to retain the services of the valuer or whether to employ another valuer.

The significance of international investment

In the past 20 years or so there has been a considerable increase in international property investment and purchases of property by foreign organisations are regularly reported. This can be of great benefit to a country as it releases home capital for further investment, it indicates foreign confidence in a country and its economy, it may be accompanied by foreign expertise also, and overall it may assist the further development of the home economy.

However, it should not be overlooked that foreign investors will invest because they see financial benefits in so doing and they will not necessarily have any particular allegiances to the country in which they are investing. If better returns can be obtained elsewhere or if more onerous investment restrictions are imposed on them, it is quite likely that they will divert their investment elsewhere. They will also be very much influenced by the economic situation in their own country as well as in the country of investment, being inescapably subject to at least two sets of economic forces which will be very influential in determining their future investment policies. If there are economic problems in their home economy it would not be an unnatural decision for such investors to seek to ensure that all is well on the home front first, which may result in a decision to realize their overseas investments.

It is therefore wise to realize that foreign investors may in fact leave the market almost as rapidly as they appear, and that they may do so not because of any problems with their foreign investments or with the country in which they have invested, but entirely because of their own problems elsewhere or the existence of better investment opportunities in other countries. The valuer should remain conscious of the possibility that although foreign investors may play an important part in a property market, in many cases it will be more likely that home investors will set the general and long term tone of the market.

The problem of unusual leasing arrangements

As observed earlier, in depressed markets, in order to let their properties many property owners have agreed leases which have given lessees benefits over and above normal occupational rights. New lessees have often been given lengthy rent-free periods, generous fitting-out allowances, and in some instances lessors even took over the leases of their new lessees previous accommodation.

Valuers may as a result have to value properties which have been subject to such arrangements, and if so they will have to determine whether there is a liability attached to a property which reduces its value. Where lessors have taken over leases of other property, generally the liability will be a personal liability on the part of the lessor which will not adversely affect the value of the newly let property. However, if the valuation being undertaken is for a single property owning company, such a liability may be an important consideration for the valuer to report on. As a normal precaution, valuers will need to carefully inspect the leases of properties which they are valuing to ascertain whether there are rent-free periods to take into account or financial liabilities of any other type which will necessitate a deduction from what would otherwise be the capital value of an interest.

Likewise, the relevance of rent review and break clauses in leases will take on greater significance if there are surpluses of accommodation and falling rental values. No longer can it be assumed that whatever happens today's rent will continue to be paid indefinitely, and it is critical for the valuer to carefully consider what is likely to happen at the time a break clause or rent review clause becomes operative. It may well be appropriate in some cases to value on the basis of future reductions in rent receivable, a possibility generally thought of as impossible in the past. This could be particularly relevant in situations in which there could possibly be legislation outlawing 'upward only rent review clauses'.

The problem of contaminated sites and properties

Two problems which valuers have had to consider in recent years have been the effect on property values of the contamination of many sites as a result of previous usage involving such things as chemicals or petroleum products, and the existence of asbestos in many buildings. These are considerations which would not even have been thought of about 25 years ago when there was no general awareness of the problems to health and safety caused by contaminated sites and asbestos.

However, an increased awareness in society of such dangers means that the valuer now has to be vigilant to identify the existence of dangerous materials in buildings and sites, and then has to make due allowance in the valuation process for the cost of remedial work. Because the valuation process involves discounting future income and expenditure to the present, the valuer may need to go further than simply allowing for currently known liabilities of this type. It may be necessary to make allowances in respect of probable expenditure which is likely to result from expectations of improved standards of safety and environment in buildings. These may merely be the result of changing consumer expectations, but they could in fact result from the threat of improved standards imposed by legislation. Such a possibility is not unrealistic as the history of the built environment in developed societies reveals ever more demanding planning and building codes in respect of such matters with the passage of time, and in this respect the future is likely to be no different from the past.

Expenditure which proves necessary because of problems of this type can be very considerable, whilst the blight caused by their existence can sometimes make properties completely unsaleable in their existing conditions. Even when the problems have been addressed by property owners, there may still be a residual stigma which reduces a property's value.

The valuer may in fact be faced with a market situation in which there may be no willing buyer for a property with problems of this type, the only course of action being for the owner to remedy the problems prior to offering the property for sale. If this is done it may be that the cost of remedial works exceeds the sum which is ultimately realized for the property, creating a situation in which the property in its affected state has in reality a 'negative value', that is it is a liability not an asset.

Valuers will need to be ever conscious in the future with regard to problems of this nature and will need to carry out very careful property and site inspections to identify whether they exist. Failure to identify such problems or to make sufficient allowance for their rectification may possibly render a valuer subject to a claim for professional negligence, and where a valuer suspects such problems exist it will be advisable either to commission or to recommend the use of a consultant who is expert in environmental matters.

The valuation of large properties

In recent years there has been a trend towards very large property developments, particularly high-rise office developments and large shopping centres. In some cases such developments were what could be termed as 'user specific' or even 'investor specific', that is they were built very much to suit the specific requirements of one user or one investor. In this respect developments of this type are very specialised, and the problem may well exist that if the original user or the original investor no longer require them there may be few or even no alternative users or investors interested in purchasing the property interests. Likewise, it may also be that there are few organizations which could even contemplate a purchase, so large would be the finance involved in a purchase.

In such a situation there is no simple solution to the valuation problem and the valuer will have to research the market thoroughly to try to determine exactly which potential purchasers there are and how much they are able and likely to be prepared to pay for the interest concerned. Indeed, there may at any point in time be no potential purchaser, or alternatively there may be such limited competition amongst would-be purchasers that only a restricted sale price is likely to be realised.

The valuer should remain aware of this possible problem as the long term value of a property of this type may be more dependent upon the existence of other potential users or investors rather than upon the existence in the short term of the first user or investor. If there are not likely to be other potential users and investors in the long term, such properties assume the nature of highly specialised investments which may have very limited value to anyone other than the original user or investor.

Concluding observations

In general it is suggested that any inability to produce reasonably realistic valuations probably results more from the inefficient application of conventional valuation methods rather than to deficiencies in the methods themselves. Valuation involves studying the future and people, and both are uncertain quantities to the extent that it will never be possible to value property interests with complete precision. It is also a fact that everyone places their own subjective valuations on properties, and the task of the valuer is therefore to try to identify who are potential purchasers, what their subjective valuations are likely to be, and whether they have the financial capability to purchase. What someone else previously paid for another similar property may influence them in the bid they make, but equally well it may have no influence whatsoever on that bid.

The valuer can at best only provide a well informed and reasonable estimate of the market value of any property interest, and no valuer can sensibly believe in the complete infallibility of his or her valuation. However, with diligent research and intensive scrutiny of the players in the market, allied to sound reasoning and decision making, the valuer can produce acceptable valuations and the best possible valuations given the circumstances of each case.

Chapter 10

Accuracy in Valuation

Notwithstanding the fact that valuations are merely, in effect, opinions of value rather than scientifically precise facts, as observed in earlier chapters swingeing criticisms have periodically been levelled at property valuers, including suggestions that their work is too inaccurate and that dated and inappropriate valuation methods are used. A combination of events in the United Kingdom property market at various times since 1970 and in other countries where there have been significant periods of depressed property values, has focused attention on the accuracy of property valuations, particularly those done for the purpose of obtaining loans or for the appraisal of the assets of major property owning organisations.

The increasing importance in the property market of institutional investors, particularly superannuation and pension funds, and the problems caused by property crashes for them and their investors, have highlighted the importance of stability in commercial property markets particularly for the 'man in the street'. Additionally, a better informed public and an ever vigilant media sector have resulted in any problems in the market place rapidly becoming well publicised. These factors, coupled with the extremely high rates of inflation of the 1970s in particular, concentrated attention on the performance of all investments, and highlighted any failure to at least provide a hedge against inflation, and, more latterly, a failure to provide reasonable periodic returns in the form of dividends.

In the United Kingdom, as long ago as 1976 *The Greenwell Report* focussed attention on shortcomings in property valuation which involves both art and science. The art is that of forming judgements, and as subjectivity is inevitably involved in that process, complete consistency between valuers is impossible. The science is the mathematical conversion of these judgements into a valuation, and at this stage precision is possible. It will not remedy any errors of judgement, but it is nevertheless essential that valuers should aim for the highest degree of accuracy possible and should use appropriate and precise mathematical methodology.

More recently, in recognition of the need to have reliable valuations, in the United Kingdom the Royal Institution of

Chartered Surveyors (RICS) established a working party chaired by Sir Bryan Carsberg, which *Chartered Surveyor Monthly* of February 2002 reported as having made 18 recommendations to the RICS (see Appendix A) on how the valuation process should be tightened up with respect to commercial property valuations.

> The working party's recommendations aim to minimise the risks of valuers' objectivity being compromised and ensure public confidence in the valuation system is maintained. ... Sir Bryan Carsberg said; 'Valuers face many of the moral and ethical hazards which confront auditors. It is essential that public confidence is maintained in the system and everything possible is done to assure the reliability of valuations. Proposals stop short of a complete separation of valuation from agency and other consulting services, as this would leave valuers less well placed to achieve accuracy in valuations.'

Recognition by the RICS of the need to constantly monitor valuation standards and to seek as great a degree of accuracy as possible in the valuation process was both appropriate and commendable.

Market value and the property market

Valuers value for many purposes, but it is frequently open market value which causes comment from both laymen and allied professions, partly because it is the concept of value which most regularly affects the general public, and partly because market valuations form a very significant proportion of the totality of valuation work. It therefore behoves valuers to consider the accuracy of valuations both in the interest of improving the reliability of valuations and professional expertise, and also to protect the valuation profession from external criticism.

Market value is the price at which an item will change hands if offered by a willing seller to a person or persons willing and able to purchase. In economic theory there is the concept of a perfectly competitive market in which, among others, the following conditions should exist:

(a) buyers and sellers must have precise knowledge of prices being paid elsewhere;
(b) the product in the market must be homogeneous;
(c) there must be perfect mobility in the market, with buyers and sellers willing and able to move to make a purchase, and the product must be mobile as well; and

(d) there must be so many buyers and sellers in the market that no
one individual on his or her own can influence market price.

Consideration of the above conditions makes it clear that the
property market is normally imperfect, indeed often incredibly
imperfect. There is rarely perfect knowledge of prices paid
elsewhere, although this situation has improved very much in
recent years in many localities and for most types of property with
the creation of computer data banks containing records of market
transactions. Also, the availability of property particulars on the
internet has made it easy to research asking prices for property,
although these do not necessarily provide reliable information on
actual selling prices, whilst there may only be a limited amount of
information about the properties advertised. The market product is
heterogeneous, there is very little mobility (the location of the
product cannot be moved, and buyers usually restrict their
searches to particular and small geographical areas), and there are
frequently few buyers and sellers.

Valuers therefore work under extremely difficult conditions as in
buoyant market conditions the distinctive features of a property
interest may create a situation in which the seller has almost
monopolistic powers – more so if the time factor is taken into
account – as, even if relatively identical units of property exist, they
will not necessarily be offered for sale simultaneously.

Conversely, the variety in the product and the great importance
of location can sometimes result in a possible buyer being
indifferent to the purchase of a particular property, giving them
great power in negotiations particularly if the market is depressed.
These considerable imperfections create a background in which
great accuracy in valuation is impossible to achieve on a regular
basis.

The great importance of location and the heterogeneity of
property interests also result in there being not one but a series of
separate property markets which are not always clearly defined,
and in which the physical and financial boundaries may vary with
time. For example, the opening of a new railway line may
completely alter commuter travel possibilities so extending the area
of accessibility to a particular shopping or commercial centre with
resultant changes in marketability and property values.

The theory of price determination and problems of price estimation

The price at which items offered on the market change hands is determined by the interaction between buyers and sellers, which should in theory result in a market price at which the number of articles offered for sale is equal to the number buyers will purchase. But it is not unusual in the market that at any particular asking price there will be some purchasers who would in fact be prepared to pay a higher price for the product. Such 'consumer surpluses' can make it very difficult to value property accurately, as if market circumstances persuade buyers so to do, they may well bid away some or all of their consumer surplus with resultant price increases which valuers might find difficult to anticipate.

Whereas in most markets suppliers can increase the supply of an article in response to increases in demand which result from buyers being prepared to bid away some of their consumer surplus and to pay higher prices, two factors operate against such a reaction in a property market. First, as no two property interests are identical it may be impossible to offer another suitable unit of property, particularly when specialised property is concerned, although with reasonably standard properties, particularly in the housing market, it may be possible to increase the supply by offering additional fundamentally similar properties.

However, the second problem is that the production period for property is such that in the short run it is usually impossible to produce other similar buildings and the supplier of the one (or few) properties already on offer may well be in a monopoly position. In such circumstances the price will be determined by demand; if demand increases the price will increase, as supply cannot be increased. With most other products production can often be rapidly increased, or existing stocks can be moved to areas of high demand, but this is not possible with property.

There are other factors which may cause demand to increase suddenly, with resultant price increases which may be very difficult to anticipate. These include:

(a) reductions in the cost of borrowing;
(b) increases in the amount of money which lenders are prepared to lend and borrowers are prepared to borrow;
(c) changes in taxes levied on property interests; and
(d) changed consumer preferences.

Conversely, unfavourable changes in demand can result in falls in value, particularly if the supplier has to sell and cannot afford to withdraw a property from the market.

In the 1970s in the United Kingdom there were great variations in the mortgage interest rate with resultant effects on residential property values. In the 1980s also in some countries mortgage interest rates rose considerably, and, for example, in the United Kingdom on 10 January 1985 the minimum lending rate was 9.5%; it rose to 10.5% on 11 January, and again on 14 January to 12.7%. In Australia in the later 1980s the mortgage rate rose at regular intervals, reaching a high of 18.5%, whereas some years later it had fallen to about 6%. These two extremes were obviously significant determinants in the amount typical potential purchasers could afford to bid for properties, their available funds being primarily determined by the amount of loan funds available and the cost of borrowing those funds. The life of the valuer in such rapidly changing and such widely varying situations is not easy, but it is uncertainty and technically difficult situations which give rise to the need for specialists and which provide them with their livelihood.

The valuation process is further complicated by other factors already referred to. Other products are supplied to markets in which there are many suppliers and a very large number of buyers, as a result of which the actions of individual buyers are barely noticeable, while even the actions of individual suppliers may only have a marginal effect on market values. However, property markets tend to be either local in nature or restricted to specialist properties. This results in each market regularly having few buyers and few sellers, and in such a market the actions of any one buyer or seller may affect market value substantially, particularly in the type of limited market which exists when very valuable properties are being sold.

The valuer therefore has not only to anticipate the decisions of a large number of people but also to predict value in a market in which the decision of one individual may substantially alter the status quo. Specialist purchasers, such as those who wish to buy a neighbouring property for personal reasons or redevelopment purposes, can confound all previous market evidence and their actions can be extremely difficult, if not impossible, to predict.

The circumstances of the buyer and the 'different faces' of a property interest

Another particular difficulty is that the heterogeneity of property means that a particular property interest can mean different things to different people. Potential purchasers vary greatly in their needs, and their expectations of a particular interest in property are likely to vary accordingly. A specific house may have varying attraction for potential purchasers as, apart from the fact that the location may be a greater or lesser compromise for different people, the accommodation may be virtually ideal for some, but a substantial compromise for others.

With an investment property, value to individual purchasers may depend very much on their own circumstances. A property offered on the market for £500,000 which produces a net annual income of £50,000 appears to yield a 10% return.

However, consider a situation in which of three possible purchasers, A will need to borrow £200,000 at 6%, B will have to borrow £300,000 at 7% and C will have to borrow £400,000 at 8% in order to pay the asking price of £500,000. The different costs of borrowing result from differences in the sums borrowed, different rates of personal risk assessed by the lenders, and different sources of borrowing. An analysis of a possible purchase at that figure by each reveals the following:

A		Annual income	£50,000
	Less	Interest on £200,000 @ 6% =	12,000
		Yield on equity of £300,000 =	£38,000
		or	12.666%
B		Annual income	£50,000
	Less	Interest on £300,000 @ 7% =	£21,000
		Yield on equity of £200,000 =	£29,000
		or	14.5%
C		Annual income	£50,000
	Less	Interest on £400,000 @ 8% =	32,000
		Yield on equity of £100,000 =	£18,000
		or	18%

So the interest would give a 10% yield to none of these possible purchasers, even though the vendor may consider it a 10% property at the asking price.

Clearly in the above situation market value is extremely difficult to predict, and this is not untypical. Even if each potential purchaser could borrow at the same rate of interest, their different borrowing requirements would result in the yields to their equity being different, whilst on the face of it the potential purchaser with the lowest amount of equity (personal funds) to put into the purchase is likely to be most attracted to the property as the above calculations show he or she would get a higher yield on their equity than would the other two interested parties. However, if A decided to borrow £400,000 and was able to do so at a 6% rate, then the yield on his or her equity of £100,000 would become 26%, an incredibly attractive investment yield. The valuer in such circumstances has an extremely difficult task in predicting an actual market value, as should the property be offered for auction or sale by tender - which are in fact the ideal selling methods where there are known interested parties and market value is difficult to assess - there is no way of predicting how each of the potential purchasers may react, and what their actual bids will be. The property could in fact fetch a price well in excess of £500,000 if A or B decided to borrow more and to bid away some of their consumer surpluses, being satisfied with a yield on their equity nearer to 10%.

In view of these variables and unknowns it would be foolish to expect consistent and incredible accuracy in the property valuation process. In the United Kingdom, in his judgement in *Singer & Friedlander Ltd* v *John D Wood & Co* [1977] 2 EGLR 84, Mr Justice Watkins suggested that valuations which fell within 10% either side of the figure which would be arrived at by a competent, careful and experienced valuer would be within the permissible margin of error. At the time, and since, this observation was criticised by some for expecting too great a degree of accuracy, and while Mr Justice Watkins's general observations in the case seemed appropriate, it is debatable whether such limits can reasonably be accepted as hard and fast rules for margins of error in valuation. Such accuracy will often, if not regularly, be impossible to achieve. To consistently value within such limits may be more than can be expected of a reasonably competent professional. However, it is certain that valuers ought to be seeking to value within such a range, indeed within a smaller range of value in most cases, and that instances in which valuations fall outside the suggested range should be rare rather than normal.

Notwithstanding these observations, it should not be forgotten that in many cases the fundamental difficulty may be to determine what value 'a competent, careful and experienced valuer' would be likely to assess.

The need for the advice of a specialist is even more important in uncertain conditions than where relative certainty exists, and the specialist valuer should be very much better informed than the layman. Even limited comparable evidence should be better than no evidence, and the systematic collection and analysis of market data should be undertaken by every valuer if they are to perform their functions in a professional way. With today's cheap and versatile computers and computer programs offering incredible capabilities, there is no excuse for not having efficient systems of data storage with almost immediate recall, while such a system should repay its costs over a very short period.

However, as indicated in earlier chapters, evidence of past transactions must be used with great caution. There is a fundamental difference between analysis and valuation, analysis being an investigation of the past, valuation entailing a prediction of the future. The rate of technological development is so rapid that the next 25 years are likely to be very different from the past 25 years, and while the events of the past may build up the professional's store of knowledge and experience, they may only be of limited assistance in predicting the future. Additionally, analysis will only suggest what appears to have happened in the past; it rarely proves anything, no matter how carefully it is done. When considering evidence we are rarely in the fortunate position of knowing all the personal circumstances of buyer and seller and what factors affected the transaction, so an element of doubt is almost inevitably attached to analysed information.

Such factors will vary both from individual to individual and with time. Add the uncertainty of the future in contrast to the relative certainty of the past, and it is clear that analysis must be combined with very sound professional judgement in the use of its results. In addition to basic skills, the accumulated store of data, a professional approach, and experience, the really competent valuer also needs to be a person of vision, and there are probably many who do not justify such a description. In that respect the valuation profession is probably no different from any other.

Even so, the valuer's fundamental skills and knowledge of the property market should equip him or her to give better advice than can be obtained from any other source, even though it may have similar imprecision to the advice given by other professional men and women. Stockbrokers will frequently have varying opinions on the prospects of particular shares, even with the benefit of an active and well documented market for guidance. Their advice will nevertheless generally be better than that of an uninformed layman, and the competent valuer can in the same way serve property investors best if he or she takes positive steps to ensure they keep abreast of all factors which are likely to affect values.

Professional development and research

This is an area in which the valuation profession was certainly not immune to criticism in the past. The high level of expertise expected of professionals and the rapidly changing world in which they work demand that they should make positive endeavours to continue their education throughout their careers, and with most professional organizations now requiring qualified members to undertake continuing education or development of some kind in order to try to maintain and to improve their professional skills and abilities, the danger of valuers not being conversant with modern practices and conditions should be less than in the past.

In addition, most firms have been progressive and have made good use of computers both to improve efficiency and to introduce new approaches to valuation. Many have paid increased attention to the compilation of data banks and their analysis, and some have set up research departments to assist their professional and commercial activities.

There has also been considerable research activity in academic institutions and in firms and professional organizations, although many possible research initiatives are sometimes restricted by lack of money especially within smaller firms or organizations. Well directed and relevant research must save money and will probably make money, whilst it should also provide a defence against criticism from others and should help valuers to keep ahead of competitors such as accountants, actuaries, statisticians, and economists.

Reporting to clients

An undoubted shortcoming in many valuation reports in the past was the failure to give reasons for recommendations or to state the assumptions which underlay valuations. Where this still occurs there can be no defence to criticism on these grounds. Most people would not accept reports with similar shortcomings from stockbrokers, accountants, builders, or mechanics, and there is no reason why they should be expected to accept the recommendations of valuers without the provision of full and valid reasons. It is the client who has to make a decision on the basis of a report, and it is only with a clearly explained report that the client can get the fullest benefit from a professional adviser. Indeed, the inclusion of stated assumptions and reasons for recommendations reduces the scope for criticism, whilst a failure to provide them may justifiably cause a client to doubt the competence of a valuer.

A report should include observations on all matters to which a client should pay particular attention before making a decision in respect of the interest concerned. Typical matters which are important and which should be reported on include:

(a) the rental growth anticipated by the valuer and the likely speed of such growth;
(b) the opportunity cost of capital or the cost of borrowing considered appropriate and used in the valuation;
(c) allowances made for future repairs, rental voids, management expenses, and other similar outgoings; and
(d) the period of years over which future income flow has been anticipated, and
(e) whether any consideration has been made for the possible need for major refurbishment or even complete redevelopment at some future date.

The presumption that an investor should take a valuer's decision as a basis for his or her own decision without adequate explanation of the rationale behind valuation advice is untenable. Investors are unlikely to make decisions without considering options, and unless they are provided with adequate information they will find it difficult, if not impossible, to make proper comparisons.

The assessment of the market value of property is difficult because it involves trying to predict the valuations of a number of different people all with different circumstances and different expectations of the future. Add to these variables the different expectations of a number of valuers and it is hardly surprising that they regularly arrive at different valuations. It would be surprising if there was not variation, as different valuers will possess different background information and, inevitably, some will be more optimistic about the future than others. In such circumstances, were the assumptions made by each valuer in arriving at a valuation figure clearly stated, each individual valuation in a range of valuations might be equally defensible.

A clear statement of the basis of valuation and of the reasons for recommendations also enables a client to consider how subsequent changes in circumstances might affect continuing investment policy. In reality no one can tell whether or how a rent will grow or what interest rates will be in the future. A client can, however, decide whether to accept the underlying assumptions and predictions made by the valuer, and consequently whether he or she is prepared to purchase or dispose of an interest. This is no different from a physician telling a patient what the likely risks and benefits of a recommended operation are, leaving the patient to decide what course of action to take in the light of this information. Clients should also be forewarned of the likely implications of any recommendations made, for every action taken will result in consequences which may not be apparent to a lay person, and which the professional should consequently bring to the client's notice.

The assessment of value to an individual

While the actual market price of an interest is difficult to predict, in valuing for a specific client very much greater precision is possible and the valuer can perform an extremely useful service by providing 'tailor made' advice for individual clients. For most clients the critical point is not 'what will someone pay for an interest?' but 'what can I afford to pay?'

Valuation for individuals involves building in their own personal specifications. What yield must they achieve, rather than what is the market rate? What rate of interest will they have to pay on borrowed money rather than some other investor who can borrow at a lower rate of interest? What growth expectations are they prepared to, or can they afford to, build into a valuation? This is not asking the client to do his or her own valuation: it is, rather, the same process a tailor goes through when he asks our requirements, takes our measurements, and then adds his professional skill and knowledge to produce a suit to fit us and our needs. It may produce a figure which is different from that which our comparable evidence suggests the market will pay, and from that which is subsequently achieved. That does not make the exercise futile but proves its worth: people would not wear suits which do not fit, and they should not be expected nor persuaded to buy properties or property investments which do not fit their own specific needs nor to pay prices they cannot really afford.

Too great a reliance on comparable evidence carries the danger that the mistakes of others may be repeated. Not all previous purchases will have been wise, and yet there appears to be great willingness on the part of many valuers to assume that figures previously paid in the market place are a completely reliable indication of what can sensibly be paid for another similar interest. What frequently appears to be an almost blind faith in the power of the comparable transaction as an indication of current market value must result in some of the mistakes of the past being repeated, rather than in valuers learning from them. This emphasises the need for careful analysis and wise application of the resultant information if valuers are to properly serve their clients.

Conclusions

It does no harm for professional people regularly to critically examine their performance and the quality of the service they provide; indeed, the process is essential if they are to maintain or improve their position in the market place by producing a service which consumers want and are prepared to pay for. In past years there has been frequent complaint from valuers in the United Kingdom, and in other countries also, about the low level of fees they receive for some work, yet the possibility that the reluctance of clients to pay higher fees may be an indication that they do not value highly the quality of service or work provided rarely seems to be considered.

Just as one cannot accurately predict the winner of a horse race, so it is impossible to introduce great and consistent accuracy in the prediction of open market value. If great precision were possible the risk would virtually disappear from property investment, no one would make losses, and conversely no one would make fortunes. What is possible, however, is that the valuation profession can ensure a high level of performance:

(a) by utilising modern technology to improve the collection, storage and analysis of a wide range of essential data, so assisting a continuous monitoring of legal, financial and property market conditions;

(b) by viewing comparables critically rather than unquestioningly accepting them as evidence of what the market will pay;

(c) by providing a service to suit the needs of specific clients rather than assuming all clients' needs are the same;

(d) by improving the standard and content of reports, explaining assumptions and recommendations fully; and

(e) by continuously educating itself, so seeking to improve its own technical ability and to provide an improved service which changes with the needs of the times.

Despite the inevitable problems of predicting an uncertain future, the well educated, well trained, well equipped, thinking, reasoning and professional valuer can provide an invaluable service and a better service than others can give in what is, and will remain, a most important area of investment. Valuers should be more than just valuers: they should be the most appropriate and most competent business and financial advisers on all matters relating to property valuation and property investment.

Chapter 11

The Valuation of Specialized Properties

Valuers will sometimes be asked to value a property which may be outside their normal range of work, in that the property is of a type built to be used for specialized purposes, or which is unusual or even rare in terms of such matters as architectural features or historical significance, a result of this being that such properties only occasionally, or even rarely, come onto the market.

In reality the majority of properties are specialized in nature, and, for instance, houses have a specialized use which is residential. However, with most types of houses there are numerous transactions in the market place with respect to both rental and capital values, and a valuer can consequently normally use the comparative method of valuation. The same applies to many other specialized properties such as offices, shops, and factories, the high frequency of transactions enabling comparisons to be made with respect to rental values, yields, and capitalisation rates, or sometimes even capital values.

However, with certain types of property there may only be a few in existence in a defined geographical area, as a result of which sales or lettings occur only relatively infrequently. There may also be a limited range of potential purchasers for a particular type of property, whilst with other types of property there may be a restriction on competition in the market place. The need for a licence to operate a particular type of business could for instance cause such restriction, whilst the difficulty of obtaining planning approval for a particular use could also restrict the number of competing properties suitable for that use.

The method or style of construction of a particular type of building may make it specialized by restricting its versatility in use, eg potteries, breweries, motels, or petrol filling stations usually do not easily lend themselves to any alternative uses. Alternatively, a monopolistic or oligopolistic situation in the market place may result in there inevitably being only one or a limited number of potential purchasers for a property or type of property, such a situation existing in many countries with respect to petrol filling stations with a few leading petrol companies frequently dominating the market place.

Determining suitable valuation methods for specialized properties

Whenever a property has to be valued which is specialized either because of the use to which it is put or because of other considerations, the valuer is faced with the problem of determining the most appropriate valuation method to use. In making a decision it should be considered who are the most likely prospective purchasers in the market place, for what prospective uses might the property be purchased, and how would potential purchasers be likely to assess its value. Having considered such matters the valuer may see fit to choose any of the normal methods of valuation depending upon the circumstances of the case.

It is worthwhile considering some of the fundamental aspects of the different valuation methods:

1. The Comparative Method can be used when there are frequent sales of similar properties in a given area and time period;
2. The Investment (or Capitalisation) Method can be used with income producing properties and it relates capital value to net income flow from a property;
3. The Contractors' Method (also known as Summation) relates market value to the cost of providing a suitable alternative property to the one being valued;
4. The Residual Valuation Method (or Hypothetical Development Valuation Method) is used to determine the value of a property which has development or redevelopment potential;
5. The Profits Method (also known as the Accounts Method or Treasury Method of Valuation) relates the value of a property to the profits which can be expected to be generated from its use for a particular activity.

It is arguable that if one can use either the Comparative Method or the Capitalisation Method to value a property it is unlikely to be regarded as a specialized property, because for each of these methods to be used there need to be regular market transactions to provide evidence of capital values, rental values, and investment yields. However, there will inevitably be some instances in which, although market transactions are infrequent, specialized properties are let to tenants as a result of which the valuation of the freehold interest may therefore require the use of the Capitalisation Method, even though that is unlikely to be the normal method of valuation for all specialized properties.

Many specialized properties that have to be valued will involve a situation in which trading profits will be generated by the use of the property, although it should not be forgotten than not all trading necessarily generates profits. However, the valuer must always remember that it is utility which creates value in any particular property together with the degree of scarcity of the type of property in the market place. In valuing specialized properties the valuer therefore has to seek to assess the level of scarcity of such properties and the relative utility of the property under consideration. He or she should ask the questions: 'How many other suitable properties are available and competing with this property in the market place?' and 'How suitable is this particular property for the type of activity for which it will be used?'

The degree to which a property is or is not suitable for a particular activity will to a large extent determine the level of effective demand, that is demand backed by the willingness and ability to pay for the use of a property. It is part of the valuation process for a valuer to ascertain the figures at which demand will in fact be effective. As practising valuers will know this is very difficult at the best of times, but it is even more difficult when properties are specialized in nature. For instance, with properties such as breweries and bottling plants there may well be changes in user demand and technology which result in buildings which are not particularly old becoming obsolescent in terms of modern production needs. In a market in which there are in any event likely to be only one or a few potential purchasers, this may result in there being either limited or no demand for a particular property, the value of the site for redevelopment purposes possibly being greater than the value of the site with the existing development which might cost too much to upgrade to satisfy modern production requirements. This type of situation can also occur with such properties as relatively new petrol filling stations when their market potential has been damaged by changes in local road patterns or by the opening of competing stations which have locational advantages. It may be that whilst in functional terms a property of this nature may remain very suitable, in economic terms it is no longer suitable for selling petrol and should be valued for possible alternative uses or for redevelopment purposes.

Whereas with many properties their suitability for a specific use is evidenced in the market place by capital values or rentals paid by purchasers and users, a significant market fact with many specialized properties is that such evidence does not exist, or does not exist in sufficient quantity or in a sufficiently reliable form for use in estimating the market value of other properties. In many cases the valuer will therefore have to assess value (either capital or rental value) by first estimating the likely profitability of the activities for which a property will be used. Such a task can only be done by one who takes great care to keep closely informed of performances in particular trading activities, and in particular with changing practices and trends in trading and profitability.

It is possible to classify the various types of specialized property in a number of broad categories.

Specially constructed buildings

Properties may be specialized by virtue of the fact that they were constructed for specialized uses, typical examples being potteries, breweries, oil refineries, and petrol filling stations. With such properties the market value will normally be the figure an alternative user would be likely to pay, this figure being related to the potential profits to be obtained from their use for the purpose for which they were designed and constructed, that is a figure reflecting the utility that potential users could obtain from them. For instance, a bottling plant will not in itself produce a separate profit unless it is used for sub-contract business, but it will provide a valuable part of a profit making production process. The utility to the user could therefore be related to the costs it saves, which could be measured by assessing how much it would cost to have similar processes contracted out to another firm.

In many cases it will be impossible for a valuation to be made using a market comparable because of large physical differences which often exist between different properties and because of significant locational differences, and the profits method of valuation will frequently be the most appropriate. However, sometimes there may be sufficient transactions with some types of property and enough similarity amongst different properties to allow the Comparative Method to be used. In other cases it will be appropriate to use the Contractors' Method (or Summation) to find the cost of a suitable alternative property, whilst if there is unlikely to be a purchaser for the existing use the valuer will have to consider what other uses might be appropriate for the property concerned, and also the likelihood of obtaining planning approval for such uses. If it is considered that a potential purchaser would be likely to demolish the existing buildings and redevelop the site the Residual Method would become an appropriate valuation method.

Properties used for specialized trades or occupations

Although not inevitably restricted to a particular user, the fact that a property is currently devoted to a specialized use may make the business and the property into a specialized valuation situation. If a valuation has to be made on a 'going concern' basis the valuer will need to value the property on the assumption that it will continue to be used by the business for which it is currently used, which will probably entail using the Profits Method of Valuation or, in some cases, the Comparative Method. Again the use of the Residual Method should also be considered if redevelopment of the site is feasible and likely to produce a higher value.

Public buildings

Buildings which are owned by public authorities such as local authorities will not normally be sold on the open market and the use of the Comparative Method of Valuation will therefore be virtually impossible. Such properties as town halls, libraries, museums, and art galleries will normally be valued using the Contractors' Method, as the most realistic method of determining what a prospective purchaser might pay for such a property would be to calculate the likely expenditure necessary to create a suitable alternative property. As indicated above, if it is likely that the existing buildings would be demolished by a future owner to enable redevelopment to take place, the Residual Method of Valuation would be appropriate.

Properties which are used for non-profit making activities

The obvious situation in which the valuation of such a property is required is when a charity is the occupier for purposes other than trading, in which case the property may only be specialized in nature whilst the charity remains in occupation. The Comparative Method may therefore be appropriate if the property is considered to be suitable for other uses for which there is good market evidence, whilst the Residual Method may be appropriate if redevelopment for an alternative use is possible. However, there are instances in which the occupier is a charity and there is also a specially constructed building involved, churches and chapels being the most obvious examples. The Contractors' Method then becomes the most appropriate method of valuation unless the existing use of the property is likely to be discontinued, in which case the Comparative or Residual Methods would be appropriate.

Properties where the use is dependent upon a licence

In the case of public houses and hotels in particular, the ability to use a property for a specific purpose may be dependent upon the issue of a licence by the appropriate licensing authority. In many countries the same will apply to gambling establishments. The possession of a licence, the likelihood of a licence being granted, or the likelihood of one being revoked are therefore critical factors in the valuation process, as without a licence the valuer has to consider the value of a property for an alternative use or for redevelopment. On the assumption that a licence will be granted or will remain in force the valuer will be likely to value on the basis of the Profits Method for the trade to which the licence applies. If a licence is unlikely to be granted or an existing licence is likely to be discontinued, a major consideration will be what alternative use is likely to be considered appropriate by planning control authorities.

Leisure and recreation facilities

Such properties may be classified as specialized for a variety of reasons including the fact that they may be specially constructed (squash courts, swimming pools, golf courses etc.), they may have special locations (eg ski lodges), or they may have a combination of both (eg marinas and ski lodges with ski-lifts). Their values in their existing uses will also almost inevitably be dependent upon high levels of management skills on the part of the proprietors. Valuation for their existing use might sometimes be possible using comparison but will probably more frequently be done using the Profits Method. In the event of a valuation on the open market for the highest and best use, it may be that alternative use value might be required using either the Comparative Method or the Residual Method, for example in the case of a sports ground which had potential for development as either a residential or industrial estate.

Properties used by the extractive industries

Properties used for operations such as sand and gravel extraction, coal mining, and the extraction or mining of other types of minerals are normally valued using the Profits Method. The valuer has to carefully estimate the likely quantities of product which the land will produce over the time period in which it is likely to be productive, from that deduce the annual profitability of the operation, and then estimate the rent which an operator would be prepared to pay for the privilege of owning the operational rights. In some cases rather than a predetermined rent being paid for such a property, returns to the owner may be in the form of royalty payments by the occupier based on the amount of product actually extracted over a given period by the lessee. Needless to say such valuations are highly complex and should only be undertaken by those with a great amount of skill, and preferably also a great amount of experience and knowledge of the particular extractive industry.

With such properties the valuer should always remember that the value may be depreciated by the need to observe strict environmental guidelines whilst using the property, and also the need to carry out what may be both extensive and expensive reinstatement works when the specialized use is discontinued. Should the particular use be nearing the end of its economic life, for example if a quarry is almost worked out, it would be necessary to determine what would be a realistic alternative use and then to value for a limited period in the existing use with a reversion to the alternative use at a realistic future date. Adequate allowances should be made for all the costs which would be incurred and any delay entailed in making the anticipated change in use

Properties subject to monopolistic or oligopolistic market conditions

Where one party is in a position to dominate either the supply or the demand side of a property market they will enjoy a monopolistic situation which may enable them to dictate market value to a very large extent. If either side of a market is dominated by a small group an oligopolistic situation will exist in that the small group will probably have a very powerful influence on market value. If two or more such groups choose to operate a cartel they may in effect create a monopolistic situation. Where such a state of affairs exists the valuer will have to be very much aware of the methods used by the monopoly or oligopoly for assessing the values of operational properties, as those methods will invariably determine value. Such a situation exists when, as is the case in many countries, a small group of petrol companies dominate the ownership of petrol filling stations, often with closely related selling prices for their products.

With properties subject to such market forces the Profits Method of Valuation will usually be appropriate using 'company' or 'industry' methods for the calculation of profits and thus of rental value also. However, a valuer should not forget the possibility of a property having a higher value if used for an alternative purpose, in which case it would be appropriate to use the Residual Method of Valuation to determine value for that other purpose.

The estimation of trading profits

When using the Profits Method of Valuation it is first necessary to estimate the trading potential of a property and it is possible that records of past trading may be available to assist in this task. However, it must not be forgotten that current capital value relates to expectations of the utility or profits to be generated in the future, and records of past activities may not necessarily be a good indication of that. There may have been a very poor trader in action in the past resulting in poor profit figures, or alternatively there may have been a 'super-trader' who achieved exceptional profit figures, both types of result being unreliable evidence for valuation purposes. There may also be the prospect of competition in the future which did not exist in the past, such new competition being likely to adversely affect future profit expectations. Different market factors may apply in the future, for example new or expected future legislation could effect future changes. There are other reasons for treating evidence of the past with caution, some of which will be referred to later.

When considering the use of the records of others, an extremely useful piece of advice from a very successful British property developer is well worth remembering. 'Never believe anything of what you hear, and only believe 50% of what you see!' It is advice which could be well remembered with any valuation, but with the valuation of some specialized properties in particular it is likely to be extremely useful advice.

Having estimated likely profits, the anticipated costs of realising those profits have in turn to be estimated. This process requires an extremely good understanding of the trading activity involved and an appreciation of all likely trading costs, but having estimated costs the net profitability of the activity for which the property will be used can be estimated.

Once net profits have been estimated the valuer can in turn estimate how much of the profits should be attributed as a return to the property rather than as a return to capital employed in the business or to the entrepreneur as a return for his or her expertize and for the business risk undertaken. Again, it is easy to indicate the process but not necessarily easy to implement it in practice, particularly as the appropriate rent share may be influenced by such factors as the other costs of property occupation (eg property rates and taxes), the amount of capital employed, the cost of such capital, trade customs, and other factors such as a high degree of personal skill required to successfully operate a particular type of business.

Once a rental value has been estimated capital value will relate to the annual rental value of the property, if capital value rather than rental value has to be determined.

The valuation survey

In undertaking a valuation the survey process is a particularly important stage. It is worth considering what is meant by the word 'survey ' as it gives a very important and relevant insight into the role of the valuer.

Under 'survey' *The Concise Oxford Dictionary*, seventh edition, says:

1. 'let the eyes pass over, take general view of';
2. 'form general idea of the arrangement and chief features of';
3. 'examine condition of (building etc.)';
4. 'determine boundaries, size, position, shape, contour, etc., of (land, coast, district, estate, etc.) by measuring distances and angles'.

Despite the disquiet on the part of some who consider the United Kingdom title of Chartered Surveyor as being misleading, these definitions of 'survey' indicate the appropriateness of the title as they describe what should really occur in a survey, and what valuers should be doing or seeking to do in all valuation surveys.

The definitions indicate a far wider range of activity than simply measuring and mapping land, which some regard as the only tasks properly relating to the term 'surveying'.

The objective of a valuation survey is to inspect a property and to find out as much as one possibly can about it and its past use, about the competition which currently exists or which may exist in the future, and about the local neighbourhood and the wider geographical area. In *taking a general view of a property* the state of the local economy should be researched, and the levels of income and spending patterns in the area considered. The effect of national and international economic factors on the locality and the trade or business (if the property is used for trade or business) should be considered, and any likely business and economic developments should be taken into account. Local population patterns and trends should be considered, and the local development proposals should also be studied to see whether there are proposals which might either assist or threaten the property under consideration. Proposals for new roads, road improvements or new traffic control schemes should be considered; such changes can have an incredible effect on the values of petrol filling stations or hotels and motels in particular. The possibility of changes in taxation or the introduction of new laws or amendments to existing laws should also be considered if they are likely to affect a property's value.

In fact the objective is to discover as much information as possible about any factors which could possibly influence a valuation, and research may need to be intensive and may need to include market surveys. It should not be forgotten that much of what is discovered will relate to past events, and accordingly it has to be used with caution as it is the future which valuers are seeking to predict in the valuation process. Beware of assuming that the future will be the same as the past as there may be new factors which will affect future property values.

The analysis of survey information

Once collected, information has to be sifted and analysed, and subsequently opinions have to be formed by the valuer. He or she has to analyse information as objectively as possible, and must determine what are the key factors that affect value, which in turn involves giving lesser weight to the less important factors. The judgemental process in which such decisions are made is very important and it has to be done as objectively as possible, although it is almost inevitable that the very process of forming opinions will involve some subjectivity. However, as a general rule the factors which are likely to be important in the future should be uppermost in a valuer's mind, as they should perforce be more important than others which might have been very important in the past but which currently are less significant. The latter may nevertheless influence the views the valuer takes of the future.

It is the formation of opinions which is perhaps the most critical part of the valuation process, and the consequent valuations must be imprecise because they result from both opinion formation and attempts to predict the future. With specialized properties where market comparisons are likely either not to exist or to be rare or imperfect comparisons, the survey process and the formation of opinions from the information so collected are extremely important and should be done with extreme care and diligence.

Insider knowledge

Reference was made earlier to the need to get to know as much about specialized trades and trade practices as possible if one hopes to become a competent valuer of the properties used by specific trades. In some trades there may be customary practices used for the valuation of such things as trading goodwill, or, for example, petrol throughput with petrol filling stations. It is essential for the valuer to be conversant with such practices and to keep closely in touch with relevant trades for such things as rule of thumb measures or customary practices do not necessarily remain static over time. Not to have up to date insider knowledge of current trade thinking and practices could result in inappropriate values being placed on properties. It is consequently extremely unwise to value properties used for specialist trades unless one is fully aware of current trade practices and customs, and the valuer who is not so informed would be wise to refer a potential client to a fully informed specialist valuer.

Large property investments

A brief reference to these is not inappropriate as many of the large investment properties developed in recent years display many of the market characteristics of what are normally regarded as specialized properties. They are few in number; they are designed for specific uses; each tends to have specific qualities of location, design, and quality of construction which make other properties imperfect comparisons; sales in the market place are infrequent, and when they are sold there are few potential purchasers because there are few organizations which could afford to purchase them or which would want to utilize them. Accordingly, it may be extremely dangerous to value such properties by reference to the Comparative Method of Valuation or a combination of the Comparative Method and the Capitalisation Method.

It is appropriate to briefly consider each of the conventional methods of valuation with reference to the valuation of specialized properties.

The Comparative Method of Valuation

Although the following observations apply to all types of property valuations, it is suggested they are even more important with specialized properties where the participants in the market place are relatively few in number. There is great danger in assuming that the next market transaction will display similar characteristics to the last transaction, as the next potential purchaser or lessee may have quite different requirements and characteristics to the last purchaser.

The last purchaser may have been particularly flush with cash, the next one may be struggling to make ends meet. The last purchaser may have been desperate to get trading representation in a locality; the next potential purchaser may already have some representation and may not be desperate to extend it, merely mildly interested in so doing. In such circumstances they are likely to be a conservative bidder for an interest. Underlying market factors may have changed since the last transaction, and for a host of other reasons great caution has to be used in analysing past transactions and in the use of evidence so obtained.

The Contractors' Method of Valuation (or Summation)

As a precaution the valuer should not forget to use this method when assessing the value of specialized properties. It should not be forgotten that a potential purchaser may have the option of buying land and building their own specialized property, and if this is the case the cost of so doing may place a ceiling value on the property under consideration. However, if this is a possibility it should not be overlooked that there may be a considerable cost resulting from the time delay involved in the planning and construction processes, whereas with an existing property the time involved in effecting a purchase is likely to be very much shorter. Despite this the possible use of a Contractors' Valuation as a check should not be ignored.

When checking or valuing by using the contractors' or summation method the valuer will need to:

(1)   estimate the cost of buying a suitable alternative site , plus
(2)   the cost of constructing suitable alternative accommodation, these costs to include all preliminary costs, fees and profit elements of development;
(3)   Total these items of cost to calculate the total cost of developing suitable alternative accommodation;
(4)   Estimate a deduction to be made from the above total to allow for the fact that the envisaged alternative property will be new and up-to-date whereas the existing property will almost inevitably suffer from dilapidation and some element of obsolescence.

It is always possible that having gone through this process a valuer will still consider that differences in site quality between the existing property and the site considered appropriate for an alternative development were not adequately reflected in the summation process. Although differences in site quality should be reflected in the cost used as the value of an alternative site, a valuer may nevertheless consider that such differences in site values may not be an adequate indication of the difference which in reality would exist between the property being valued and the envisaged alternative development, and in the circumstances he or she may adjudge that a further adjustment for this factor is necessary.

The allowance for obsolescence which the valuer must make is critical as there is a significant difference in value in use between a property which is right up to date in design, construction and fit-out, and a property which is dated and less efficient in use. There are various reasons why a property may be adjudged obsolescent, which include the following.

Physical obsolescence exists when a building has become so dilapidated that it is no longer physically capable of properly or efficiently fulfilling its intended uses. A typical example would be a building in which brick and mortar walls were in a dangerous condition, or one in which timber floors were worn and unsafe. In each case the obsolescence allowance would be the sum needed to reinstate the buildings to conditions in which they were physically safe for use and strong enough to fulfill their original purposes.

Economic obsolescence occurs when a property ceases to be suitable in economic terms for its use, and such obsolescence will often occur much earlier than physical obsolescence. A car production factory constructed 20 years ago is by now likely to be obsolescent when current production needs are considered, even though it may still be in relatively good physical condition. In valuing such a building using the Contractors' Method it might be necessary to make allowances for both types of obsolescence, one allowance being the cost of physical reinstatement to an 'as new' condition, the other being the cost which would be incurred in updating the property so that it was in line with modern technical requirements in terms of design, construction and fit-out. The latter figure could be very substantial indeed.

A building could become out-dated by virtue of legislation and this could be referred to as *statutory obsolescence*. This might be the case if stringent new health and safety legislation was introduced which made, for example, certain residential hotels and motels unusable until works were undertaken to bring them in line with the new requirements. What is referred to as *environmental obsolescence* is similar in that changes in attitudes to certain activities may result in the need to spend money on a property to bring it up to the requirements of current environmental standards; this might include work for such purposes as reducing or refining emissions produced as a result of processes carried on within a property, or the installation of air conditioning plant in a building to improve the working conditions of employees.

When using the Contractors' Method a valuer would need to make an obsolescence allowance which in such circumstances would be the cost of complying with the new requirements or the proposed new laws if they were not yet enacted.

The Residual (or Hypothetical Development) Method of Valuation

As earlier observed, a valuer should never forget that a specialized property may in fact be more valuable if used as a site for redevelopment, or if a change of use in the property occurs. Such a possibility should therefore always be considered and a valuation on this basis undertaken if appropriate.

It is often the case that the current use of a property is far from its most valuable use, the current use continuing perhaps as an accident of history or because of inertia or lack of knowledge on the part of the present user. A valuer should therefore always consider whether there is a more valuable use to which a property could be dedicated, and should indicate any higher value to a client after allowing for any necessary costs which would be incurred in converting the property to the alternative and more valuable use. In reality the costs incurred may sometimes be substantial and may result from the need for extensive adaptation works or even total redevelopment. In considering a property for an alternative use or uses a valuer should always consider whether it would be necessary to obtain planning approval for the anticipated change, and also the likelihood of such approval being forthcoming together with consideration of any conditions likely to be attached to an approval.

Even when total change of use or total redevelopment is not appropriate, a valuer should always give thought to the possibility of partial change of use, the extension of existing uses, the addition of new uses, the intensification of existing uses, or partial development or redevelopment.

There may be surplus land which can be used for development purposes without disturbing the existing trade, there may be surplus accommodation which could be used for other purposes or converted to increase total value, or the addition of more buildings might enable existing activities to be extended or new and profitable activities to be added.

Use of the Residual Method of valuation should therefore always be considered by a valuer to research whether a property is currently under utilized and whether development potential exists which makes it more valuable than might at first appear to be the case.

Summary of approach to the valuation of specialized properties

The overall process, as in all valuations, should be one of detecting as much information as possible, the consideration of that evidence, the discarding of irrelevant evidence, the weighting of the relevant evidence, the formation of opinions, and the subsequent application of fundamental valuation principles to convert that evidence and the judgements made into an opinion of value. The result can be no more than an opinion of value, although hopefully if the above processes are rigorously undertaken it will be an acceptable and reliable opinion of value.

The process is in fact no different to any other valuation exercise, but such factors as the infrequency of transactions, the scarcity of similar properties, the specialized nature of design and perhaps construction, and the customs of the players in the market place, create a situation in which generally only the specialized property valuer can value such properties with justified confidence. Probably the most important thing for that valuer to do is to be so familiar with the market place as to know who is most likely, or what type of purchaser or lessee is most likely, to actually acquire the property interest should it be offered on the market. The valuer then needs to be able to assess with a reasonable degree of accuracy the price they are likely to pay for the priviledge.

To know the needs, likes, dislikes, attitudes, and financial capacity of potential buyers is absolutely critical, and such knowledge can only be obtained by being very close to the market and those operating in it on a regular basis. There is no substitute for knowledge of the market particularly with specialized properties, which is why in many cases their valuation tends to be restricted to a few highly specialized, and often very experienced, people or valuation groups. This is particularly so in the case of properties such as public houses, hotels, and petrol filling stations. However, by working from basic valuation principles, fully researching a situation, thinking laterally, and working systematically, a competent valuer should be able to value a specialized property if sufficient market information can be obtained through these processes.

Chapter 12

The Valuation of Assets

Background considerations

'Assets' are defined in *The Concise Oxford Dictionary*, seventh edition as 'property of persons or company that may be made liable for debts'.

In company balance sheets two broad categories of entry are detailed – assets and liabilities – the assets representing the value of the various items owned by a company and the liabilities representing its indebtedness to others. The excess of its assets over its liabilities represents the net value of a company. If its liabilities exceed its assets a company is technically insolvent and may go out of business unless a change in the current situation is anticipated and the company is in a position to continue trading until the position is reversed.

The value of assets is therefore very important, and the valuations of individual assets are likewise, as their collective value will help to determine the financial position of a company. The valuation of property assets is, accordingly, very often a most important process in the assessment of a company's total assets values, particularly when companies have substantial sums invested in either freehold or long leasehold properties which are used for operational purposes.

It is worthwhile considering the generalities and some historical aspects relevant to the valuation of assets which led to the development of international standards for the valuation of assets for the purpose of financial reporting. The International Assets Valuation Standards Committee approved on 24 March 1994 International Valuation Standards, since which date it has, in general, been essential for individual valuers doing valuations for financial reporting to work at all times with reference directly to the most recently approved standards relevant to the member country in which they are valuing. The International Valuation Standards are under regular review, and at the time of writing the latest set of international standards was issued in 2001 with another set of revised Standards imminent. Each time the International Valuation Standards are revised there may well be resultant revisions to national standards in different countries which have adopted the Standards.

The value of property assets

When the values of assets are considered, any interest in property has at any point in time at least two values, namely:

(1) Market value, and
(2) Value to the owner.

'Market value' in broad terms is the value of the property in exchange, that is the figure that is likely to be obtained for an interest in property if it is offered for sale in the open market by the existing owner.

'Value to the owner' is quite simply the value placed on an interest in property by the current owner which should indicate the utility of that interest to the owner, that is its value in use. One would normally expect this to be at least as high as market value, otherwise an owner could make a profit by selling the interest, and in most cases value to the owner will be in excess of market value. If this were not so many more properties would normally be on the market for sale than is generally the case, although in the case of small businesses there are often quite a lot which would be sold at any point in time if purchasers for them could be found in the market place.

It is often the case that in holiday towns, for instance, many business properties are in reality available for purchase if a purchaser can be found. This happens because people who visit attractive locations whilst on holiday often become captivated by the thought of working and living in a locality. As a result they purchase a business believing it to be relatively easy to make money and also believing that they would benefit from a change of life-style, only to find out in due course that making a living that way is not as easy or as rewarding as they originally anticipated. They therefore decide to put their business and property up for sale because its value in use to them is far lower in reality than they originally thought it would be. Despite this, such properties are often difficult to sell because, even though they may be disenchanted, the owners still place a higher value on the property and the business than do potential purchasers in the market place, that is their assessment of value to the owner exceeds the market value.

Companies regularly own property from which they pursue business activities, in which case the properties are both assets of the companies and operational necessities. For the latter reason in good trading conditions the properties generally will be worth more to a company than to other potential purchasers. Consider a retailer who owns a shop which could be let at a net rental of £30,000 per annum and which would be valued by investors on a 9% yield basis.

Market Valuation:

Net rental value	£30,000	pa
Year's Purchase in perpetuity at 9%	11.11	
	£333,300	

On these figures it is likely that the property would fetch about £330,000 if offered for sale on the open market.

However, the retailer, through the use of a shop as a trading asset, is able to make a net annual trading profit of £120,000 per annum after allowing for all expenses of trading, including an allowance for interest on capital employed, this to include interest on capital tied up in the ownership of the freehold property. Clearly, this is an instance in which after estimating returns for the risk involved in trading and for his own skill and expertise, the trader may consider the rental value of the property to him in his current business as being in the region of say £50,000 per annum, or even more, a considerably greater figure than the open market rental value. The capital value of the property in use to the business is therefore such that the property would be retained in use as an asset of the business, and its sale would only be contemplated for sound operational reasons such as the possibility of moving to another location where even higher profits could be achieved. Certainly, a sale would not be contemplated on the basis of the open market value of the property being attractive enough to make a sale preferable to the retention of the property in the business.

Many traders and companies were in the past not really aware of the market value of their property assets (although in general they have become much more aware of such matters in recent years), as a result of which they often did not really know whether their property assets were 'earning their keep' in a business. Consequently some businesses used properties to make annual trading profits of say £25,000 when by ceasing trading and leasing the property to another trader they could in fact have made a rental income in excess of this without the labour and risks of running their own business.

In the past it was common to do 'going concern valuations' of properties which took into account the value of a property interest or interests for the purpose of a business which operated from the property; the property was valued as part of a business which was a going concern, that is it was an active and viable business operation. There were different views expressed as to the objectives of such valuations, but they should have included the objectives of showing

(1) the value of the property in use for the purposes of the business,
(2) the open market value of the property, and accordingly
(3) whether the property would have been of greater value if it remained in use in the business or whether it would have been more valuable if offered for sale on the open market to other would-be users.

Problems experienced in the past

Businesses often became subject to takeover bids because their owners were unaware of the true total open market value of all of the separate assets owned by the business. In particular the owners frequently did not realize that the property interests owned and used in their businesses were in fact worth very much more on the open market than they ever imagined. There was therefore unrealized value in many of the properties owned by some businesses which anyone who took them over could realize by selling the properties on the open market. Purchasers often obtained far more for the properties than they had paid for them as part and parcel of the businesses they had bought, indeed they often realized far more for just some of the properties alone than they had paid for the entire business, including its property interests, goodwill, stock, and other assets.

Such activities as taking over undervalued businesses and selling off the undervalued property assets often resulted in going concern businesses which were making profits going out of business once they were taken over as a result of the asset stripping which occurred subsequent to the takeover. Many takeover specialists made huge fortunes through such activities, and it became particularly important for companies which wished to avoid becoming the prey of takeover specialists to ensure that all their assets were regularly valued and that the annual balance sheet contained true representations of the current market value of the company's assets (including its property assets), particularly as part of the company as an existing business. This was especially important for public companies which were listed on a stock exchange, when a takeover might occur following the purchase of blocks of undervalued shares.

In many cases it had been the practice for property assets to be represented in balance sheets at 'historic cost' sums, that is at the prices at which they had been bought originally. Such sums could easily be 20 or more years out of date and consequently generally very much less than the current value of the assets, even allowing for wear and tear and other depreciation and after allowance for any element of obsolescence. Other balance sheet figures were often estimates of the current values of properties made by a company's directors who frequently were not skilled in property valuation, as a result of which many such values were regularly inaccurate and unreliable. In times of rapid inflation historic cost figures and directors' valuations were often well below market value and companies whose balance sheets included such figures were often prime targets for takeover bids.

In other cases in which takeover bids did not occur many businesses would continue to trade, but because their owners were unaware of the true current values of the properties from which they traded, they would continue to use those properties in a way which represented an inefficient use of capital. There was frequently a resultant uneconomic and extravagant use of resources, often by companies which might have been borrowing money to trade whilst sitting on underused but valuable property assets which could have produced a capital surplus for them if sold to realize their true value.

It therefore became important for a number of reasons for owners and those responsible for running companies to be aware of the true values of property assets, whilst the development of property companies also gave rise to a need for the regular valuation of property assets. In the 1960s and 1970s in particular, property companies became very important sectors of the overall corporate scene in the United Kingdom. They were different from most other listed companies in that whereas most other companies existed to pursue production and trading activities using properties for operational purposes, the major objective of property companies was to hold property to let to others to use, the returns to the property companies being the rents received for leasing out their properties. In many cases properties may also have been developed and built by the property company, which also received returns represented by the development profits and the increased capital values of the properties owned. The regular and accurate valuation of the assets of property companies was clearly very important if existing and potential investors in them were to have an accurate indication of their current net value at any point in time.

The valuation of property assets

There is in fact a need for the valuation of property assets for a number of reasons which include:

(i)   to inform current owners of the true values of property assets;
(ii) for inclusion in company accounts for the information of share-holders and would-be investors;
(iii) to provide an accurate assessment of assets and liabilities when seeking to borrow money;
(iv) for taxation purposes, particularly with respect to depreciation allowances on such items as fixed plant and machinery, and on buildings where taxation laws permit depreciation allowances being set against income to reduce net tax liabilities;
(v)   for inclusion in prospectuses in the event of a private company being floated on a stock exchange, this enabling those interested in bidding for shares in the newly-floated company to have an accurate indication of the value of the company's assets;
(vi) for inclusion in balance sheets drawn up on the occasion of a takeover bid being made for a company, this enabling the directors of a company for which a bid has been made to negotiate or to oppose a bid on the basis of accurate assessments of the current value of the company's assets;
(vii) for the regular valuation of the assets of property trusts and property companies whose total asset values are generally almost entirely based on the current value of their property assets.

In the past there were conventional approaches to the valuation of property assets, but much was left to the judgement of individual valuers, with the result that considerable discrepancies might exist between the practices of different valuers and the resultant valuation figures given by them for the same properties.

As already observed, in the 1960s and 1970s in particular there was considerable publicity given to the activities of 'asset strippers' who took over companies with undervalued assets and sold those assets off to make substantial profits. Quite frequently such activities resulted in unemployment for those who had previously worked for the companies which had been taken over, and resultant local social problems often caused 'asset-strippers' to be unfavourably regarded even though their activities could regularly be defended on financial and economic grounds.

The development of valuation standards

The importance of asset valuations was recognised by the Royal Institution of Chartered Surveyors (RICS) in 1973 with the formation of the Assets Valuation Standards Committee (AVSC) which has been responsible for the publication of Guidance Notes and Standards on Asset Valuation matters.

Valuation: Principles into Practice
edited by WH Rees (Estates Gazette, 1988)

At the same time a close association was established with the various accountancy bodies in the United Kingdom which had also shown concern over such matters and which had established an Accounting Standards Committee, asset valuation standards being developed through co-operation between these two committees. There was also close co-operation with the Stock Exchange and the City Panel on Take-Overs and Mergers, the Incorporated Society of Valuers and Auctioneers (now merged with the RICS), and the Rating and Valuation Association (now the Institute of Revenues Rating and Valuation).

Over the ensuing years a number of sets of Valuation Standards were published and The International Assets Valuation Standards Committee (TIAVSC) was established in 1981; with effect from May 1995 its name was officially changed to the International Valuation Standards Committee (IVSC) which has international headquarters in London, England. TIAVSC first issued standards in 1985 which have since been revised several times, the latest IVSC Standards at the time of writing being those published in 2001. Membership of the IVSC is through national valuation societies, and the current membership includes valuers from over forty countries. Background information about the IVSC is available on the internet at www.ivsc.org.

TIAVSC standards dated 1 June 1994 were described as representing 'the best consensus of 40 participating nations'. TIAVSC stated its principal objective as being:

> ...to formulate and publish, in the public interest, valuation Standards and procedural guidance for the valuation of assets for use in financial statements, and to promote their world wide acceptance and observance.

The second objective was described as being:

> ...to harmonize Standards among the world's states, and to make disclosure of differences in standards statements and/or applications of Standards as they occur.
>
> It is a particular goal of TIAVSC that international valuation Standards be recognized in statements of international accounting and other reporting standards, and that Valuers recognize what is needed from them under the standards of other professional disciplines.

In 2003 these objectives remain the objectives of the International Valuation Standards Committee (IVSC) which repeated the desire that 'international valuation Standards be recognized in statements of international accounting, ...'. This acknowledged the fact that the Standards have been devised through co-operation between a number of different professions and their representative bodies, and it is also indicative of the fact that valuations of property assets are required for a wide range of reasons and are relied upon in important decision making processes by many people and many professions.

The IVSC as an international body, liaises with the International Accounting Standards Committee, the International Federation of Accountants, the International Auditing Practices Committee, and the International Organization of Security Commissioners. There is therefore liaison both between different professional organizations and also between nations in the hope of achieving widely accepted valuation standards which will be practised and understood on an international basis, and which will be understood and usable by different professional groups.

Members of the IVSC support the Standards and guidance published by the IVSC and use their best endeavours to secure recognition of the Standards where appropriate in their respective Member States, but there is acceptance of the fact that detailed regulations may vary from state to state because of variations in law and cultures in different countries. It is therefore very important for valuers to consult the most recently published Standards for the country in which a property is located when they are required to make assets valuations for use in financial statements. It is essential that valuers should always act in compliance with the laws of the relevant country and the valuation standards of that country. This is particularly important if valuers are not to leave themselves open to legal action on the basis that they have not operated in an appropriate manner for a competent professional.

Much of the content of the Standards ought to be routine knowledge and practice for competent and professional valuers, but it is probably because there are some valuers for whom that is not the case that there is a need for standards to be drawn up and officially endorsed by professional organizations. Many if not most laws, rules, and regulations are in reality only required because of the actions of a minority of people – often a small minority – the burden of compliance nevertheless being imposed on the majority most of whom may already behave and operate to acceptable standards.

Whilst there appears to be some repetition in the IVSC Standards, it is likely that the international body thought that certain fundamental matters were so important, and perhaps so often neglected by some valuers, that repetition for emphasis would be highly beneficial. The repetition of certain requirements in different Standards also allows for the possibility that individual Standards may sometimes be read in isolation from the others.

Whether the international standards or national standards are considered, there are a number of fundamental matters which are likely to be central to all sets of standards. These include the specific definitions provided for the most common types of value which valuers may be asked to assess, the three most important probably being *Market Value*, *Existing Use Value*, and *Depreciated Replacement Cost (DRC)*. Other important matters covered in the standards are *Valuation Bases*, *Reporting Requirements*, and the *Responsibilities of the Valuer*.

Some of the Standards will be considered below, the intention being to give an overview of their objectives, their requirements, and the appropriate valuation approaches necessary to satisfy the Standards. Whilst the IVSC Standards are international, as noted earlier valuers should always operate under the standards applicable in the country in which they are valuing.

For example, in Australia valuers would operate under the Standards approved by the Australian Property Institute (previously the Australian Institute of Valuers and Land Economists), which standards recognize both the IVSC Standards and Australian legal considerations.

In Europe valuers operate under the European Valuation Standards 2003 (EVS 2003) drawn up by The European Group of Valuers Associations (TEGoVA), departure from those Standards only being permitted in order to comply with national compliance requirements when they differ from the requirements of the Standards. The European Standards comply with the IVSC Standards but are adapted to take into account European considerations, particularly directives of the Council of Europe. The Standards and guidance notes are contained in *European Valuation Standards*, fifth edition, (Estates Gazette, London, 2003) and they contain an introductory statement that:

It is the recommendation of TEGoVA that EVS 2003 should be adopted and applied within Europe, except where explicitly stated to apply to European Union States only, where such use is compatible with existing national legislation. ... The purpose of EVS 2003 is

(i)   to assist valuers to prepare coherent reports for presentation to their clients by providing clear guidance;

(ii)   to promote consistency by the use of standard definitions of value and approaches to valuation;

(iii)   to enable users of valuations to know and understand more fully what is meant by particular terms and definitions so that they are better able to utilise the valuations which have been prepared as a result of their instructions;

(iv)   to provide a quality standard in terms of a validation of recognised qualifications and best practice as a benchmark for users of valuations. This will be further enhanced by the scheme of certification that has been introduced by TEGoVA ....;

(v)   to provide an accurate basis for economic analysis of the efficient use of scarce land and building resources;

(vi)   to inculcate in valuers, both a client-orientated and a task-orientated approach to valuation;

(vii)   to increase the awareness of the role of the valuer;

(viii) to institute procedures which are likely to lead to clearly set out, accurate, unambiguous certificates of value which are consistent with national and supranational legislation and with valuation and accounting standards;

(ix)   in the investment sector, to use procedures intended to promote consistency in valuations that are used to build indices which represent financial performance; and

(x)   promote coherence in national regulations and recommendations of best practice.

They also contain the statement

> Where compatible with EU Law and practice and EVS 2003, TEGoVA
> recommends that the International Valuation Standards published by
> the International Valuation Standards Committee (IVSC) should be
> complied with to further global consistency in best valuation practice.

Whilst the previous and subsequent observations are in no way a
substitute for reference to the actual Standards, it is appropriate to
further consider some of the more important provisions of the
Standards, with reference to the TEGoVA Standards 2003 in
particular.

Valuation Standard for the market basis of valuation

The introductory notes to the IVSC Standard (which became
effective on 24 March 1994 as a TIAVSC Standard), said the objective
was to provide a common definition of Market Value, and this
definition is perhaps the most important item in the Standards in
view of the fact that much valuation work involves the assessment
of Market Value. Even though this definition is specifically for the
purpose of Financial Reporting, it is likely to become a basic
standard for other purposes also, and may well be referred to by
courts in instances of litigation. In the United Kingdom the Financial
Reporting Standards and the normal Valuation Standards of the
RICS have for some years been amalgamated and officially
endorsed by the Institution, and it is likely that in the course of time
standards which are consistent over the whole range of valuation
work may be approved in more countries. Indeed the change of title
of the international group from International Assets Valuation
Standards Committee to International Valuation Standards
Committee in May 1995 would appear to have recognized the
desirability of agreed standards which apply to all property
valuation situations rather than simply to the valuation of assets.

'*Market Value*' is a representation of value in exchange or the
amount a property would bring if offered for sale in the open
market at the date of valuation under circumstances that meet the
requirements of the definition. The most recent IVSC/TEGoVA
approved definition is:

> Market Value is the estimated amount for which a property should
> exchange on the date of valuation between a willing buyer and a
> willing seller in an arm's-length transaction after proper marketing

wherein the parties had each acted knowledgeably, prudently and without compulsion.

(SeeTEGoVA Standard 4.)

The 'date of valuation' is that on which the property is deemed to be sold.

It is anticipated that valuation methods and procedures that reflect the nature of a property and the circumstances under which it would most likely trade in the open market will be applied by the valuer, and approved methodologies include the comparison of rental values, the comparison of sales, the Income Approach based on the capitalisation of income, the Discounted Cash Flow approach, and the Cost Approach (or the Depreciated Replacement Cost Method). It is also stated that:

> The Residual Method is used to arrive at a value for a vacant site or a site or a building that is ripe for redevelopment.

The valuer should consider each method in every market value exercise and should decide which methods are most appropriate in the circumstances.

However, it is specifically stated that the Cost Approach or the Depreciated Replacement Cost Method (DRC)

> is most commonly used to estimate the Market Value of specialised properties and other properties that are very seldom, if ever, sold or let in the market.

and this approach will be considered more fully later in this chapter.

In the definition of Market Value, 'the estimated amount' refers to the money which the valuer expects would be payable for a property interest in an arm's-length transaction, that is in circumstances in which there is no special relationship between the parties to the transaction. It is the best price which could reasonably be obtained by the seller and the most advantageous price reasonably obtainable by the buyer in accordance with the realities of the current market and with current market expectations. It must be remembered, however, that there will in fact be no sale as the valuation is only for asset valuation purposes for inclusion in financial statements.

Negotiations beneficial to both parties have to be assumed, as a result of which there is neither an inflated nor a deflated value assessed. The buyer is not assumed to be over eager to buy nor the seller over eager to sell, but the present owner is included amongst those who constitute the market. This should therefore mean that market value cannot be assessed at a figure lower than the value to the current owner, who logically would only sell if at least that value, and preferably a higher figure, could be obtained in the open market. However, it has to be assumed that the property is unoccupied at the date of valuation, as a result of which the value assessed cannot be influenced in any way by current occupation. Both parties to the assumed transaction are taken to be reasonably informed about the nature and characteristics of the property interest, and they are both assumed to act prudently judged by the state of the market at the date of valuation, not judged with the benefit of hindsight at some later date.

The Standard provides that Market Value shall not be '…inflated or deflated by special terms or circumstances such as financing which is not typical…' *Special Value* is likewise to be excluded. Special Value relates to an extra element of value over and above Market Value which could be paid in the market place because of special value to an adjoining property or to a particular user, but it would not be an element of value which would be paid by those who did not own an adjoining property or who did not have other special reasons for wishing to purchase a property. It would in fact result in the total value of a property being in excess of Market Value by a figure which would depend upon the circumstances of the case. In reality it is an element of value which might be achievable on an actual sale in special circumstances, but which might equally as well not be obtainable if those circumstances did not apply at a specific point in time.

Market Value has to be assessed as at a specified date, and the value will reflect the state of the market as at that date assuming that the property asset has been offered on the market in the most suitable way to bring about its disposal at the best price which can reasonably be achieved. This means that value has to be assessed on the basis that appropriate methods of marketing must be envisaged for the property interest concerned, and that an appropriate marketing period must also be envisaged. With some types of property an appropriate marketing period might only be a few weeks or a few months, whilst with other types of property a very much longer marketing period would need to be envisaged. The question that has to be determined is what is the best figure that would be obtainable if both appropriate marketing methods and an appropriate marketing period were utilised. Market Value is also understood as the value 'without regard to costs of sale or purchase, and without offset for any associated taxes'.

If the market is so disrupted at any time that Market Value might be impossible to assess, the valuer should clearly indicate this to be the case, and should also disclose all circumstances considered, all the criteria used in the valuation process, and the basis for assumptions made in doing a valuation. Clearly, the circumstances in which such a decision will be made will depend very much upon the judgement of the valuer concerned.

Certain types of property attract relatively few potential buyers at any particular time perhaps because of market conditions or unique factors, and the sale of such properties generally requires a longer marketing period than with other properties. Such might be the state of affairs with a particularly expensive property for which few people or organizations may have sufficient capital to be potential purchasers, or in circumstances such as those which applied in the mid 1960s in the United Kingdom when government imposed credit restrictions prevented banks from lending for property purchase except in extremely limited circumstances.

When a number of similar assets in one ownership have to be valued it would be clearly inappropriate to value each of them on the assumption that offering all of them on the market at the same time would 'flood the market' to the extent that their individual values would be depressed. In such circumstances the valuer ought to value on the basis that at any one time only one of the assets would be offered by the owner onto a market which was normal in other respects. The assumption ought to be made that the owner would adopt a sensible marketing programme in order not to depreciate the value of any individual property offered for sale, as otherwise the collective depreciation of a number of property assets might seriously understate the true value of a company's assets.

Some valuation bases other than market value

The Standards recognize that there are circumstances in which bases of value other than Market Value are required. They identify such bases of value, distinguish them from market value, and establish standards for their application. They provide definitions of a number of types of value which have been commonly referred to by valuers in the past, but for which there have previously been no officially approved definitions, with the result that there may frequently have been misunderstandings as to the precise objective of a valuation made on a particular basis, and also of the implications of such a basis of valuation.

Specialized, special purpose, or specially designed property is rarely, if ever, sold on the open market, except as part of a sale of the business in occupation. Oil refineries, power stations, churches, and similar properties, or properties located in particular geographical locations for operational or business reasons (for example a lighthouse), fit into this category. As such properties are rarely sold the *Depreciated Replacement Cost (DRC)* Method of valuation (see TEGoVA Standard 4) is commonly used in their valuation, the procedure requiring the estimation of the replacement costs of the property to be valued. With respect to this approach, the Standards state that the DRC approach:

> is most commonly used to estimate the Market Value of specialised properties and other properties that are very seldom, if ever, sold or let in the market. This means that the Cost Approach is only ever used when a lack of market activity precludes the use of the comparative method and when the properties to be valued are not suited for valuation by the income approach.
> ...as the Cost Approach is not a market driven method it must not be looked on as a primary valuation method. TEGoVA recommends that it must normally only be used when there is no market driven method available.

Construction costs should, however, be determined by reference to the market and an analysis of market based costs, whilst allowances for depreciation can also be estimated by reference to the market.

DRC is based on an estimate of the current Market Value of the land on which the property stands for its existing use, plus the current gross replacement costs of improvements on the land, less allowances for physical deterioration and all relevant forms of obsolescence. This method of valuation is akin to the conventional Contractors' Method of Valuation, or Summation as it is otherwise known. The specialized nature of the property or its location make it inappropriate to value by comparison with other properties because of the scarcity or complete non-existence of reasonable comparables as market evidence, hence the adoption of the DRC approach.

The Standards state that the DRC procedure is '...unsuitable for use in respect of properties that are held for the purpose of investment, or are surplus to the operational requirements of the company that owns them'.

Market Rental Value has the same definition as Market Value except that the expression 'estimated rent' replaces 'estimated amount', 'lessor' replaces 'buyer', and 'lessee' replaces 'seller'. (See TEGoVA Standard 4.)

The expression *Highest and Best Use* which is used by the IVSC is common in North America and is also frequently used in Australia. It is defined by the IVSC as:

> The most probable use of a property which is physically possible, appropriately justified, legally permissible, financially feasible, and which results in the highest value of the property being valued.
>
> (See TEGoVA Standard 4.)

Existing Use Value is an adaptation of the Market Value definition and is based on the assumption that the property continues to be used for its present use. This will not necessarily include the highest and best use which would be included in the normal assessment of Market Value but which in some cases could only be obtained by offering the property for sale in the open market which would of necessity involve discontinuance of the present use. Market Value for the Existing Use is, therefore, similar to the concept of Going Concern Value as considered earlier in this chapter. *Going Concern Value* is referred to in TEGoVA Standard 5 which says it

> ...relates to the total value of an enterprise based on financial performance of the business, which incorporates intangible as well as tangible assets, goodwill and other non-property market considerations.

The approved TEGoVA definition of Existing Use Value is:

> Existing Use Value is the estimated amount for which a property should exchange on the date of valuation based on continuation of its existing use, but assuming the property is unoccupied, between a willing buyer and a willing seller in an arm's-length transaction after proper marketing wherein the parties had each acted knowledgeably, prudently and without compulsion.
>
> (See TEGoVA Standard 4.)

The essential elements of this definition appear to be that a property has to be such that it would have a value on the market for its existing use, the valuation envisaging the continuation of that use even though it may be lower than the highest and best use value.

Value in Use is the value a specific property has for a specific use to a specific user, that is the value it contributes to the enterprise of which it is a part. It envisages value to the current user, and is not assessed on the basis of the property and the continuing operation being offered for sale on the market. The TEGoVA Standards state:

> Value in use is the Present Value of estimated future cash flows expected to arise from continuing use of an asset and from its disposal at the end of its useful life. The discount rate should be a pre-tax rate that reflects current market assessments of the time value of money and the risks specific to the property. The discount rate should not reflect risks for which future cash flows have been adjusted.
>
> (See TEGoVA Standard 4.)

It is warned that Value in Use should not be confused with *Existing Use Value,* the former relating to a situation in which marketing a property is not envisaged, whilst the latter relates to circumstances in which the market value of a property is assessed on the basis of it continuing to be used for its existing use, although not necessarily by the existing user.

Valuations for the purpose of financial reporting (see TEGoVA Standard 5)

The following observations will cover some of the more important provisions of this Standard, but they are in no way a substitute for reference to the Standard itself, as the intention is merely to provide a summary of the main considerations regarding valuation for financial reporting. Additionally, depending upon the country in which a valuer operates, there may be national valuation and accounting rules which have to be complied with in addition to the Standard. For those operating in the European Community there is also the need to comply with rules imposed by the European Council, although the TEGoVA Standard has been drawn up taking its requirements into account. In particular, it appears that the IVSC/TEGoVA definition of *Market Value* (TEGoVA Standards 4 and 5), The European Commission definition of *Market Value,* and the accountancy term *Fair Value* all have the same effect in practice and would each result in the same estimation of value.

It is necessary for the valuer to define each property to be valued into one of four categories, and then to determine whether each property is a *specialised property* or a *non specialised property.* The four categories or classifications are:

(i)   Owner-occupied – for the purpose of the business;

(ii) Investment for the purpose of generating income or capital gain;
(iii) Surplus to the requirements of the business; or
(iv) Trading stock, designated as current assets.

Specialised properties are as defined earlier in this chapter, that is those '...that are specialised and are rarely (if ever) sold, except as part of the business in occupation.' Any property which is not determined as being specialised will automatically be considered to be a non-specialised property.

Indications of whether assets are essential to an enterprise or not will generally be obtained by the valuer from the directors of a company, as will an indication as to whether assets are regarded as investments. The valuer should therefore obtain from the directors a list of those assets to be valued as existing use assets, surplus assets, or investment assets.

These categories and classifications are important as they determine the valuation base to be used by the valuer. Properties which are surplus to the operational requirements of a business have to be valued on the basis of Market Value, as do properties held as investments. However, surplus properties should only be valued on the Market Value basis if they could be sold on the market without detriment to the continuing business operation; for example, a surplus building might be sited among other operational buildings as a result of which its sale on the market would be physically impracticable. In such circumstances it might be adjudged by a valuer to have a small incremental value to the continuing business, or even no value or a negative value if it is no longer used because of non-compliance with, for example, health and safety standards.

Properties which are occupied by the continuing business should be valued on the basis of *Existing Use Value* as defined earlier in this chapter, which is similar to the accountancy concept of *Fair Value*. The effect of these provisions is that a building which is adjudged to be essential to a continuing business operation has to be valued on the basis of value to that business. Should it subsequently become surplus to the requirements of the business and be physically capable of sale on the open market it could have a substantially higher value if its highest and best use resulted in a higher market value being achievable. In assessing such higher values, a valuer must take into account all underlying market conditions including the legality of alternative uses and the likelihood of planning approval being given for such uses if required. All costs of disposal and of changing to an alternative use should also be deducted from the Market Value assessed in such circumstances. Should valuation procedures suggest that the highest and best use would exceed the value of a property to a business operation, this should be separately noted in the valuer's report.

In assessing Existing Use Value it has to be assumed that the property asset could be sold in the market for that use, and it also has to be assumed that it could be so used for the foreseeable future, that the existing use complies with all legal requirements, and that the property is vacant and available for use on the date of valuation. The last point means that the occupation of the current occupier has to be ignored, but they can be considered as a bidder in the market. This means that the concept of *deprival value* to the existing business operation is an important consideration, this value equating to the amount it would cost the business to replace the asset. The concept of existing use means that any element of value which relates to possible alternative use has to be ignored, as does hope value which could only be achieved by discontinuing the present use.

Properties could be adjudged to be trading stock in some circumstances, such as those in which a property development company had operational buildings and also buildings which it was developing for subsequent sale. In the case of the latter properties they would be valued on the basis of Market Value, with deductions being made for the costs which would be incurred on their sale.

Properties which are adjudged to be specialised properties must be valued on the basis of Depreciated Replacement Cost if there is no market evidence which would enable them to be valued on the basis of Market Value. The references earlier in this chapter to this approach are relevant, and as it is a non-market approach the value determined must be reported as being

> … subject to adequate potential profitability or long-term viability and service potential of the enterprise … compared to the value of the assets employed. The assessment must also be separately itemised in the certificate of valuation.

In using this approach the valuer will have to make allowances for the fact that the property to be valued is an existing property which will almost certainly be subject to depreciation in physical terms and also to elements of obsolescence, whilst the assessment of the Gross Replacement Costs necessary to provide an alternative property will envisage a brand new, modern facility, existing at the date of valuation. However, it should not be overlooked that such an alternative replacement building might be cheaper to provide than the identical replacement of the existing building, if more efficient building techniques could be employed and a more efficient building could be designed.

Valuations for bank security purposes

TEGoVA Standard 6 covers this topic, for which purposes it defines *Market Value*:

> Market Value shall mean the price at which land and buildings could be sold under private contract between a willing seller and an arm's-length buyer on the date of valuation, it being assumed that the property is publicly exposed to the market, that market conditions permit orderly disposal and that a normal period, having regard to the nature of the property, is available for the negotiation of the sale.

This definition is the same as that contained in Article 49(2) of the European Council Directive, and is referred to in the Standards as the EU definition. Whilst the wording differs slightly from the TEGoVA definition as in Standard 4, the concept is similar. It is assumed that the EU definition is used for loan purposes because the major banks of most countries now operate on an international basis. Consequently, an accepted international definition would be appropriate should legal action ever be necessary with respect to loans made with property as a security. The Standard further defines *Mortgage Lending Value*:

> Mortgage Lending Value shall mean the value of the property as determined by a valuer making a prudent assessment of the future marketability of the property by taking into account long term sustainable aspects of the property, the normal and local market conditions, the current use and alternative appropriate uses of the property. Speculative elements may not be taken into account in the assessment of the Mortgage Lending Value. The Mortgage Lending Value shall be documented in a transparent and clear manner.

It is specified that the use of Market Value provides an assessment of value at a given point in time, and that the valuer should, 'as part of the risk appraisal process and subject to the specific circumstances…' also prepare a *forced sale value, an alternative use value, and forecasts of future value*.

A *Forced Sale Value* (see TEGoVA Standard 7) requires the market value approach, but it recognizes that the sum that would be received from the sale of a property might be depressed because of an inadequate marketing period resulting from the circumstances of the sale. It envisages a situation in which the current owner does not have the liberty to sell in the most favourable way but has to sell a property as a matter of urgency. One would expect such a value to be below that which would normally be estimated under the Market Value concept, when a longer selling period would enable a more favourable figure to be achieved.

In valuing for loan purposes, therefore, the emphasis appears to be upon assessing the market value of a property with particular regard being paid to its long term value and specific allowance being made for any doubts that might exist regarding its future value, with the exclusion of any speculative element of value, and taking into account the fact that a possible forced sale of a property may not allow it to be marketed in the most favourable circumstances.

Abnormal or temporary market conditions should be ignored and the property valued as if normal circumstances existed, although presumably this would not result in a valuer ignoring the problems that might result from a possible forced sale in adverse market conditions. Unjustifiably high passing rents, unrealistically favourable capitalisation or discount rates, and any other unusual factors which might result in a high current value at the time of valuation which the valuer considers may be unsustainable in the longer term, would result in a valuer having to make a downward adjustment in value to more realistically reflect what could be regarded as true long term value.

The Standard specifically states that Mortgage Lending Value is not an appropriate concept for the valuation '...of incomplete development projects and wasting assets.'

With wasting assets it is suggested that if a valuation is required particular attention needs to be paid to the relationship between the rate of wastage and the proposed loan arrangements. Clearly, if the value of an asset is depreciating rapidly, the security of loan funds secured against that asset could be at risk particularly if the term of the loan exceeds the likely useful life of the wasting assets or if the rate of depreciation is likely to result in the value of the property becoming less that the amount of the loan at any time during the loan term.

However, it is appropriate when valuing for loan purposes to take into account value for alternative use subject to the provisos that such use would have to be legal, possible in planning control terms, and practicable taking into account market considerations.

It is suggested that owner-occupied properties should be valued on the basis of vacant possession and on the basis of highest and best use, which would exclude any special value to the owner from the value assessed. This is logical, as when property is sold to realize a debt it will invariably be on the basis that the owner has vacated the property.

It is suggested that great caution should be exercised by a valuer if properties to be valued for loan purposes are specialised properties, as their specialised nature may reduce their marketability and thereby their quality as security. Great caution also needs to be observed in valuing a property which would normally be valued by reference to the trading profits produced in it, for if an existing business should experience trading problems it could well be that the value of the property as security could also be threatened, as other business occupiers might experience similar difficulties. In both cases it may be appropriate to prepare valuations on the basis of value with vacant possession for an alternative use, and valuers should report to their clients any misgivings about the value of such properties as security for loans.

The above is a brief summary and commentary on the Standards as they relate to valuation for loan purposes, and the writer would stress the need for loan valuers to fully understand the Standards and the accompanying Guidance Notes which contain detailed guidance with respect to agricultural properties and loans, and the valuation of mortgage portfolios for securitisation purposes.

Professional considerations

The Standards specifically require that a valuer shall have appropriate qualifications, and sufficient knowledge, experience and competency to complete a valuation, or alternatively that any deficiencies should be disclosed to a client before an assignment is accepted. This responsibility of disclosure is very important and is fundamental to the credibility of a valuer and his or her valuations, and indeed to the credibility of the valuation profession. Valuers must be seen to be independent and to have 'no conflicts of interest which are actual or possible and which could be foreseen at the time that the instructions are accepted'. Valuers are also required to comply with 'all legal, regulatory, ethical and contractual requirements related to the assignment' and also to have 'appropriate professional indemnity insurance cover'.

The Standards also require that a valuer must agree certain matters with a client before undertaking a valuation and should consequently also include these matters in his or her report. Among these matters a valuer should adequately identify the property to be valued, the property interest, the basis or bases of valuation to be adopted, the purpose and intended use of the valuation, any limiting conditions, and the effective date of the valuation.

It is required that valuation certificates and reports must not be misleading, and that they should clearly identify the effective date of the valuation and the date on which property inspections were made. The purpose and function of the valuation should be stated together with such other information as is relevant and appropriate to ensure that there can be no misunderstanding on the part of those reading a report. If a valuer has not been in possession of all necessary information required for a valuation, this must be made clear in the certificate or report, as must any specific assumptions made by the valuer. Appraisals should be set out in a manner that will not mislead, and the valuer must provide sufficient information to enable those reading and relying on the report to fully understand its contents and the findings, opinions and conclusions.

Valuation certificates or reports should contain a provision prohibiting the publication of the certificate or report in part or in whole or any references to the certificate or report without prior written approval of the valuer as to such use and the manner in which the material is used. This requirement is clearly intended to prevent, or minimise the possibility of, the misrepresentation of the report or parts of it by third parties, or its use for the wrong purposes by anyone.

'When valuations are made by an "internal Valuer" ...there shall be a specific disclosure in the valuation certificate or report of the existence and nature of any such relationships'. The insistence on the need to indicate when the valuer is valuing for his or her employing organization or when other special relationships exist is repeated in other standards. This is an important provision, as rightly or wrongly some may perceive that a company valuer might value a company's assets more favourably than an external valuer would do, and this knowledge forewarns third parties of the possibility of such an occurrence.

Furthermore, it is made quite clear that a valuer should perform adequate and relevant research, perform competent analyses, and should draw informed and supportable judgements. There will be no more relying simply on '...my 20 years experience and a "gut feeling" that this is the value...', and if market data are scarce the valuer will have to reveal that fact in the report. In cases in which the valuer has to rely primarily on judgement, the report must make that clearly evident.

Valuers have to pay particular attention to market evidence when market circumstances are unusual, such as when there is a rapidly rising, a rapidly falling, or an unstable market, when properties or the so-called comparables are specialized, or when there are substantial differences between the property being valued and the supposed comparables.

Concluding observations

The TEGoVA Standards contain much other useful information for valuers including Standards relating to *Estimates, Forecasts and Other Appraisals, to Valuations for Investment – Insurance Companies, Property Unit Trusts, and Pension Funds, Etc.*, and to *Valuation Reporting*. In addition there are almost 200 pages of very useful Guidance Notes together with eight Appendices which also include helpful information. They should therefore be essential reading and reference material for any property valuer.

In reality the matters included in the Standards relate to standards and procedures which competent professional valuers should automatically observe. They incorporate many considerations which should be fully covered in a well designed and well taught valuation course, and they should cause no concern for those who wish to operate as truly professional valuers.

The fact that they are detailed and recorded as Standards has the benefit of them being seen to be approved by groups of professionals so emphasizing their importance, with the added advantage that they represent standards agreed on an international basis. In addition the recording and agreement of these Standards should assist valuers as they provide an approved basis of valuation for many important situations; as long as valuers operate according to the Standards they should be able to argue that they have operated as a reasonably competent professional valuer normally would. This should provide a good defence in the event of litigation, but on the other hand the existence of the Standards may provide the rope with which those who do not observe them may be hung.

In the case of those valuers who were already competent and professional in approach the main significance of the introduction of the Standards will be that the approaches and methods of different valuers will be standardised, which should introduce greater certainty into the valuation profession, whilst practices adopted in different countries will be standardised as much as national laws and customs permit. This should assist valuers and those using valuers' services in particular, whilst it should also, through demanding higher standards of them, improve the performances of poorer valuers or see them go out of business, at least in respect of assets valuations for financial reports.

Most importantly, these Standards should ensure that valuers provide a high level of service to their clients and society, and that has to be to everyone's advantage.

Chapter 13

The Valuation of Retail Property

Introduction

In developed countries in particular there are substantial amounts of retail property space in which very significant amounts of total retail turnover occur each year, a healthy retailing sector usually being an indication of both a prosperous country and a prospering economy.

For example, in Australia in 1995 there were approximately 40 million square metres of retail space with sales in excess of $110 billion per annum, and there were about 180,000 separate retail premises. There was therefore a separate retail outlet for approximately every 100 people in Australia at that time and an annual retail expenditure of about $5,900 per capita. The stock of retail properties comprised a significant part of the total sum invested in property in Australia, which in turn represented a significant proportion of the total capital investment of the country. The relatively recent introduction of compulsory superannuation contributions in that country is likely to result in even more investment funds being channelled into retail property investments, with the result that the importance of retail property to the average Australian is likely to increase.

Indeed, The Australian Bureau of Statistics report *Retail Industry Australia 1998–99* stated that

> …at the end of June 1999 there were 98,289 employing businesses (management units) operating in the retail trade industry; by then they …generated a total income of A$169.3 billion and at 30 June 1999 employed just over 1.1 million persons.

These figures indicate that there was on average a separate retail business – as opposed to retail premises referred to in the previous paragraph – for about every 190 people, whilst approximately 5.8% of the total population was employed in the retail sector at June 1999. Additionally, by 30 June 1999 retail expenditure per capita of the total population had risen to approximately $8,900 per annum. Such statistics suggest that the retail sector has become an even more important sector of the Australian economy, with a large increase in retail turnover between 1995 and 1999. This represents a

153

significant increase over a short period of time, but it is not particularly surprising and it appears to be a feature of developing economies with rising standards of living that the retail sector becomes increasingly more important as the population's disposable income increases.

In the United Kingdom the Office for National Statistics (ONS) figures indicated that in 2001 retailing turnover was estimated at £226.07 billion, which equates to about £3,840 per capita annual retail expenditure for the total estimated population of almost 59 million. The ONS Annual Business Inquiry estimated that for 2001 in the United Kingdom 3,154,000 people were employed in 'Retail Trade, except Motor vehicles and motor cycles; repair of personal and household goods', which was approximately 5.3% of the total population and 12.5% of the total working population. Furthermore, a report from the Office of the Deputy Prime Minister entitled *Commercial and Industrial Floorspace and Rateable Value Statistics 2000* indicated that in 2000 there were 105,094,000 square metres of retail floor space in England and Wales (not the United Kingdom) with 573,533 separate retail hereditaments. On these figures there was therefore a separate retail hereditament for approximately every 91 people in England and Wales which had an estimated combined population in mid 2001 of 52,084,500.

These statistics indicate the importance of the retail sector in modern economies particularly in highly developed countries, whilst in developing countries growth of the retail sector is likely to be a significant aspect of a country's economic development, the sector becoming increasingly more important as standards of living increase with resultant increases in retail expenditure.

The values of retail properties and the valuations performed by valuers will therefore be extremely important in that the increasing stock of properties and trends in retailing will probably result in substantial future changes in the values of at least some and probably the majority of retail properties. In addition the significance of retail property valuations to financial institutions and their investment policies is likely to increase as the monitoring standards applicable to financial institutions and companies become stricter, as they almost inevitably will, particularly those which relate to organizations responsible for superannuation savings and pensions.

It is appropriate first to consider the conventional approach to retail property valuation, and then some fundamentals of property valuations because, just as sportsmen often fail as a result of ignoring basic principles of their sports, it is all too easy to pay insufficient attention to the fundamental determinants of value.

Indeed, many negligence claims arise because of the neglect by professionals of fairly basic considerations. A lot of the large negligence claims which have been determined by the United Kingdom courts have not been determined on the issue of whether the valuer made the right value judgement, but on the basis of the neglect of the valuer to address fundamental issues which were relevant to the valuation task in hand. A 'whole new industry' which goes under the title of 'due diligence' has arisen because of the failure of professionals in many instances to observe fundamental procedures and to consider important and essential basic facts, due diligence procedures relating to a series of investigations which ought in reality to have been undertaken in the past as a matter of course by all true professionals.

With respect to methods of valuation, a United Kingdom article written in 1995 ('Evaluating Valuations', *Estates Gazette* 9540:62) began with the statement 'During the recession, valuation methods were tested under fire and found wanting'. As observed in Chapter 9, it is open to debate whether the methods were tried and found wanting, as possibly what actually happened was that too many valuers were found wanting in the way they applied those methods. Whatever the truth of the situation, it is suggested that many of the criticisms of valuations in the past could have been avoided had valuers in general been more diligent in the investigation of fundamental valuation considerations.

The conventional approach to retail property valuation

In the Australian text book *Land Valuation and Compensation in Australia* by Rost & Collins (Australian Institute of Valuers and Land Economists 1993) it was stated that:

> Rentals of retail premises are frequently expressed at so much per week for each metre run of street frontage occupied. The unit value per metre frontage will vary for shops of greater or lesser depth and/or frontage than is normal in the locality.
>
> For some premises ... the extent of the space occupied is frequently of more importance than the actual length of street frontage.
>
> In determining the rental value of a shop with dwelling, the rental value of the shop itself is estimated by reference to the units of rental value in the locality. The rental value of the residential section is then added.

The rental value of the upper floors of retail premises can be expressed in and compared at amounts per square metre of the available selling area. Analyses of rentals in the locality paid for single storied premises and rentals paid for those which have upper floors may indicate the rental value per square metre of areas in the upper sections.

There was in total less than one page to cover retail property valuation even though by 1993 retail property was a major economic and investment asset, and the entire emphasis was that valuation should be based on the unit of comparison found by analysing other transactions. That is the valuation would be based upon the figure found from the analysis of other market transactions, with adjustments to the figure per square metre being made if shops were either bigger or smaller than the normal sized unit of occupation. The approach briefly indicated in Rost & Collins is based on finding an average rent per square metre for the entire shop unit, that is it assumes that space at the back of a shop is just as valuable as the space at the front of a shop, which may well be correct in some cases but which is likely to be a false basis for valuation in others.

The Appraisal of Real Estate, eighth edition (The American Institute of Real Estate Appraisers 1987), devoted about two pages to retail properties, but did not actually say much about how to value them. However, in the section on 'Community Shopping Centers' it was stated:

> Sales potentials may be estimated from various surveys of consumer buying patterns, which are conducted by the U.S. Department of Commerce, certain universities, and private and trade organizations. Studying historical patterns and changes in the number and types of competing establishments helps an appraiser to determine the market share of a particular center.

It therefore referred to historical patterns and also to sales potential, and the latter point, it is suggested, is very important. In a later section there was reference to the use of units of comparison, namely price per square foot and price per foot front. Again, this was relatively scant coverage of retail property valuations for a country which almost certainly has the most retail property in value terms of any in the world.

A later edition, *The Appraisal of Real Estate*, twelfth edition (The American Institute of Real Estate Appraisers 2001), devoted approximately seven and a half pages specifically to retail properties. This expanded coverage includes sections on retail districts; descriptions of types of shopping centres; functional utility in shopping centres; emerging trends in shopping centre design; important factors in demand analysis; and forecasting demand. Coverage is at what might be described as a macro level rather than a micro level, discussion concentrating on factors that determine general levels of demand and the relative values of shopping centres or shopping districts, the market analysis of existing retail areas, and the analysis of demand for new property. However, there appears to be little or no consideration of what actually determines the rents which are likely to be paid for individual shop units or how they should be valued.

The United Kingdom valuation texts devote much more space to the valuation of retail properties and *Modern Methods of Valuation* by Tony Johnson, Keith Davies & Eric Shapiro (Estates Gazette, 2000) devoted about nine pages to it, whilst in *Valuation, Principles into Practice* edited by WH Rees (Estates Gazette, 2000), coverage extended to 20 pages. In devoting so much more space to this topic these texts acknowledge the complexity of the modern retail scene and the importance of retail property valuation.

The determinants of property values

The value of an article is the representation in money terms of the utility of that article, market value being determined as a result of the sale by the current owner to a willing purchaser. In property markets there are two distinct types of value; rental value is the figure which represents the utility of a property for periodic use over a temporary and generally predetermined period, whilst capital value represents the utility of the property to the owner of the freehold or superior leasehold interest in the property. That capital value may indicate the utility to an owner occupier or to an owner investor, in the latter case utility being the ability to generate an adequate net investment return.

As already suggested, rental value represents what an existing or a potential user is prepared to pay for the periodic use of a property, and that value is likely to be almost entirely determined by the user's perception of the likely value in use of that property for a specific purpose, in this case for a retailing activity of some specific kind. In addition to the likely value in use of the particular property, rental value will normally be very much influenced by the supply of other suitable retail properties onto the market. If there is competition amongst suppliers of properties, retailers will rent properties from the cheapest supply source. However, they will only do this if such a decision does not adversely affect their retailing potential; the net profits expected from retailing in a cheaper property should therefore not be less than those expected from retailing in a dearer property. Overall the major determinants of retail rental values are likely to be the perceived potential profitability of various retailing activities on the part of those considering leasing them, and the amount of property suitable for those purposes which is supplied onto the market.

Despite this second factor, in an open market the most important determinants of retail rental values are likely to be the perceptions of potential retailers with respect to anticipated profitability. The rent a retailer is prepared to pay represents his or her assessment of the utility of that property to the business in current circumstances and in the reasonably predictable circumstances of a relatively short term future. This will certainly be the case if leases can only be obtained for periods of three to five years as is the case in some countries because of a reluctance on the part of landlords to let properties for longer terms. In effect the assessments by retailers of their ability to make profits is probably the major determinant of retail rental values, as if a retailer does not believe he or she can make profits from an outlet at a specified rent, then they will be foolish to rent it at that figure.

On the other hand, the capital value of a retail property is determined essentially by the perceptions of investors – and sometimes of owner occupiers – of the long term quality of the property as an investment. However, as that long term assessment is influenced by the capacity of the property to generate rental income, it is therefore also influenced by retailers' assessments of its shorter term quality as a retail outlet. If retailers are only prepared to pay a relatively low rental then the capital value will automatically be depressed, while if a property does not reveal the potential to produce high rent levels coupled with the likelihood of future increases in rent levels, then investors are unlikely to regard it as a favourable long term investment proposition, as a result of which they too will regard it unfavourably. The value perceptions of investors are likely in reality to be very much influenced by the initial value perceptions of retailers who are the potential users of retail properties. If a property is attractive to a range of retailers and likely to remain so, it is also highly likely to be attractive to a property investor.

The return to an investor owner will be the rental which is paid by a retail lessee less the owner's expenses and outgoings, and only if a property is attractive to a potential trader will it have a rental value in the market at any point in time. Whatever the age, location, design or physical condition of a retail property may be, it is the ability and willingness of a retailer to pay a rent for it which is the essential element in the value of that property. As already indicated, it is the present and future trading potential of a property which determines its present rental value, and in the same way it is the anticipation of future rental returns which determines the present capital value of a property. Investors contemplating the purchase of a retail property should first estimate what rental returns they can expect immediately and in the future, and should relate their capital bids for the property to those rental estimates in a way which, in their view, adequately reflects both the good features and the bad features of the property. They should also take into account future economic expectations and the relative quality of the investment when compared with other potential investments.

Although investors may be influenced by the past performance of an investment, the major factors determining the bids they are likely to make should be the current performance and their expectations of future performance. Their bids will be determined by their predictions of the rental flows likely to be produced by a property and their judgement of the future investment risks likely to be associated with that property.

General factors affecting retail property values

A major factor affecting the value of retail properties is *the location of a property and the suitability of that location for a particular type of trade*. Locational suitability will vary from trade to trade, and a valuer will need to understand trading needs and to estimate what particular type of trader is likely to be attracted to specific properties. Where there is likely to be competition between a number of types of trade for one specific location, it is probable that the trade with the greatest profit potential will be able to secure the outlet by outbidding other traders, although this may not necessarily be the case when an enlightened landlord is seeking a retailer who will help to create a good mix of outlets in a group of shops, so improving the overall variety of goods on offer to shoppers. What trade is likely to be most profitable in a particular location will depend upon many variables, including accessibility, the size of the local population, their purchasing power, their propensity to spend and their consumer preferences. Location is probably the most important determinant of retail property values and requires very careful consideration by valuers.

Accessibility for customers is closely related to location, and the existence of good road, rail and bus access together with ease of parking is likely to very much enhance the value of any particular retail unit. A major attraction of modern shopping centres is the ease of access to them provided by purpose built access roads and the proximity of ample parking space close to the shops, although some centres are now becoming so large that there is no guarantee that shoppers can in fact park close to the shops they wish to visit.

The physical features of the premises are also very important and are likely to determine their suitability for particular types of trade and also their value to the trade for which they are best suited. The number of floors, whether they are usable or surplus to requirements, the overall size of the accommodation, its subdivision into rooms and the sizes of individual rooms, the length of the street frontage, the suitability of window display space, the adequacy of ceiling heights, the load bearing capacities of floors, the existence or otherwise of pavement display areas, the existence of necessary storage space, the quality of access for service and delivery vehicles, the state of repair and maintenance, the cost of the same and of necessary adaptations and refurbishment, are all likely to be important to a potential lessee and likely to affect the rental bid.

New shops are invariably let as 'shells' with the lessee having to provide all internal finishes even including the provision of services from the mains throughout the unit. Whilst this may result in a unit being more easily adaptable to the needs of a particular trade, it will also result in considerable cost for a lessee which will be reflected by that lessee in the rental bid made for a unit. It requires considerable capital outlay for a lessee to fit-out a modern retail unit for discretionary shopping, and if, for example, a lease offered is only for five years, the annual equivalent cost of a fit-out of £100,000 in such circumstances would be well in excess of £20,000 taking into account interest on capital employed. In addition to this annual equivalent cost, the lessee will also have to pay rent and other property outgoings such as charges for the provision of services and tenant's rates and taxes where applicable. The higher the total of all these additional costs of occupation, the lower will be the amount a potential lessee can afford to bid as rent.

The status of the tenant and the type of trade can be important valuation factors particularly in respect of the security offered by a letting, and in general leases will be considered less risky when the lessee is a well established and reputable chain of national or international repute, and more risky when a letting is to a small trader who may not be well established and who may be more likely to fail in business. However, the reputation and market power of chain lessees may be such that the bargaining power they possess is likely to result in them negotiating lower rent levels, and in some cases the rents major lessees pay are so low that, even when capitalised at a secure yield, the capital value of their lease represents a low figure when compared with the replacement cost of the property. This is frequently so in the case of department stores, discount stores and supermarket occupiers when they are the magnets – that is dominant attractions – in major shopping centres, the property owners having given them leases at low rents in their anxiety to secure them as lessees.

However, in general terms it is true that a letting to a major and reputable tenant will normally be considered much less risky by investors than will a letting to an individual trader, and these relative risk levels will be reflected in lower capitalisation rates being adopted for the capitalisation of income flow, and consequently in higher capital values.

Lease terms and conditions will have an important bearing on the value of let properties. The effect on value of the length of a lease; the existence or otherwise of rent review clauses; the frequency of reviews; the existence of break clauses which might allow a lessee to terminate a lease at an early date; the basis on which rent is to be reviewed; the responsibilities of the parties for outgoings (such as rates, taxes, insurance, and management expenses), and for repairs and maintenance; and the existence of restrictive covenants and the details of the trading covenants attaching to a lease, should all be carefully considered by the valuer and reflected in the valuation process.

In the United Kingdom in particular the valuation of retail properties is often done using the 'Zoning' approach, this approach acknowledging that the window display area and the front area of a shop is often the most valuable space in that it enables goods to be displayed and so assists in attracting potential customers into a shop. Accordingly it is regarded as more valuable than back space and space in basements or on upper floors which may often be used for such purposes as storage, consequently being regarded as less valuable to potential tenants. It is possible to analyse lettings to try to determine what 'natural zones' of value are revealed by market transactions, and it is often found that valuations are done on the basis of perhaps '7 metre zones with halving back'. The effect of this would be that with an 8 metre wide shop which is 18 metres deep with a 'Zone A' value of £800 per square metre the rental valuation would be:

Zone A rental value = 8m	7m	£800 =	£44,800	pa
Zone B rental value = 8m	7m	£400 =	£22,400	pa
Zone C rental value = 8m	4m	£200 =	£ 6,400	pa
Rental Value =			£ 73,600	pa

Using such an approach, the analysis of market evidence and the judgement of the valuer are both very important, and the rate applied to basement space and upper level accommodation will both be dependent on these. In general such space is likely to be valued at a Zone C rate or lower value, although circumstances may in some cases dictate that it commands a higher or lower relative value.

The Zoning approach is likely to have limited or no application to the valuation of the type of retail accommodation generally occupied by department stores, supermarkets and other trades which require large amounts of space, the rental value of such space generally being consistent throughout the entire retail unit so used.

Zoning has been considered to be particularly useful when there are units of varying width and varying depths, the zoning approach making allowances for the effect on rental values that such variations may have.

Valuation by Comparison

Reference to the past has been made but the importance of present circumstances has also been stressed, and, more particularly, the importance of future expectations. However, the convention with many valuers (as confirmed by quotations earlier in this chapter) is to value by use of the Method of Comparison whenever possible, that is whenever there is evidence of comparable transactions on which to base current valuations. In using the comparison approach one makes the fundamental assumption that what happened in past property transactions provides a good indication of what is likely to happen currently and in the future, whilst it is quite clear that a valuation made today should represent value based on expectations of what will happen in both the immediate and the more distant future. What has happened in the past may in fact be completely irrelevant, and yet a large proportion of the valuations made in the market are probably firmly based on the past rather than being assessed through looking to the future.

What the author frequently refers to as 'the love affair with the comparable' holds many dangers for valuers, particularly in a world which is changing as rapidly as the modern world. The concept that comparables will indicate what the likely rent of a vacant property will be is based on the assumption that today's most likely tenant, when assessing the property currently available, will be influenced in his or her business decision by what another trader, possibly in a different line of business, with different personal and business circumstances, paid for a different shop, in a different location, at a different point in time, and with underlying economic conditions which may have changed significantly since that transaction occurred.

When looked at realistically it can be regarded as a somewhat extreme suggestion, as ridiculous as suggesting that you or I will be primarily influenced in our expenditure decisions by what others have decided in the past, rather than by our own needs, desires, constraints and perceptions.

Comparables are not to be ignored, as if they are available they are evidence which should be considered, but comparables have to be used extremely carefully. They tell what happened in the past in different circumstances, many of which the valuer relying on a comparable will be unable to determine precisely because of the limited availability of information relating to many comparable transactions. In any event the valuer's task is to try to estimate current value which is dependent on future expectations. Comparable evidence is likely to be helpful in giving an indication of the general level of values; alternatively, it may be helpful in indicating trends in value if the comparable transactions are sufficient in number and sufficiently comparable to be acceptable evidence and to give a reliable indication of either general levels of value or trends in value.

The use of comparable evidence as the main basis for the valuation of retail properties was probably far more acceptable in the past as market considerations were generally very different. In shopping developments in the past there was often a greater similarity in the size of shop units, whilst, with the multiplicity of landlords which generally existed in most street shopping locations, there was more competition on the supply side, which competition more than likely generally resulted in many lessees getting what amounted to a consumer's surplus in the rent agreed. That is lessees were able to negotiate on a number of potential properties as a result of which they often did not have to bid up to the maximum economic rental they could afford to pay before eating into the desirable net return from their proposed retailing activity.

It is suggested that that situation has been changed considerably by a number of factors:

(i)   large blocks of retail property in any locality are now frequently owned by one supplier – that is by shopping centre owners – which results in a quasi monopolistic supply situation in which retail lessees may have extremely limited bargaining power;

(ii) the turnover rent system applied in many areas results in landlords having 'insider information' regarding retailers' businesses which enables them to press for the maximum possible rent from a retailer which they, the landlords, believe could be paid by that particular retailer;

(iii) the objective of many institutional retail property owners of achieving ever increasing returns from their investments to make them competitive in the open market for property trust units and shares, results in them expecting and seeking increased rents as frequently as annually, irrespective of economic or retailing conditions. With the more traditional type of landlord it was regularly a major objective to keep good relationships with an existing lessee to maintain long term occupation and hence long term income flow, landlords in such circumstances being content with what they regarded as a fair rent agreed for several years in advance.

The quest by some modern property owners for annual rent increases which often results in them taking a bigger share of retailers' gross turnovers irrespective of the net profits achievable by retailers, and the other factors referred to above, create a situation in which comparable evidence is not necessarily a good indicator of what the next potential lessee may be able to afford in terms of rent for a vacant shop, and what rent is in reality likely to be paid immediately and also over the longer term. What a potential lessee can in fact afford to pay in rent is directly related to the potential turnover of a specific trading activity, the likely costs needed to produce that turnover, and the risk attached to the proposed business operation. Returns to different retail activities vary greatly, as confirmed by quotes from the Australian Bureau of Statistics publication *Retail Industry Australia 1998–99*:

> At 30 June 1999, the 67,561 businesses in food retailing and personal and household good retailing operated from an estimated 89,039 locations … with the average retail sales being $5,568 per square metre. This varied from a high of $7,666 per square metre in the Supermarket and grocery stores group to a low of $383 per square metre in the Household and repair services group.

If one takes into account the fact that the above figures refer to averages in groups, some supermarkets will have produced turnover in excess of $7,666 per square metre, whilst some outlets in the household and repair services group will have had turnover below $383 per square metre. Clearly with such widely varying turnover figures the ability of different types of retailers to pay rent will vary enormously. Based on the Australian figures quoted above, to use a comparable rent from a supermarket operator to justify a rent demanded from a retailer in the household and repair services group would therefore generally be quite absurd.

The estimation of rental value

It is likely that the use of comparables for the estimation of retail rental values will rarely be a reliable basis of valuation in the modern retailing scenario. The ability of any retailer to pay rent will be directly related to the ability to make profits from a specific retail outlet, and to the expected level of those anticipated profits. The higher the profit potential in any location, the higher will be the rent a trader can afford to pay.

In estimating the rent they can afford to pay for any retail unit, a retailer will use the following calculations:

		Anticipated gross takings from the business.
Less		Cost of purchasing stock
Equals		Gross profits from business
Less		Trading expenses
Equals		Net profits from the business
Less		Allowance for interest on capital employed,
	Plus	Allowance for the labour and expertise of the retailer,
	Plus	Allowance for the risk attached to the business
Equals		Balance available to pay the costs of Property Occupation (Rent plus other property outgoings).

The rental value of any retail outlet is clearly directly related to the ability of potential occupiers to generate business income in that location, the residue of income available for property rental and the payment of other property occupation costs being directly related to the initial income less the overall costs of trading. Total deductions must include an allowance for interest on the capital a trader employs in the business, be it borrowed capital on which the trader actually has to pay interest, or the trader's own capital which could be earning interest if invested other than in the business; an allowance for a salary for the trader who could otherwise work in other employment to produce a salary commensurate with both the labour provided and the level of expertise of the trader; and an allowance for the risk which an individual takes by going into business rather than seeking employment elsewhere at a lower level of risk than that which attaches to the retailing operation. Without allowances to the business person for all of these items there can be little reason for anyone entering into a business activity.

If valuers are to make realistically reliable valuations of retail properties, it is essential that they have an understanding of the turnover potential and the trading costs which would be applicable to average traders – that is typically competent traders – in a range of retail trades, and that they keep themselves fully aware of developments which affect any of the constituent parts of the above calculation.

Anything which adversely affects the profit potential of a trading outlet is likely also to adversely affect the ability of a retailer to pay a particular level of rent. Adverse factors might include:

(i)   A deterioration in overall economic conditions both nationally and locally;
(ii)   competition from other retail outlets be they in the same locality or in other competing localities;
(iii)   unsatisfactory or deteriorating standards of shopping centre management;
(iv)   management policies which permit too much competition within a specific trade in the same centre;
(v)   the development of new competing shopping areas or new methods of retailing;
(vi)   increases in the costs of trading imposed on retailers by such things as adverse movements in the value of the pound or the dollar (that is in the currency of the home country);

(vii) increased charges which suppliers seek to pass on to retailers; and

(viii) increases in operating costs including statutory increases in such things as the wage rates of employees, superannuation contributions, payroll tax and other statutory contributions, or other cost increases resulting from new or more onerous legislative provisions which affect the retail operation.

All of the above are factors which could reduce the profitability of retail outlets and which could therefore create situations in which retailers could not afford to pay a previous level of rent. It appears that some property owners and property managers sometimes ignore such considerations, their demands for higher rents at times of adverse retailing conditions themselves being a threat to the long term security of some retail property investments.

It is clear that many factors which are likely to adversely affect trading returns, and hence rental values, are completely outside the control of both retailers and retail property owners, and the valuer therefore needs to be conversant with developments and trends in the economy and society in general, and to consider their likely effects on retail property values. Difficult though it may be, the valuer has to try to make reasonable (and reasoned) predictions of the future.

The Profits Method of Valuation

Before considering in more detail some of the factors which are likely to affect rental levels, it is appropriate to comment further on the rental equation referred to above. Such an approach to valuation has been used for many years and in the United Kingdom it is known as the Profits Method of Valuation. However, while it is a traditional method of valuation, its use in the past was by convention generally restricted to situations in which there was an element of monopoly attached to a trading activity, such monopoly usually being related either to the need to have a licence in order to pursue a particular type of business activity, or, more rarely, to situations in which a unique or extremely unusual geographical location gave a business property a locational monopoly. This convention was probably based on the assumption in the past that the comparative method would in most cases provide reliable valuation information, but if there could be no true comparable because of monopoly considerations, value had to be assessed from basic principles.

Whilst one should not throw out convention without careful consideration, because conventions usually exist for good reasons, one should nevertheless regularly question conventional methods as changing circumstances may well call for changes in approaches. It has already been suggested that there are good reasons to use comparable evidence with extreme caution, as a consequence of which it becomes essential to consider what alternative approach might be more reliable. It has also been intimated why the Profits Method can be considered an appropriate indicator of potential rent levels for retail outlets. It is also a fact that in modern shopping centres in particular, the control which owners and managers have over the location of various types of traders and the control which they can exercise through covenants in leases, actually results in many retail outlets (and their lessees) being in a similar situation to that of the licensees for which this method of valuation has regularly been used. However, whilst these factors may be interesting, the main reason for recommending the use of the Profits Method has to be, quite simply, that when used by a well informed valuer it is likely to produce the best estimates of rental values of retail outlets, and certainly more reliable estimates than those obtainable from the use of comparable evidence. In any case, comparable evidence is frequently not sufficiently comparable to be completely reliable, and frequently not available in sufficient numbers also to do anything other than provide a general indication of levels of value.

In case anyone should believe the suggested use of the Profits Method of Valuation for valuing retail properties to be new and radical thinking, it is appropriate to remember that this is exactly the same theory as that propounded by David Ricardo in *The Principles of Political Economy and Taxation* published in 1817, whilst in *The Economics of Real Property* by Ralph Turvey (George Allen & Unwin, London 1957) the author said (page 14):

> It follows that the only practicable method for a person to estimate the value of a shop to himself or his firm is to start by estimating the turnover which can be obtained if the shop is run in the normal manner … the various cost items can be forecast fairly accurately by reference to the experience of other similar shops. Thus rental value can be ascertained residually …

In looking further at issues affecting retail property values, it is appropriate to remember that capital values are a function of annual values, and that with respect to the profits estimation process there are a number of variables which determine the bottom line figure. Anything which affects, or is likely to affect in the future, any one of those variables is therefore a relevant valuation consideration. The likely gross turnover from a business activity is extremely important, as the higher the potential turnover the greater is the ability to pay rent, unless when increased turnover occurs there is a more than equivalent increase in the costs incurred. The cost of purchasing stock, the trends in trading expenses (which include a large number of separate cost items), and the cost of interest on borrowed money (including that borrowed from the retailer, that is the retailer's equity), are all important variables which valuers should carefully consider.

It should also not be overlooked that the residual figure is available to pay the total costs of property occupation, which has to be split between rent, management and service charges, and property rates and taxes. Any increases in management and service charges and in property rates and taxes therefore reduce the ability to pay rent, unless such increases are matched by increased returns and increased retailing profits, whilst the converse also applies.

The retail property valuer therefore needs to be an observer and analyst of many variables, and it is appropriate to consider some of them more fully.

Variables which affect retail property values

Economic Conditions

Ultimately, business turnover is determined to a very great extent by the general conditions of an economy, returns to most retailing activities being higher when an economy booms and lower during periods of recession or depression, all other things being equal. Valuers therefore have to be practising economists, and this, sadly, is an area in which many members of the valuation profession have probably not been particularly good in the past. An awareness of the current state of a number of key economic indicators and of trends in the same, and of their likely implications for retailing activity, and hence for retail property values, is an essential underpinning for competent and professional valuations.

Trends in productivity, in import levels, in price competitiveness between imports and home produced products, in employment levels and wage levels in general but in particular in the local area, in levels of disposable income, in interest rates which affect the latter, and demographic considerations, are all particularly important factors affecting retail property values, and should be carefully studied by valuers.

Comforting though the myth that you cannot lose in property investment may be to those who sell real estate, it is indeed a myth, and the valuer should in particular be conscious of trends which are likely to adversely affect values; this is especially important because of the dangers of litigation and in view of the high cost of professional indemnity insurance. The valuer should not be ultracautious but he or she should be realistic enough to recognize that economic reality dictates that retail property rent levels and capital values do not automatically rise from year to year, neither are they in any way immune from falls in value, particularly value in real terms.

Competition

The turnover of any retail undertaking will be very much affected by the level of competition both within a particular line of trade and also for retail expenditure in total. Whilst the number of competitors in the same type of business and the strength of competition they offer when competing for sales of a particular type are likely to play an important part in determining the turnover of a specific retailer, so in the long term will competition which results in expenditure in total being diverted from that retail trade to another form of expenditure, be it in retailing or elsewhere. So for instance, whilst total expenditure may not be reduced and the wish of people to spend may remain the same, if incomes remain unchanged but payments for superannuation, tax or house purchase unavoidably are increased, the ability of people to spend on other things will be reduced, and so the turnover of individual retailers is likely to fall. A consideration of the effects of competition should not therefore be restricted to competition within the same line of business, but should take into account competition from other types of businesses and all other forms of potential expenditure, including items controlled by government, such as taxation. What is happening outside retailing may be more important than what is happening within it!

Retail competition

Obviously, what is happening within retailing is very important, and when there is extensive shopping development occurring in the form of the development of new centres and extensions to existing centres it is likely to impact upon the performance of other existing centres. Whilst analysts may maintain that there will be adequate retail expenditure to support all new developments, such predictions appear to be based on the assumption that the ability and the propensity to spend of the population will remain unchanged, and that alternative forms of retailing will not have an adverse effect on shopping streets and shopping centres. In addition, some predictions do not appear to allow for the significant change in age distribution of the population which will occur in the relatively near future in many developed countries. It should also not be overlooked that it is in the interests of many analysts themselves to make optimistic forward predictions, for their incomes, or those of their firms, are frequently directly related to the amount of new development which is proposed. In such circumstances there is likely to be a propensity to support predictions which encourage growth in retail property development.

Valuers will need to carefully consider whether there will in reality be sufficient total retail expenditure to support the levels of rents which have been paid to date in existing centres, and which are predicted for centres yet to be developed, because if this is not the case both rental and capital values are likely to suffer in at least some existing centres as well as in some newly developed centres.

It is probable that extensions to some existing centres are not always as successful as anticipated by the developers, and it appears that in some extended centres all that seems to occur is that new units are let to retailers who increase competition for existing traders within the same centre. It may well be that rather than there being an increase in the range of goods available to shoppers in many centres, all that happens is that more shops of the same type compete for a total market which may in reality be inadequate to support all the retailers in the enlarged centre. The result may be that keen price competition ensues to the benefit of shoppers, but because of the keen competition there are under performing retail outlets which ultimately spell danger not only for the retailers, but for rent levels overall and consequently the capital value of the centre.

Too much competition in one area of retailing may be detrimental to all the retailers concerned, and may in effect be detrimental to the overall success of a centre and to an owner's interests.

In reality, therefore, the long term result of some planned retail development may be a surplus of retail outlets which adversely affects both many rental and capital values, the only winners perhaps being builders and developers who have been fortunate enough to get a development profit before values slump, and shoppers who benefit from intense retail competition which results in lower retail prices. Valuers will need to keenly monitor developments in retailing, occupancy rates, and rental trends if they are to be able to accurately forecast trends and values, particularly in those areas which are most subject to development activity.

Trading covenants

It is customary, and good management practice, for owners and managers to seek to control the balance of retail activities within a managed shopping area by use of covenants which both permit and restrict specific types of retailing, and the rental value of an individual outlet is likely to be very much dependent upon the type of retailing activity the property owner will permit it to be used for. It is clear that the type of goods or services which an outlet is entitled to sell under the terms of a lease will affect the anticipated total turnover which can be expected from a business, and it is therefore essential for any valuer to study the lease which applies to any property interest to be valued, and then to consider what the likely turnover will be on those specific lease terms.

Whilst it is critical to consider such covenants in valuing individual outlets, it is also very important to be aware of what trading covenants are being granted to other traders. When, as in the case of enlarged centres, more retailers are granted similar trading covenants to existing lessees, or when the covenants of other traders are extended to allow them to increase the competition to existing traders in a particular line of business, clearly the balance of rental values is likely to be disturbed. Total rental values and pro rata rental values may also be decreased if there is insufficient trade available to adequately support all those ultimately permitted to trade in the same line of business. Changes in policy with respect to trading covenants may in reality result in excessive competition and adverse effects on total rental value in just the same way as the overdevelopment of properties may do.

The effect of increased competition which results from allowing variations in trading covenants may be extremely important when it results in major tenants who pay subsidised rents being permitted to compete with specialty traders, this new competition often resulting in specialty traders being unable to continue trading profitably. Such competition is in effect often subsidised, as many major tenants are allowed to occupy space at rental levels which provide an inadequate return on capital because they are regarded by property owners as magnets, that is they are major attractions which draw shoppers to a centre, whilst the specialty traders regularly occupy space at far higher rental levels. Valuers and property managers should appreciate that whilst management decisions such as this may keep major tenants happy, they may also seriously damage the total rental value and hence the capital value of a centre if they result in poor trading conditions for the specialty traders who regularly pay the major part of total rental income.

The effect on specialty traders of allowing supermarkets to extend their operations into the sale of meats, delicatessen products, bread, and greengrocery items may be that the purchasing power and low rents paid by the supermarket operators enable them to undercut the prices charged by the specialty traders to the extent that many of the latter may be forced out of business by price competition which they cannot match. Whilst initially the consumer may benefit, in the longer run they may be left with a limited choice of retail outlets and higher prices which result from reduced competition, whilst the property owners may be left with vacant retail units and reduced income flow. In addition, if the number of empty retail units is significant it may adversely affect the attraction of a centre overall, causing its further deterioration as an investment.

A covenant which requires specialty retailers to open for unduly long hours may also adversely affect the ability to pay rent if there are inadequate increases in turnover to compensate for the increased operational costs which will almost inevitably result from longer opening hours. Such a possibility can be clearly illustrated by consideration of the Profits Method of Valuation.

Location, retailing, and value

As every valuer knows well, location is a critical factor in the determination of value. In retailing in particular, success in business is largely affected by the quality of location, whilst locations which are suitable for one trade may be quite unsuitable for another type of business. This is another major reason why the use of comparable evidence in the valuation process has to be treated with great caution, because the actual rental value of any retail outlet at any point in time will ultimately depend on the type of trade undertaken by the most probable lessee. Once a property is let it will be the actual lessee rather than the probable lessee, and the valuer therefore has to be closely in touch with the market place to be able to make reasonable predictions of probable occupiers of properties to be valued.

The probability of a particular retail trade locating in a specific property will depend on many variables, some of which have already been considered. The characteristics of the shopping population, the number of shoppers regularly visiting a retail location, their levels of affluence, their propensity to spend, the number of existing traders in the same line of business, the current levels of success of those traders, and the management policies of property owners are all important factors in determining the most probable occupier. The valuer should seek to consider all relevant factors and then to predict which type of retail trade is most likely to locate in a specific property, and should then use the Profits Method of valuation to assess its likely trading performance and hence the likely rental value of the property. Because of the varying turnover and profit capabilities of different retailing activities, at different points in time the relative rental values of retail units may vary because of a different balance of existing retailers, and possibly also because of changes in expenditure patterns. This may result in the most likely occupier of a specific unit varying from time to time as and when it becomes vacant.

The control of location of various retailing activities in managed centres is therefore a particularly important determinant of both individual rental values and total rental value. The maximum rental income for a centre may not necessarily be achieved by letting to the highest bidder whenever a unit becomes vacant, as the maximum overall attractiveness to shoppers of a centre is likely to depend upon its having a complete and well balanced mix of retail outlets. From the valuation viewpoint it is therefore important to carefully study the shopping mix in a centre and the effect of that mix on both individual rental values and total rental value, both in the long term as well as the short term. The valuer should be a professional adviser, not merely a technician, and it may well be that there will be occasions on which he or she should indicate to a client that although, for instance, the highest bid for a vacant shop is from a jeweller, acceptance of a lower rent from an alternative type of retailer may in the longer term result in a better performing and more valuable centre, perhaps because there are already sufficient jewellers in the centre whilst other trades are currently absent.

It is important that valuers should remember that although location is a most important determinant of value, locational criteria will change over time and will vary depending on a wide range of frequently changing variables.

Outgoings

Outgoings which have to be borne by retailers are also important considerations in the valuation process, as any variations in the level of outgoings will, all other things being equal, affect the residual figure available to cover the costs of property occupation. It should not be forgotten that the residual figure has to cover rent, property rates and taxes if applicable, and other property outgoings such as repairs and service charges, and, if a property is located in a managed centre, probably a share of centre promotional costs also dependent upon the lease terms. Variations in any of these items will affect the capacity of a lessee to pay actual rent, and if a landlord seeks to pass on the responsibility for various outgoings to a lessee, that lessee should in fact reduce his or her rental bid by the anticipated annual cost of the property outgoings for which they are being given responsibility. Valuers should therefore study leases to determine the responsibilities of the parties to a lease for the various property outgoings, and should then be able to make reasonable estimates of the annual cost of those outgoings. In like manner they should also consider clauses which place a responsibility on a lessee for sharing the promotional costs of a managed centre. It should not be forgotten that if a sound business is to be run from a leased shop the lessee must contain all costs of property occupation within the bottom line figure produced by the Profits Method of Valuation.

Chapter 14

Retailing in the Future and Retail Property Values

The current situation

In view of the significance of retail expenditure to the economies of most countries, the large numbers employed in the sector, and the large amount of capital investment represented by the stock of retail property, it is appropriate to consider the future of retailing and thereby of retail property. Just as in the period since World War II there have been enormous changes in retailing, so there may well be big changes in the future. Moreover, it is likely that any changes will occur more rapidly than in the past, and quite possibly they may be more significant than those of the past.

Over the past 30 years or so, in most countries there have been substantial changes in retailing which have resulted largely as a result of the emergence of a more affluent society and the ever expanding ownership and use of the motor car. This has given rise to the development of modern, enclosed shopping centres at neighbourhood, local and regional levels which to a significant extent have supplanted the traditional 'high street' shopping locations in terms of retailing importance.

Prior to the advent of modern, self-contained shopping centres most retailing was done through traditional shopping streets, complemented to a lesser extent by postal shopping through catalogue purchases. The development of an increasingly more affluent population with more people financially able to spend on discretionary goods rather than merely on essential subsistence goods, has resulted in there being a consumption orientated public which has assisted the growth of retailing especially in the discretionary and luxury goods categories. Ever increasing car ownership has made it possible for consumers to shop at centres other than their own local town centre, and a combination of the greater purchasing power of people and their greater mobility has been the stimulus for the development of modern shopping centres which have often been developed away from town centres in locations in which there was previously no retailing activity.

Currently the modern shopping centre appears dominant in retailing to the extent that many believe other types of retailing to be of minor importance and even that the traditional shopping street is now of limited significance in many areas. However, it is only in the relatively recent past that the modern shopping centre has attained its current dominant position. Such is the pace of change in the modern world that its current dominance is not necessarily secure, and valuers should therefore consider what future developments in retailing are likely to occur, for today's retail property capital values are very much dependent upon future prospects.

There is little doubt that the large amounts of capital required for the development of modern shopping centres and the high costs of running them result in a situation in which relatively high returns to their owners are required if they are to be financially successful. However, the high returns required by developers and owners result in their seeking high rents from occupiers, and the higher the rental levels demanded of occupiers, all other things being equal the lower will be the returns to those occupiers. It will therefore be surprising if retailers do not consider alternative means of retailing which may allow them to reduce operational costs and to retain a higher share of turnover as profit for themselves. This must be a logical consideration for any business operator, and in the area of retailing it naturally leads to consideration of a number of possibilities including a return to traditional shopping street locations, market retailing, the development of factory and warehouse type retailing, the further development of catalogue shopping by post, the development of TV shopping, and the development of computer shopping including the use of the internet.

There are also other factors which might in the longer term result in shopping centres losing some of their current market dominance. Their success to a large extent is based on their convenience for shopping by car, but the sheer size of some of the larger centres results in some of their convenience being reduced as shoppers cannot necessarily be ensured of being able to park near the shops they wish to use, whilst the very use of some car parks is often quite daunting because of deficiencies in their design. As the proportion of older people in a population increases, as is already happening in many developed countries, it may also be that older people will be less attracted to larger centres with a resultant reduction in their overall popularity, particularly in view of the security problems experienced in some of the large multi-storey car parks attached to some centres and even within some centres themselves.

The problems of pollution are also increasing with each year, and both society in general and governments have become very much aware of the need to control pollution and to improve the quality of the air we breathe. One of the major causes of pollution is the internal combustion engine, and it is far from impossible that there may in the future be a reduction in the dependence of the average person on the private motor car resulting either from controls on its use in some areas, or on disincentives to its use caused by taxation or pricing policies enforced by environmentally aware governments.

The Government of Singapore has for many years sought to restrict the use of automobiles in central Singapore by means of charges, whilst a similar system has recently been introduced in central London in the United Kingdom, fees being charged to drivers of vehicles wishing to enter the restricted area in the centre of the city. These measures have been largely the result of efforts to reduce traffic congestion in the city centres and thereby to increase average traffic speed for the remaining traffic, but future controls in other centres may be introduced because of both congestion and other environmental considerations. Any reduction in the number of people visiting an area as the result of such schemes is likely to have an adverse impact on retailing activities in the area concerned, so retailing patterns and retail property values are likely to be affected by the introduction, or even the likelihood of the introduction, of such restrictive schemes.

The increasing use of charging systems for road use is likely to result in the cost of car usage increasing for some motorists. It now appears to be more common for tolls to be charged for the use of major roads in a number of countries, the rationale for the tolls often being to raise money to finance road construction on a 'user pays' basis. However, tolls could also be used as a means of discouraging vehicle usage in order to relieve congestion, as a result of which their use may become even more common. If travel to regional shopping centres and out of town complexes becomes more expensive as a result, the attractiveness of such outlets to shoppers may decrease in comparison with what may be a cheaper and easier trip to a local shopping area. Should developments of this nature affect future shopping patterns, then the relative values of retail properties are also likely to be affected.

Any retail property valuer should consequently give careful consideration to the possible future relevance of the alternative forms of retailing referred to earlier, whose importance may get a further stimulus if dependence of the average person on the motor car is in any way reduced, even if this is caused simply by government action resulting in the cost of car usage increasing as a consequence of increased taxes on fuel, vehicle ownership, or vehicle usage.

Traditional shopping streets

Whilst these are often currently underoccupied in many towns and cities because of the difficulty of competing with rival enclosed shopping centres, there are still some areas in which they are thriving and competitive. Even where they are not currently very successful, if retail rent levels demanded in shopping centres reduce retailing profits below levels acceptable to retailers, the latter may decide to revert to street locations. These have the advantage of being readily available in many cases, and with building structures already in existence there is often only a need for modernisation and refurbishment, which can frequently take place relatively rapidly and within acceptable cost limits. If progressive local authorities recognize the need for the maintenance of and the renewal of the urban fabric, the combination of high occupation costs in shopping centres and local urban renewal programmes may result in the revival of some traditional shopping streets, particularly as rental levels in such locations are frequently below those in shopping centres. Their easy availability as alternative retailing outlets may therefore result in them regaining some lost popularity, with a resultant increase in the values of retail units in such locations.

Catalogue shopping

For many years purchasing from mail order catalogues was probably the only major alternative to shopping in traditional shopping streets, and to some extent it seems to be enjoying a revival in some countries. In the longer term this may assist the development of other types of retailing such as the development of selling by use of video tapes, compact discs, and the internet, as many very well produced catalogues would easily convert to video tape or CD storage or to publicity on the internet. Some major companies are placing considerable emphasis on catalogue shopping with orders placed by telephone or mail: for example, considerable publicity has been given in Australia by the major department store group Coles Myer to their mail order arm, the Myer Direct facility. Such a method of retailing has the advantage of not requiring additional expensive retailing outlets as it can be based in relatively cheap warehouse accommodation, and if occupation costs in shopping centres become too high it may have a considerable cost advantage for retailers and could enable competitive prices to be charged without destroying retailing profits.

Postal or catalogue shopping is clearly of great value to those who live a great distance from major retail centres, and if purchases over the counter become too expensive other consumers may resort to such a form of shopping. The United Kingdom produced paper *The Weekly Telegraph* issue number 174 of 9 November 1994 to 15 November 1994 reported on page 33:

> Every day in Tokyo, some 200 shoppers bypass department stores, high street shops and the local grocer and buy their clothes and children's toys, even their food, in a library. This is the mutating world of catalogue shopping. And it is big business in Japan – so much so that the government set up a library in the capital which subscribes to 1,500 different catalogues from around the world. Three quarters of them come from America, but an increasing number are British.
>
> 'Catalogue shopping of all sorts is getting very popular' says Mr Kiyotaka Hishida, Mipro's (The Manufactured Imports Promotion Organisation) assistant director, 'and because of the high yen, more and more people tend to buy through foreign catalogues to get something which is good value.'

Not only is such a development evidence of the perceptiveness of purchasers and their desire to get value for money, it is also evidence of the continuing globalisation of markets. Just as overseas retailers are now well represented in the major retail areas of most major cities, so may overseas catalogues become used in other countries as already happens in Japan. It was estimated at the time of the above quote that 1.5% of Japanese retail sales were done through home shopping, the equivalent figures at that time being for America 6% and for Europe 4%.

There is clear potential for a considerable expansion in home shopping, and while many consumers do not like to purchase without inspecting the goods they are buying, there are those for whom home shopping is more convenient than a trip to the shops, whilst if catalogue prices are more competitive than shop prices other consumers may well be attracted to such a method of purchasing.

From the valuer's standpoint the existence of such an alternative form of selling means that high occupation costs in modern shopping centres could persuade at least some retailers to transfer their operations away from them, which has implications for the long term security of some centres as investments, particularly if current lessees are not committed to long periods of occupation.

Factory and warehouse outlets

High property occupation costs must inevitably make any retailer consider cheaper alternatives whatever type of property is currently occupied, and factory and warehouse outlets provide a very much cheaper type of accommodation for retailers than do shopping centres because of a combination of cheaper site costs resulting from their off-centre locations, and because of cheaper construction costs resulting from the ability to use buildings constructed to lower specifications. Such accommodation has become quite popular with retailers in the USA, the United Kingdom, and Australia – and probably in many other countries – and it enables goods, including those of high quality, to be sold at very competitive prices largely because of reduced overheads. Such outlets are also ideally suitable for a combination of on-site selling and distance selling by catalogue, TV or computer. Apart from providing cheaper space than shopping centres they can also reduce labour costs and accommodation needs by enabling the warehousing and retailing operations to be based in one property. Largely because of their relative cheapness to construct and occupy, such centres are particularly attractive for the sale of bulky goods which require large areas of accommodation for storage, and consequently the sale of such goods is tending to move from shopping centres and town centres to these more convenient and cheaper new shopping areas.

There must be retailers seriously considering such a form of retailing as being a cheaper alternative to shopping centre retailing, particularly if they are also interested in developing TV or computer selling. Indeed, in Australia there is already a considerable number of prominent retailers carrying out substantial retail activities in this type of accommodation, some of it being fitted out to quite high standards, despite which it still remains relatively cheap. One of the major attractions has to be the ability to rent substantial areas of space at very much cheaper rates than would apply in modern shopping centres, where the high development costs make it essential for owners to seek relatively high rent levels if they are to achieve an adequate return on their invested capital.

Television retailing

To date this has had only limited impact in many countries not being helped by the fact that it often uses unpopular viewing time for transmission, whilst in some countries its cause has probably not been helped by the financial failures of some of its pioneer retailers. However, such problems are not uncommon with new methods, and it is likely that its importance may grow, particularly through cable television networks. In Australia there are a number of regular selling programmes shown on terrestrial television at convenient viewing times, and it is certainly a very relaxing way to shop if one is able to sit in one's own house, sipping tea or coffee, viewing products for sale displayed on the television which can then be ordered over the telephone. Even if it does not make a major inroad into total retail sales, such a retailing method will nevertheless inevitably divert some sales from more conventional types of retailing, and the increasing costs of retail space in shopping centres may persuade more retailers to try it as a price competitive alternative.

Somewhat similar to television retailing is retailing through video catalogues, and it is already possible to slot a video into one's VCR and view goods on one's TV screen whilst enjoying home comforts, this also enabling one to view products at a time of one's own choosing. Although it obviously has the disadvantage of not permitting the purchaser to inspect goods before purchase, the major attraction of such a form of shopping for the purchaser has to be its ease and convenience.

Computer shopping

This is steadily developing as a retailing format in many countries, and the potential exists for such a form of selling to make big inroads into overall retail turnover. In most developed countries a surprisingly large proportion of homes now have home computers with many being connected to the Internet, this providing a substantial base from which computer shopping can be further developed. Whilst such a form of retailing may not at present be seen by many as a major threat to conventional forms of retailing, one only has to consider how rapidly people have adopted modern technology in the form of computers, facsimile machines, mobile telephones and other developments which were unheard of only a few years ago, to realize that retailing through computer networks offers incredible possibilities, particular with the high quality of graphic and pictorial presentation now available.

The United Kingdom produced *Weekly Telegraph* issue 174 referred to above under catalogue shopping also reported in November 1994:

> About 5,500 consumers have experienced an early taste of hi tech home shopping. Philips, Barclays Bank, the travel company Page & Moy and catalogue company Freemans have completed a trial based on Philips's CD-I interactive player, a combined games machine and digital video player ... The project ... gives a preview of the marketing techniques of the future. Participants received three interactive CDs designed to sell products in a more attractive and interactive manner than conventional catalogues. The CDs could be used by consumers with no computer literacy ...

This type of retailing is clearly an area which may in the relatively near future see enormous developments, the major problem for valuers and retail property investors being to predict just how big an impact it may have on traditional retailing methods and therefore on the values of retail properties. The fact that such substantial organisations are interested in this type of shopping suggests that computer based selling techniques may be a retailing force to be reckoned with in the not too distant future.

It is probably true to say that shopping through the internet has not developed as rapidly as many commentators had expected, and this may be because many shoppers still like to be able to inspect goods before they buy them. Others who research goods on the internet may be put off actually purchasing through it because they fear it provides the opportunity for the fraudulent use of credit card numbers. It is also probably true that to many there is still the 'thrill of the chase' to be obtained from going on a shopping trip, particularly if it is to a lavishly equipped modern shopping centre or to a more traditional town centre shopping area which has character and a good range of retail outlets.

However, there are in many instances cost savings to be made by shopping over the internet, whilst for those whose free time is limited there is also the great convenience of being able to place an order rapidly from the convenience of one's home, with goods subsequently being delivered to the doorstep. Most retailers who have internet sites are taking great care to try to ensure the security of customer details provided to them over the internet. As shoppers gain more confidence with this method of purchasing there could be substantial increases in both the number and value of such transactions, which, all other things being equal, would adversely affect other forms of retailing. Internet shopping has to be particularly attractive for the purchase of such things as well known branded products which are regularly purchased, such as grocery and other household items, especially for those who lead busy lives with limited spare time available for traditional style shopping.

There is little doubt that there is the potential for a very substantial increase in internet shopping, which makes it possible to shop in an international market place, but with greater ease than catalogue shopping provides. In February 2003 the 'Nielsen/Net Ratings' Global Internet Trends Survey reported that as at the fourth quarter of 2002, 580 million people across the globe had internet access, with very high percentages of the population in some of the leading economies having access to it. The report gave the following percentages of the population as having internet access, namely 85% in Sweden, 79% in the USA, 73% in the Netherlands, 72% in Australia, 70% in Hong Kong and 68% in the United Kingdom, whilst in each of Spain, Italy, Germany, and France internet access was available to over 50% of the population.

There is clearly enormous potential for a considerable increase in internet shopping as the annual rate of increase in those having access to the internet is considerable in many countries.

The implications of developments in retailing methods

At the end of the day shoppers seek a combination of quality, service and price competitiveness, whilst for many ease of shopping is also very important. The combination of an ageing population, the desire on the part of many to have what is commonly referred to as more 'quality time' (that is time at home with one's family or enjoying recreational activities), increasing traffic congestion which makes travel more of a chore than a pleasure, and the possibility of increased costs of travel particularly if taxes on carbon fuels and vehicle usage increase, may result in the novelty of a trip to the local shopping centre disappearing and other forms of shopping being adopted both because of their relative ease and their price competitiveness. Whatever the total impact of alternative forms of shopping may be, it is possible that shopping centres may face threats to their current dominance and they will have to be well managed and will have to enable retailers to operate efficiently in a very price competitive market if they are all to continue with the levels of success which most enjoy at present.

It is difficult to believe that the success of at least some shopping centres will not be seriously dented by alternative means of retailing within the foreseeable future. At the World Valuation Congress held in Vancouver in June 1995, Blake Eagle – the well respected American property analyst of the Frank Russell Co – repeated the International Council of Shopping Centers prediction that '300 malls will go dark by the end of the decade' in the USA. If this has indeed happened in the USA, because of the large number of shopping centres there it will not necessarily be particularly drastic except for the owners of the doomed centres, but it will nevertheless have considerable implications for the value of retail properties in general. The adverse effects of the over provision of shopping space in some localities and the development of alternative forms of retailing should be seriously considered by valuers when they value retail space.

Indeed, it is possible that in some areas retail property values may come under threat from what might be termed destructive competition, and in some cases 'self-destructive competition'. Many companies seem to be obsessed by the need to increase short term profits in particular, and in their anxiety to do this many seem to assume that an increase in the size of an existing superstore or shopping centre will automatically ensure increased profits. However, it is suspected that in many cases the percentage return on the additional capital expenditure required for an extension is often inferior to that obtained from the original unextended outlet. If the extension of a centre results in greater competition within it for existing retailers, the end result may well be that although there is more retail space the centre may be less attractive, because there may be no greater retail variety than previously, whilst the underperformance of retail outlets which results from the increased competition may also result in a lower level of service and decreased shopper satisfaction. It is suspected that in some cases the result may be both a relatively unsatisfactory return on capital for the property owner accompanied by bigger retail outlets which are in fact less attractive to shoppers, this threatening their security as investments in the longer term.

It is therefore suspected that in some cases property owners construct new retail space which in fact competes with their own existing retail investments rather than competing with rivals. Where rival retail areas also expand to compete with what they may perceive as an increased threat to their own market share, or new competing retail areas are created, there is the danger that an excessive area of retail property will compete for a given total of retail expenditure. Reduced percentage returns to retailers may result, and if this is the case there must inevitably be an adverse impact on retail property values in the affected localities.

The capital value of retail accommodation

Such considerations go right to the heart of the capital valuation of retail property, because whilst the immediate short term rental values of many retail outlets may seem secure, the capital values of those centres is very much dependent upon long term security of income.

In Australia in many shopping centres owners have pursued a policy of only granting specialty occupiers leases of about three, five, or six years duration, with six years being the exception rather than the rule, the reasoning apparently being that such a policy provides flexibility in management. At the same time specialty occupiers are regularly responsible for the payment of 75% or more of the total rent roll, and there is therefore a situation in which 75% or more of the current rental value of many centres is in fact secured for less than five years. In reality this is a somewhat insecure state of affairs in that there is no long term guarantee that the bulk of the rent will continue to flow, and it is therefore difficult to see how any valuer can capitalize such income situations at the low yields which have frequently been used to date. The flexible management policy of only offering short term leases to lessees may in the longer term result in a situation in which space may rapidly be vacated if it becomes too expensive and if alternative forms of retailing prove to be more attractive to retailers and shoppers, or if there should be a downturn in economic activity.

In the United Kingdom it has been the custom for many years for retail landlords to prefer lettings with lease terms of 20 years or even longer in order to provide long term security of occupation and thereby of income also. The problem experienced when inflation resulted in rents that were fixed for long terms becoming low in comparison with current rent levels at any point in time, was overcome by the introduction of regular rent reviews. These provided for the upward revision only of rents, thereby ensuring that not only was occupation secure for a long period of time, but that rent income was also very secure in real terms.

There has been resistance by many lessees to what are often regarded as 'landlord's leases', that is leases in which the lessees seem to have very limited rights and in which their interests seem to receive little attention. At a conference organized by the Royal Institution of Chartered Surveyors and the Office, Shop, and Business and Industrial Agents Societies on 'Property in the Economy' held in Cardiff, Wales in May 1994, Sir James Blyth, the then chief executive of The Boots Company plc, one of the largest multiple retail chains in the United Kingdom with well over 2,000 group retail outlets, was reported by the *Chartered Surveyor Monthly* to have said:

> The finance-driven property industry of the past two decades had led to rigidity in lease structures, except where change had been necessitated by short-term recessionary pressures. Occupiers were not standard, so why should the 'standard institutional lease' predominate? ...

It is not out of the question that the resistance of retail lessees to leases which commit them to long periods of occupation without any escape clauses allowing them to vacate after say five years or at various intervals during a lease term, together with the possible introduction of legislation banning rent review clauses which only permit the upward revision of rent, may have substantial implications for the very low yields which have often applied to United Kingdom retail properties. All other things being equal, a resultant increase in these yields because of the greater uncertainty of future rental income would result in depreciation of the capital values of retail investment properties so affected.

As suggested earlier, it is possible that the long term security of some shopping centres may be suspect, and it may well be that those which are most suspect may in fact be in localities which are currently very popular with developers who, because of the success of existing shopping developments, seek to develop further large areas of shopping space. Not only will the existing developments be subject to the competition of new retailing methods, they will also be subject to the competition of many local competitors, for in many cases development is most intensive in densely populated areas where the next centre is only a few miles or kilometres away.

There is in any event a fundamental problem in estimating the capital values of many modern shopping centres, their very size creating a market in which only a few possible purchasers have the capacity to bid for them. When this is the case the purchaser is likely to have as much bargaining power as the vendor, and if the vendor is anxious to sell but the potential purchaser is indifferent, then the latter may well have extremely strong bargaining power. With substantial investments of this type it is therefore most important for the valuer to have very good market knowledge to the extent that he or she needs to be able to identify potential purchasers with reasonable accuracy. They need to be able to estimate not only how much they can afford to pay but, more importantly, how eager they are to bid and how much they are likely to bid. In seeking to identify potential bidders the valuer will need to identify organizations with enough capital to bid; to consider whether their current commitments are such that they would be in a position to bid; to consider whether their existing portfolio holdings are such that a property of the type on offer would enhance their portfolio and therefore be attractive to them; and also to consider that organization's current overall policies, its current gearing, and its investment and expansion policies in particular.

The sheer size of many investments of this type means that they are not necessarily going to attract a bidder at any point in time, and this makes the valuer's task a very difficult one. If such centres suffer from increased competition from new developments and from new forms of retailing the task will be even harder, and in such circumstances it is difficult to envisage anything other than an increase in the yields which in the past have been applied to the valuation of some centres.

Valuers should remember that property values are not only affected by events in the property market, investment properties in particular being affected by what is happening in markets for alternative investments. In October 1994 the AMP Society, an Australian based organization, purchased the Hammerson Australian property investments which included the Warringah Mall shopping centre in northern Sydney, at that time the second largest shopping centre in Australia. Some commentators believed that the purchase price indicated a capitalisation rate of about 6.5% for the Warringah Mall shopping centre at a time when long term bond yields were about 3% higher. Such yields for property can only be justified by the belief that the future growth in the real value of the property investment will be such as to justify a purchase at a reverse yield gap of that nature, or that the property investment is merited as representing beneficial portfolio diversification for the investing organisation. If adequate growth is unlikely or there is no investment diversification justification for a similar yield being adopted in other circumstances, then the use of such a transaction by a valuer as comparable evidence could be dangerous.

The long term prospects for retail properties

There are likely to be changes in retailing which will have a substantial effect on many retail property values, and there could well be an increase in vacant retail space with some retail outlets suffering reduced values in real terms. It is possible that only the better located, better designed, and better and more sensibly managed centres will continue to prosper and to increase in value in the way that has happened in the past. The ageing of the population in many countries is likely to result in many shoppers being more discriminating in their purchases because of reduced disposable incomes, which is likely to result in changed retail expenditure patterns in the future. Some local and neighbourhood centres may also become more popular in relative terms than the larger regional centres which can be daunting to older shoppers.

Similarly, with respect to shopping streets it is likely that there will be a concentration of retailing in the better locations, which is already tending to occur. Those may well prove to be streets where there is a management system introduced as a result of co-operation between a local authority, property owners and retailers with the objective of improving the urban fabric and providing a vibrant town centre with an attractive shopping environment to compete with planned shopping centres. At the other extreme, some areas which offer bargain shopping, such as market areas, are also likely to continue to survive by virtue of the price competitiveness of the products offered.

Retailers, being business people in close contact with their customers, will study their needs and will trade from locations that both suit those customers and that enable the retailers to provide the level of service required, at the right prices for customers, and at a profit to themselves. To value effectively valuers will need to closely monitor the needs of both retail customers and retailers, and to closely follow developments and trends in retailing, for at the end of the day it is the combination of the actions of customers and retailers that are the major determinants of the value of retail properties.

Chapter 15

The Landlord and Tenant Relationship

A lease is a letting of lands or tenements by a landlord to a tenant. It is a contract for the exclusive possession of the premises by the tenant for the period of the lease, usually in consideration of the payment of a rent

Landlord & Tenant
by Sir Raymond Walton & Michael Essayan (Estates Gazette 1982)

The creation of a lease creates a relationship between two parties, and this relationship of landlord and tenant is very important in the modern world in which many properties of all types are owned by one party and leased by another for use for residential or operational purposes. A great amount of economic activity occurs in properties which are leased, and it is therefore important that the relationship between the parties should be beneficial to both in a way which facilitates the efficient and viable provision of properties to let by developers and property investors, and efficient and effective use by those who lease them and operate in them.

In reality, both landlords and lessees should have some similar operational objectives which ought to include, as a primary objective, the maximization of the utility and of the value in use of a property. If this is achieved both the landlord and the lessee should benefit. The aim in theory should be for the two parties to work together, the landlord providing a property that best suits the lessee's needs, and the lessee then using the property to maximum efficiency that will enable the rent paid to represent a good return to the landlord's investment. The ideal landlord and tenant relationship should in effect be in the nature of a partnership, with each party realising the importance of the other to the achievement of their own objectives and recognising the mutual benefits to be derived from co-operation.

Despite this fairly fundamental fact there regularly appears to be considerable conflict in such relationships, so much so that in many countries governments have found it necessary to intervene and to enforce legislation designed to control landlord and tenant relationships, such legislation frequently being primarily designed to protect lessees in situations in which they are perceived to have inadequate rights and powers when compared with those of landlords.

Any departure from a partnership situation that results in the development of adversarial attitudes and situations is only likely to be detrimental to the overall success of both landlord and tenant, and there will be occasions in which sensible long term management policies should result in a willingness on the part of landlords to make concessions to lessees which might include the acceptance of static levels, or even reduced levels, of rent. Though short term returns might be adversely affected by such a policy, there are likely to be rewards in the longer term as individual businesses prosper or as overall business performance improves. The creation of trust and goodwill and a spirit of co-operation between landlord and tenant that ought to result from such actions is likely in the longer term to result in a better performing property, whatever its use may be, and hence a more valuable investment for the owner.

To further consider the landlord and tenant relationship particular focus will be given to business leases with the emphasis being given to leases of retail properties, although many of the considerations that apply to business properties may also apply to other types of property such as residential and agricultural properties.

The length of leases

Leases can usually be agreed at any length by negotiation between the parties (unless there is statutory intervention which governs the length of leases), but this is a matter on which the wishes of the landlord and the lessee will frequently be quite different. In general, if a person or organization is adjudged suitable as a tenant, most landlords will seek to let a property for a long term of years providing there is a rent review incorporated in the lease to ensure that the rent passing is periodically revised to keep pace with changes in rent levels in the market place. By securing a lease for a long term of years the landlord hopes to ensure that the property will produce a good return over that time period, whilst the costs of marketing and reletting will likewise be deferred for a substantial period of time, so helping to minimise the landlord's administrative costs.

However, the desire of a landlord to let for a long term may conflict with that of a tenant who will usually want to have security of tenure for a reasonable time period, sufficiently long to establish a business and to get the full benefit of expenditure on fitting out a property and other establishment costs. However, most tenants will probably also wish to retain flexibility to move to other premises should, for example, successful trading require a move to larger premises, or should the local economy change to the extent that a move to another location would be likely to prove beneficial. At the other extreme, in the event of a business not developing satisfactorily a lessee will not wish to be committed to a lease that results in a liability for rent for a long period of time when a reduction in the size of the business or even closure of the business would be the best course of action. Accordingly one will often find that a landlord wishes to secure a lease for perhaps 20 years with four yearly rent reviews, whilst a potential lessee would really prefer a lease for five years with an option to renew the lease for a further five years if with the passage of time this proves desirable. In such circumstances it might be that a lease for 20 years with rent reviews every five years tied to the lessee's right to terminate the lease at each rent review might prove a suitable compromise to enable a lease to be agreed between the parties.

However, in the past many landlords in the United Kingdom have been reluctant to agree leases for as short a period as five years, even though such leases are not uncommon in other countries such as the USA and Australia. In recent years, and particularly since the recession of the early 1990s, commercial reality has forced more landlords to accept that the highly desirable 20 or 21 year lease with upward-only rent reviews every four or five years is not so easily achievable, as a result of which shorter lease terms are now more common together with more concessions to lessees than were given in the past.

Rent

The rent of a property represents the gross return to a landlord for the investment in that property, whilst to the lessee it represents part – and often a substantial part – of the total cost of occupation of a property. Other occupation costs might include the cost of fitting out the property, the periodic costs of maintenance of the property, rates and taxes relating to occupation, and the cost of building insurance, whilst there will also be the normal costs in use such as lighting, heating and cleaning the accommodation.

With regards to rent, the basic situation is one in which a

landlord will normally seek to obtain the highest achievable rent for a property in order to maximize the investment return, whilst a lessee will seek to rent at the lowest possible figure in order to minimize the operational costs of his or her business, which in turn would help to maximize the business profit. There is, therefore, an area for possible conflict as the objectives of landlord and tenant in the assessment of rent appear to be opposed. This does not mean that there will necessarily be conflict in rent negotiations, for in many instances a landlord, in setting an asking rent that will provide what he or she regards as a satisfactory return on an investment, may in fact ask for a rent that will allow a potential tenant to trade at acceptable costs and thereby to make a satisfactory business profit.

The need to sometimes offer lessees assistance in the form of low rents when trading conditions are difficult is quite regularly recognized by landlords in that they frequently allow lessees setting up new businesses to have periods of low rent – or even no rent – in the early stages of a lease, acknowledging that to overburden a new lessee with a large rent payment before a business is properly established may well result in a short lived and failed business, this probably being to the disadvantage of the landlord as well as the lessee.

Despite this fact, there is a strong belief on the part of many tenants that the major objective of some landlords is simply to maximize rent returns at all costs, irrespective of the effect on lessees of such a policy. This is illustrated by a belief of some lessees that landlords who insist on turnover rent schemes when letting retail properties do so primarily to obtain details of business turnover figures in order to gain information that will enable them to extract as much rent as possible from tenants without actually sending them out of business.

A turnover rent exists when the rent paid by a lessee is directly related to the turnover of a business run in a rented property. The concept recognizes that a lessee's ability to pay rent for a business property depends upon their current level of success, and if sensibly implemented the system should encourage landlords and tenants to work together in a way which benefits both groups. In theory such a rental arrangement should encourage landlords to employ management policies that positively assist those renting properties from them to run successful businesses that make healthy profits.

A typical arrangement is one in which a base rent is fixed that is paid whatever happens to turnover levels, additional rent being paid once turnover exceeds a specified level, the extra rent being an agreed percentage of the increase in turnover. The base rent ought to be set at a level which would enable an average tenant to trade without any financial pressures caused by the requirement to pay that level of rent, and which would not cause financial pressures for the tenant if a rise in operating costs or a deterioration in economic conditions resulted in an unavoidable fall in profits. The concept is that a lessee is only committed in advance to a realistically assessed base rent, but as business turnover increases the rent paid should also increase, allowing the landlord to receive an increased return which is the reward for providing a property that helps the business to prosper. This is an example of the landlord and tenant relationship being a partnership, in that in theory the use of such a rental basis ought to encourage a landlord to take positive steps to make it easier for a lessee to run a successful business in the rented property, because both parties will benefit from the business person's success.

There is, however, as already observed a perception on the part of some lessees that some landlords do not accept that the businessperson should get the major part of increased profits that result from running a successful business, and they believe that turnover figures are used by landlords to try to extract the maximum possible rent at each rent review. The resultant levying of high base rents on lessees may well impair their ability to operate efficiently, and unless tenants are able to reap benefits from a turnover rent system there can be no sensible reason for them to agree to pay rent on such a basis. Furthermore, unduly large increases in rent which are imposed following increases in turnover may in reality operate against a landlord's long term interests, for they may frustrate a lessee's efforts to improve profit in that location as a result of which they may also be a disincentive to continuing to lease the property concerned.

The apparent abuse of the theoretical objectives of the turnover rent concept was well illustrated in Australia by the fact that in the mid 1990s a major national retail multiple reported that although many of their leases were based on the turnover rent approach, the base rents insisted upon by landlords were so high that in no case over a five years period did they have to pay an additional turnover rent element. In such circumstances it is not surprising that many retail tenants believe that the key objective of some landlords in requiring lessees to reveal turnover figures is to enable the landlords to determine base rent levels at the maximum figure a lessee could possibly pay, rather than to implement a system that should benefit the lessee as well as the landlord.

This perception of lessees was reinforced by the fact that some landlords insisted upon lease clauses that required lessees to reveal turnover figures even when rents paid were not based on the turnover system. Apparently the landlords in such cases argued that the figures were required to enable them to manage their shopping centre more efficiently. However, it is not unrealistic for lessees to believe (as they often seem to) that the major objective of the landlord is to gain inside information of the lessee's business that will enable the landlord to demand higher rents whenever a trader receives higher retailing returns, even though the increased returns may result entirely from the lessee's expertise in business, whilst the higher rent may also represent an inequitable share of the retailer's profit.

A problem that may arise for lessees with a turnover rent system may result from the apparent assumption that increased business turnover automatically results in increased business profitability. It may well be that in some circumstances lessees need to increase turnover simply to maintain profits at previously attained levels, perhaps because increased competition has resulted in decreased profit margins, or alternatively because increases in other operational costs have put pressure upon profit levels. Should reduced profit margins result from increased competition which is in fact new competition within the same shopping centre, it would appear more than a little unjust if a lessee had to pay increased turnover rent to a shopping centre owner despite having a static net profit level, or perhaps even a reduced net profit level.

Situations such as these can only cause distrust of landlords by tenants, and in the longer term they are likely to do much to cause deterioration in the landlord and tenant relationship to the disadvantage of both parties, and, in the case of retail lettings, perhaps to the shopping public also.

An admirable and sensible management policy was well illustrated in a statement made by Mr Ted Johnson, MEPC Investments' Managing Director, with reference to the Eagle Centre in Derby, England, which MEPC purchased in January 1994.

> Our objective is to increase rents, but we have to increase turnover in order that retailers can afford to pay those rents, and to do that we must attract more shoppers to the centre.
>
> *Estates Gazette* 9411: 126

This observation indicated a clear recognition of the desirability of landlords assisting tenants to be successful, and of the need for tenants to make higher returns before they can pay higher rents. A sensible management policy should recognize that both parties have to gain benefits from the system if it is to work to its maximum potential.

1994 was part of a period in which returns to property and to business activity in general had been under severe pressure for a number of years as a result of the worldwide recession of the early 1990s, which in some countries was so severe as to reach depression levels. It is probably an unfortunate fact of life that some fundamental policy issues receive greater consideration when times are bad for both landlords and tenants than may generally be the case in times of economic boom, and at about that time the question of rent levels and other lease terms received considerable attention in the property press in the United Kingdom.

The agreement of rent is clearly an area in which there is great potential for disagreement between the parties, for from the landlord's point of view it would generally be preferable to have a rent that increases annually, whilst lessees would normally prefer as long a period of occupation as possible at an initially agreed rent. There may be disadvantages with annual reviews from the landlord's perspective also, as the cost of annual reviews if undertaken by professional consultants, and the cost of resultant legal documentation might substantially reduce, or even exceed, the increase in rent, particularly in the case of smaller properties or when rent increases are small. This problem has been minimised in some cases by agreeing annual rent increases which are tied to increases in annual cost of living indices, but the disadvantage of such an arrangement is that changes in annual rental values may in fact be quite different to the change in a cost of living index, with the result that an unrealistic rent increase might result.

Clearly the agreement of the time periods at which rent reviews will occur is an area for potential disagreement between landlord and tenant, for whereas a landlord will welcome regular rent increases, a lessee is likely to be less enthusiastic about such an arrangement, for it will result in business planning having to be done against a background of constantly rising overheads for property occupation. If rising rent is accompanied by rising property rates and taxes, the cost of property occupation is likely to operate against profit growth, the latter being a major objective of most businesses. Accordingly, the vast majority of lessees are likely to prefer longer intervals between rent reviews than landlords would choose. They would also usually wish to have a rent review arrangement that incorporates the possibility of a decrease in rent rather than the landlord's preference for a review which only allows either an increase or at least the continuation of the existing rent.

Whatever rent may be agreed and whatever the basis of rent review, most landlords will seek an arrangement in which rent is paid at regular intervals and in advance of the period of occupation to which it relates, the practice of rent being paid in arrears now being unusual rather than common as it was in the past. Payment of rent in advance offers an element of insurance to a landlord in that should a lessee suddenly disappear at dead of night without warning, or should a lessee become bankrupt, the landlord would at least have received rent for the period in which the problem arises. Payment of rent in advance is therefore normal practice in many countries together with the payment of a bond (a money deposit) against which a landlord may draw in the case of a lessee vacating a property without satisfying all financial commitments to the landlord.

Other costs of occupation

Apart from rent there are a range of other costs associated with the occupation of property which will vary depending upon the property and the country in which a property is located. These typically include property rates and taxes, the costs of redecoration and repainting both internally and externally, the cost of regular maintenance of the internal and external structures of the building, the cost of essential periodic refurbishment and renewals – such as rebuilding chimneys, re-covering a roof, or replacing an obsolescent elevator or heating or air conditioning system – and the insurance of the building.

In the United Kingdom there has for many years been a practice by which those letting properties have sought to pass the liabilities for as many as possible of these outgoings to lessees, the objective being to ensure that the gross rent received by a landlord is not significantly reduced by any of these liabilities. The desirability of leases in which 'full repairing and insuring' liabilities were passed to a lessee (FRI leases) arose in the late 1950s and the 1960s when periods of increasing prices resulted in the increased annual repairing and insuring costs of some let properties eating very substantially into the rents of properties that had been let on leases for lengthy periods of time at fixed rents. This was a major problem for landlords as at that time the practice of having periodic rent reviews in leases was unusual if not rare. Indeed, this problem together with periods of significant increases in rental values were the stimuli for the introduction of regular rent reviews into leases of any significant length, the objective being to ensure that the net annual income from let properties remained secure in real terms and was not devalued by inflation, and also that it remained a realistic return on rising capital values.

To pass the liability for all repairs to a lessee may, however, not always be the best management policy, for it presupposes that a lessee will become aware of repairs which are required and will attend to them regularly. Lessees are not always competent at identifying necessary maintenance work, whilst many of them will not be particularly interested in carrying out repair work. This will not only be because their main interest is the business they run and not the state of repair of the property – that is unless disrepair begins to adversely impact upon business efficiency – but also because expenditure on maintenance will defray their business profits, whilst repair work may also disrupt their business operations. It is therefore essential, even if a property is let on FRI terms, for a landlord to make regular property inspections and to issue dilapidations schedules to a lessee to ensure necessary work receives attention, whilst reinspection of work done is also necessary to ensure an adequate standard of repair has been undertaken. This involves considerable work and expense on the part of a landlord, whilst there will be no direct quality control of repair work done by the lessee. It is arguable that in many instances it would be preferable for a landlord to both detect and implement all repair work in order to ensure that work is done timeously and to the landlord's satisfaction, with either the rent arrangement reflecting the landlord's liability for such work or the lessee being responsible for reimbursing the landlord's costs.

From a lessee's point of view it is critical to study any undertaking to repair a property very carefully, for there is the possibility of accepting a liability with very substantial financial implications, particularly if a property to be leased is old or in a poor state of repair. The shorter the lease a lessee accepts the more careful they should be in this regard, for whilst it may be reasonable to accept responsibility for putting a property into a good state of repair at considerable cost if one is anticipating occupying it for 20 years during which you as occupier will reap benefit from such expenditure, it would generally be unwise to accept a similar responsibility if entering into a lease for a short period of time. Whatever repairing responsibility is accepted by a lessee, their rental bid should be reduced to reflect the annual equivalent cost of that expenditure over the duration of the lease, especially if it is likely to involve substantial initial expenditure.

In any event, whatever the property outgoings that are made the responsibility of a lessee, the rent offered by the lessee ought to reflect the burdens undertaken by him or her. If the responsibility for all repairing and insurance costs becomes a lessee's burden, then they are likely to bid a lower rental figure than if the landlord agrees to cover those outgoings. It is therefore particularly important that valuers should determine exactly who is responsible for the range of property outgoings before assessing either the rental value of a property or its capital value, and also that they should ascertain this information when using rents as comparable evidence if valuing other properties.

Service charges

This is an expense which is likely to arise when a landlord supplies services of any type to a lessee in addition to the demised property. It is most likely to arise when the property concerned is part of a larger property holding, for example a flat in a block of flats or a shop unit in a shopping centre. In such cases a landlord may often supply such things as heating; hot water; air conditioning; cleaning services to reception areas, hallways, staircases and passages; lifts and their running and maintenance; gardening services and other similar services. They are generally provided on condition that in addition to the agreed rent the lessees of individual properties will pay a specified proportion of the total costs incurred by the landlord in providing those services.

There is nothing wrong with the concept of a service charge levied on lessees for services that they would otherwise have to pay for directly and individually, but it is important that the basis on which such charges are levied is equitable both between the landlord and the lessees, and also between individual lessees. To take an extreme case, it would be inequitable for a lessee to be charged a higher rent for a ground-floor flat in a multi-storey block on the basis that it was easy of access being at street level, and for that same lessee also to be charged an element of service charge in respect of providing and running high speed lifts to the upper floors, which lifts would be of no direct benefit to them.

Individual lessees ought to ensure when agreeing lease terms that any service charge clause is equitably phrased in that periodic charges will only include services from which they will benefit, and that the basis of charge will not leave them bearing an unreasonably large proportion of the total charges. In this respect there have been occasions on which lessees of shops in shopping centres have expressed disquiet that some of the promotional costs of which they have been required to bear a proportion, have in fact been used to promote the overall business activities of the shopping centre owners rather than the retail activities of the centre in which they rent a property. There has also been concern expressed by lessees in some shopping centres that there has been included in the service charges an element to cover the property owner's central administrative expenses, such really relating to the running costs of the property owner's firm rather than to the running of a specific shopping centre. When such a charge is levied it is really passing on a proportion of the property owner's investment management expenses to individual lessees, resulting in them defraying the running cost of the property owner's organization rather than those of the shopping centre in which they are located. It is extremely difficult to see such a charge as being in any way equitable or justifiable.

A problem with service charges from the lessee's point of view is that it is necessary to budget for an uncertain figure as the actual charge levied is only known in arrears. This may be the case with other business costs, but for the most part the size of most cost items will either be known in advance, such as rent, rates and insurance premiums, or their size will to some extent be controllable by the lessee in that they will have the ability to shop around for competitive prices for some items of expenditure, whilst with other expenditure it may be possible for a lessee to control costs by exercising economies. However, even though tenants may have representation on a management committee, direct control of service costs is likely to be in the hands of property owners and managers, and not with lessees. There may therefore be a further problem for tenants with service charges in that a shopping centre or a multi-occupation building management team may not have as strong an incentive for efficient and economical management as individual lessees may have in their own business activities. Service charges may therefore not only be known only in arrears, but economies in them may be completely outside the control of individual lessees. Inefficiencies in management may in fact be passed on to lessees without them having any effective right of redress.

Covenants permitting and restricting various activities

Conditions in leases determine the rights and liabilities of landlord and tenant, and each party will logically seek to ensure that their own best interests are served by the inclusion of appropriate covenants. A covenant which is particularly important for many, if not most, business people is that which indicates what uses are permitted in a property, and also any covenant that indicates which uses are prohibited. Such covenants determine what business activities can be carried on, and with retailing it is usual for them to indicate what items may be sold from a particular outlet or what services may be provided.

From a lessee's perspective it may also be particularly important to ensure that not only does a lease permit the lessee to do that which the property is being leased for, for example the sale of a specified range of goods, but that there is a covenant on the part of the landlord not to lease another property for similar activities in a locality which is likely to offer serious business opposition to the lessee. It seems quite common in shopping centres in particular to see what appear to be too many shops selling similar goods in circumstances in which stricter control of the number of competing outlets by the landlord might result in fewer but more financially successful shops, and a higher total rent roll for the landlord. Despite this, there nevertheless seems in some areas to be a tendency to let larger retailers, and chain retailers in particular, sell ranges of goods which are in direct competition with smaller specialist retailers, their ability to undercut the prices of the latter often causing serious financial problems for smaller retail outlets. For this reason it is particularly important for a lessee to seek carefully worded lease covenants to ensure that such a situation cannot cause them unnecessary financial problems both at the time a lease is taken and during the period of the lease.

Legislation affecting the landlord and tenant relationship

The best business relationships operate by agreement between the parties. The need for legislative intervention to govern the relationships between different parties or groups of people will generally only be recognized and accepted if there are frequent examples of such circumstances as the strong bargaining position of one group of people being used in a way which operates adversely to the interests of another group in an inequitable way, or which operates adversely to the interests of the general public. The need to legislate to regulate agreements between landlords and tenants has been accepted for many years in some countries, and when shortages of property occur because of such things as the destruct-ion of properties through war or natural disaster, a population that is increasing more rapidly than the supply of properties, or the ownership of the stock of property by a few owners who can control the supply offered onto the market, it is likely that governments will intervene to protect the consumer of property, that is tenants, against exploitation by any landlords who use (or might be tempted to use) their strong bargaining position in an inequitable way.

The existence of such legislation implies that a government has accepted that there has been a definite need to intervene in the market in order to provide a legal framework to regulate relationships between landlords and tenants, and generally an inspection of such legislation will reveal that a major part of it is devoted to the protection of the interests of tenants. That is not to say that landlords do not also need protection, as there are plenty of examples of the exploitation of landlords by tenants. The recognition of the need for landlords to require rental bonds and guarantees to protect them against unreasonable loss at the hands of unscrupulous lessees is an example of the legislature accepting that landlords often also need protection.

In England and Wales there has been legislation that has affected the relationships between landlords and tenants of business properties since 1927. The Landlord and Tenant Act, 1927 was:

> An Act to provide for the payment of compensation for improvements and goodwill to tenants of premises used for business purposes, or the grant of a new lease in lieu thereof...

It recognised the fact that tenants often spent considerable sums of money on improving their landlords' properties, and that they also created business goodwill that regularly improved the value of a property. The Act therefore provided for a tenant

> at the termination of the tenancy, on quitting his holding to be paid by his landlord compensation in respect of any improvement ... made by him or his predecessors in title ... which adds to the letting value of the holding,

providing such improvements were not done in pursuance of a statutory obligation or in pursuance of a contractual obligation.

The Act also provided for compensation to be paid in respect of goodwill created by a tenant.

Such compensation payments are not always provided for in other countries, and, for example, in New South Wales, Australia, lessees may be required to vacate premises without having any rights to compensation even though the premises may have been enhanced in letting value by improvement work done by them. This state of affairs appears particularly unreasonable when it occurs as a result of a landlord exercising the right under a relocation clause in a lease to insist upon a tenant moving to another outlet after perhaps only two or three years occupation of the unit originally leased in which the tenant had carried out expensive improvement work. In such circumstances it is suggested that equity could be served by the landlord either compensating a lessee for the costs incurred in improving the vacated property, or by the landlord being responsible for the fit out costs in the unit to which the lessee has been relocated, and for any other costs incurred by the lessee as a result of the relocation. It would probably be unusual for this to occur in the absence of legislation enforcing such action.

In England and Wales the provisions of the 1927 Act were enlarged upon by The Landlord and Tenant Act, 1954 which was described in its preamble as

> An Act ... to enable tenants occupying property for business, professional or certain other purposes to obtain new tenancies in certain cases; to amend and extend the Landlord and Tenant Act, 1927...

Part II of the Act provided security of tenure for business professional and other tenants, and a tenancy to which the Act applies does not come to an end unless terminated in accordance with the provisions of the Act. Even when the landlord seeks to terminate a tenancy the tenant may apply to the court for a new tenancy. Grounds for opposition by the landlord are strictly limited by the Act and, unless the landlord can convince the court that an application for the termination of a lease should be upheld, the court may grant a lessee a new lease of up to 14 years duration. The terms of a new lease under the Act can be agreed between the parties or determined by the courts in the absence of agreement between the parties. The Act provides that the rent for such a lease will be the market rent applicable at the commencement of the new lease excluding any element of rental value applicable to improvements done by the tenant – unless they were done as an obligation under the terms of the original lease – or to the goodwill of the tenant's business.

The recognition in the legislation applicable in England and Wales of the fact that goodwill created by the tenant can be an important element of rental value is significant. In New South Wales there is only limited recognition of and protection of a tenant's goodwill. Indeed, the situation is such that landlords can demand rent increases which, if paid by a tenant, result in the tenant paying rent for goodwill that has in effect been created primarily by the tenant's efforts, although some legislation now requires the effect on rent of the lessee's previous occupation to be ignored when assessing 'market rent' for rent review purposes. However, the effect on market rent does not have to be ignored for the purpose of new leases, and should the lessee refuse to pay the increase demanded and vacate the property in preference, the landlord may well receive an enhanced rent from another lessee part of which is in fact rent attributable to the goodwill created by the outgoing lessee. There is in such circumstances no provision for the payment of compensation for goodwill created by a lessee when the latter takes a new lease of the premises or when they vacate a retail unit, as a result of which a slice of value passes directly to the landlord even though its existence may be entirely due to the skill of and the expenditure of money and energy by the vacating lessee.

In England and Wales, where an order for a new tenancy is precluded on grounds which in general terms do not relate to failings on the tenant's part, the tenant shall be entitled on quitting the holding to recover compensation from the landlord, such compensation being determined by statutory provision current at the termination of the tenancy. Such compensation is commonly referred to as 'compensation for disturbance' and is additional to the compensation items provided for by the 1927 Act.

The effects of this legislation are that business tenants are able to trade from a property in the knowledge that generally at the end of their current lease they will be able to continue trading from that same property, unless they have defaulted on the terms of their current lease or unless the landlord can establish the right to reclaim possession. The grounds on which a landlord can reclaim possession in general relate to the intention to redevelop the property or the need in certain specific circumstances to obtain possession in the interests of good property management, or because of shortcomings in the lessee's behaviour during the lease term. Should they lose possession of their properties, the financial burdens of tenants are normally reduced by the receipt of compensation for improvements done by them, and by compensation for being 'disturbed' when required to leave the property, unless their disturbance resulted from their own failings during the lease term.

Whilst landlords cannot remove tenants from their properties without good reason, the Act does not protect bad tenants, so a landlord is in fact faced with a situation in which only tenants adjudged to have been responsible during their occupation can claim the right to retain possession. The Act also provides for a landlord to receive the full market rental for a property under a statutory lease, so landlords should in theory be no worse off financially than if they obtained vacant possession of their properties and relet them on the open market.

Comparison with countries without legislation to protect lessees

The situation in Scotland is often referred to by those who propose the abolition of the landlord and tenant legislation which applies to business properties in England and Wales. In Scotland, which has a different legal system from that in England and Wales, the 1927 and 1954 Acts do not apply, negotiations between landlords and lessees of business properties being done on an open market basis without the existence of any landlord and tenant legislation to protect the interests of either party. However, there is a significant difference between many of the local business property markets in Scotland and those in many parts of England in particular.

In Scotland for many years there has not been large population growth, indeed in many areas there has been either a relatively static level of population or even a decreasing population, the latter being particularly true of Glasgow. There has also been a considerable amount of new business property development in Scotland since the end of World War II, this occurring both in the new towns which were developed there and also as a result of the efforts of such government sponsored bodies as the Highlands and Islands Development Board (HIDB) and the Scottish Development Agency (SDA). These bodies were established to encourage more economic activity both in specific parts of Scotland and in Scotland generally, and business regeneration was encouraged through the provision in particular of industrial property which was often offered on the market at very competitive rents. It is probably true that in many Scottish business property markets there has not been a situation in which lessees have had to negotiate leases at a disadvantage to the landlord because of a shortage of alternative properties. Indeed, in many local markets the opposite has sometimes been the case, with an excess of properties and a shortage of would-be lessees because of limited business activity, this being one of the reasons for the establishment of such bodies as the HIDB and the SDA. It is suspected that the relatively static population and the general absence of markets in which there has been an excess of would-be tenants in comparison to the number of properties available has resulted in a situation in which there has been no real need for legislation similar to that which protects business lessees in England and Wales.

The situation could well be different were the supply and demand situation to change, and it is interesting to note that in the residential property market in Scotland there has been legislation largely designed to protect the interests of lessees and would-be lessees.

Those who would argue that there is no need for legislation that is primarily designed to protect the interests of retail lessees might also point to the USA where there appears to be no legislation of this type. It seems that landlord and tenant negotiations with respect to retail properties are in most – if not all – States of the USA regarded as normal commercial transactions, lease terms being determined as a result of bargaining between the parties with no 'landlord and tenant' legislation to influence negotiations. However, it is understood that such a state of affairs results in large multiple retail organizations being able to strike harder bargains with landlords than can 'mom and dad tenants'. It is also believed by some commentators that the latter type of tenant may in fact end up paying higher rents on a comparative basis than do many more substantial tenants, probably also having less favourable lease terms in other respects.

There may be other factors that result in the lack of protective legislation in the USA having only limited adverse effects on lessees of retail properties. It is understood by the author that the approach to property development in most parts of the USA by public authorities, including planning authorities, is in general terms much more 'laissez faire' than in the United Kingdom or Australia, with developers consequently having more opportunity to develop new properties to compete with existing properties. In contrast, in the United Kingdom the operation of the planning control system tends to severely restrict the development of new, competing properties. The lack of such a severe fetter on the supply side of the retail property market in the USA would in all probability result in more competition amongst suppliers of retail property, which in itself would strengthen the bargaining positions of potential tenants, even the sole proprietor single outlet businesses, so that they would not necessarily be at a disadvantage when negotiating with landlords.

Another feature of the retail property market that should assist tenants in their bargaining with landlords, is that the traditional shopping street still seems to be alive and thriving, at least in some parts of the USA. In some areas there is considerable development still occurring in traditional strip shopping streets, and one would assume this indicates that such locations are still strong rivals to modern shopping centres. Possibly as a result of a less restrictive planning system, shopping centres are also meeting competition from factory or warehouse style shopping developments, many of them recently constructed, which provide further competition to the modern shopping centre. It is therefore quite possible that the different features of the retail scenario and a competitive retail property supply sector in the USA results in less need for legislation to protect retail tenants when compared with the situation in the United Kingdom and in Australia, where planning control results in there being a limit to the amount of possible competition especially to modern shopping centres.

The effect of landlord and tenant legislation on property development and property investment

There are some who maintain that the existence of such legislation is a deterrent to property investment and that it impacts adversely on landlords. However, despite the existence for many years in England and Wales of legislation regulating the relationships of landlords and tenants of business properties, there are extremely active property development and property investment sectors there, and there is keen competition in the property investment market from both United Kingdom based and overseas investors. Apart from the occasional recessions which afflict property markets throughout the world, retail properties in the United Kingdom have consistently been sought after as investments producing good income flows and good capital growth.

It is interesting that there are many who suggest that the exist-ence of similar legislation in Australia would result in investors not being interested in retail property in particular, and that developers would cease to develop new retail properties. As a result there is strong opposition in some quarters to the possible introduction of legislation to strengthen the relatively limited protection already given to most business lessees in most parts of Australia, where different laws may apply in different States and Territories.

However, the existence of legislation which is essentially designed to protect tenants of business properties and to give them rights which they would not possess but for the legislation, does not appear to have deterred Australian property investors from investing in the United Kingdom. It is interesting to note that such legislation did not deter the Australian company Lend Lease Corporation (through Lend Lease Global Investment) becoming involved in the major development scheme at Bluewater, Dartford, Kent, where they developed the largest shopping centre in the United Kingdom with 1,625,000 sq ft (150,962.5 sq m) of retail and leisure space. It seems clear that Lend Lease were not put off by the security of tenure and compensation provisions that affect the letting of retail properties in the United Kingdom. Other major Australian property and investment groups have likewise not been deterred from investment in England and Wales by the existence of this legislation, Westfield Holdings being a significant investor in United Kingdom shopping centres. It is therefore arguable that reasonable landlord and tenant legislation does not deter property development and investment in property, and even if it does so the effects would appear to be relatively insignificant.

As suggested earlier, the best business arrangements are those that are agreed by negotiation between the parties, but there are certainly circumstances in which the public interest and the interests of important minority groups can only be properly protected by statutory intervention.

It is suggested that, despite the quite strong arguments from various interest groups against the landlord and tenant legislation which applies in England and Wales, strong arguments can be put forward for the retention of legislation that has in general prevented the unacceptable exploitation of lessees for so many years and which has given them rights to reasonable compensation in justifiable circumstances. At the same time the legislation has been reasonable enough to have allowed the healthy operation of a vibrant and large property development industry and property investment sector as those that operate in many, if not most, parts of England and Wales.

The importance of realistic investment policies and objectives

Objectives are only worthwhile if they are capable of being achieved, and whilst it is a logical and not unreasonable objective of property owners and managers to seek to maximize the returns from each investment, such a policy becomes unrealistic if it fails to accept that specified objectives which may be achievable in one economic environment or one locality, may not be achievable in another economic environment or another locality. In this respect the objective of maximizing returns from retail property investments is laudable and defensible. But if such an objective is translated into a target of, for example, a 5% rental increase per annum from every property in a portfolio irrespective of the state of the national and local economies and irrespective of geographical location, then such a policy is likely, at some point in time at least, to be very much flawed. It may in fact be flawed to the extent that it may well be extremely counter-productive over the longer term. Whilst economic growth in excess of 5% per annum subsists such a target might be achievable, but once economic growth is below 5% per annum it is likely to be more difficult and perhaps impossible to achieve an overall growth rate of that level from, for example, a portfolio of retail property investments.

It is rapidly apparent to any observer of the stock market that the values of equities vary with time, there often being quite dramatic fluctuations in value over very short periods of time. The values of stock market investments are influenced by a wide range of factors including variations in the state of the economy, the availability and the cost of finance, the performance of the companies in which stock is held, the performance of other companies which makes their stock a more attractive alternative investment or vice versa, the relative attractiveness or otherwise of other forms of investment such as property or government bonds, and the attitudes and levels of confidence of investors in general.

Even when national economies are strong there are likely to be areas in which local economic conditions are not good or are even particularly bad. Likewise, when general conditions are not really bad, some local property values may be adversely affected if they become less attractive investments than the investment opportunities available in other more prosperous areas. As a result, it is not impossible for some income producing properties to under perform others to the extent that their value does not increase as rapidly.

They may even under perform to the extent that, whilst other properties increase in value, they actually fall in value because of their diminished attractiveness in relative terms, notwithstanding the existence of reasonable economic conditions. Property investments are not immune to the vagaries of the investment markets in general. Despite this, there appear to be some in the property investment and management sectors who consider that constantly rising business rents and constantly rising property values on a universal scale are realistic expectations and achievable objectives.

It needs to be stressed that, as with any investment situation, attempts to ignore the realities of the market place in an effort to ensure the occurrence of given levels of increased value in property investments, may in the long run be counter-productive to the extent that they may result in reduced values rather than enhanced values if the resultant high occupation costs cause lessees to vacate properties. The resultant void properties are likely to be liabilities rather than assets, with no income produced even though there remains a continuing liability for the property owner to pay such outgoings as property rates and taxes, maintenance costs, and property insurance premiums. Indeed, the latter would probably increase substantially because of the increased risk normally adjudged to be attached to vacant properties.

The development of adversarial attitudes between landlords and tenants may well arise if unreasonable management practices are adopted, and they are only likely to be detrimental to the overall success of both parties. Accordingly, there will be occasions on which sensible long term management policies should result in a willingness on the part of a landlord, for example, to accept reduced levels or static levels of rent. Though short term returns may be adversely affected by such a policy, there are likely to be rewards in the longer term as individual businesses prosper or as overall business performance improves. The creation of trust and goodwill and a spirit of co-operation between landlord and tenant ought in the longer term to result in a better performing property, and hence a more valuable investment for the owner. The acceptance of a conservative rent for a period of time may well be a much cheaper sacrifice than the cost to a landlord of an empty property producing no rent but incurring holding costs combined with the associated relatively substantial costs of marketing and re-letting the property.

In the case of such properties as shopping centres it is also important for landlords and their property managers to recognize that the total rental value is the sum of the individual rents paid in respect of each of the retail outlets, and that the objective of sensible investment management should be to maximise the total rental income. This may not necessarily be achieved by seeking to maximise each individual rental as vacancies occur. The inter-dependency of various retailers and the importance of getting the correct trading and retailer mixes in a centre may dictate that, in the interests of maximising the appeal of a centre to shoppers and thereby creating a situation in which a high total rental value may be achieved, some retail units may have to be let at lower pro rata rent levels than others.

Positive property investment and management policies can greatly influence the business performance of lessees and hence the consequent performance of property investments. At various times prominent figures in the United Kingdom retail property environment have stressed the need for good and enlightened management policies.

The *Estates Gazette* of 19 February 1994, Issue 9407, reported a strong warning from Mr Vincent O'Doherty, the then president of the British Council of Shopping Centres, on the dangers of unenlightened centre management policies. At a conference on 'Shopping Centre Performance in the 1990's' he is reported as having stated:

> We are likely to see 10% vacancy in the short- to medium-term in our centres and this means that we will require more dextrous management. We must focus harder on satisfying shoppers and building sales by providing the optimum tenant mix, even if this means sacrificing rental income or security in order to bring the most appropriate retailers into the scheme.
>
> Our valuation rules suggest that proactive management is not right, but we are not optimising performance because we are permitting ourselves to be bound by rigid management conventions.
>
> Our conventions are not founded on consumer demand and our centres are in danger of becoming dinosaurs within five to ten years.

At a conference organized by the Royal Institution of Chartered Surveyors and Office, Shop, and Business and Industrial Agents Societies on 'Property in the Economy' held in Cardiff, Wales in May 1994. Sir James Blyth, the then chief executive of The Boots Company plc, one of the largest multiple retail chains in the United Kingdom with well over 2,000 group retail outlets, was reported by the *Chartered Surveyor Monthly* to have urged the property industry to recognise the pre-eminence of the customer. Property as land or physical structures had little intrinsic value – its real value lay in its economic use by occupiers. The finance-driven property industry of the past two decades had led to rigidity in lease structures, except where change had been necessitated by short-term recessionary pressures. Occupiers were not standard, so why should the 'standard institutional lease' predominate? Why were rents reviewed by reference to 'comparables', frequently not directly comparable at all? What of the tenants ability to pay or the importance of maintaining a tenant mix that attracted shoppers? ... Sir James blamed agents for insulating landlord and tenant from each other, rather than fostering the development of their relationship.

With respect to the ability of different traders to pay specific levels of rent, it is interesting to note that the Australian Bureau of Statistics report *Retail Industry Australia 1998–1999* observed that

> ... average retail sales ... varied from a high of $7,666 per square metre in the Supermarket and grocery stores group to a low of $383 per square metre in the Household and repair services group.

Clearly with such widely differing levels of turnover per annum the ability to pay rent will also vary widely.

Sir James was in fact emphasising a number of the points made above, and in *Estates Gazette* of 12 November 1994, Issue 9445, it was reported under the title 'Virgin issues warning to shop landlords', that

> Simon Burke, managing director of Virgin Retail, warned shopping centre landlords last week about the likely consequences of inflexible leases. 'The institutional lease can be like a strait-jacket and it is becoming more and more out of step with our business. The leases we are offered are increasingly important in our choice of sites ...' Burke said rents should be more closely related to the profit-making capacity of the location. And he attacked shopping centre landlords for their tendency to compromise on tenant mix in times of recession.
>
> 'In the mix of shopping centres we would seek to control assignability of leases. Far too often, when the money is tight, landlords feel tempted to take in a rag bag of tenants' Burke said. 'This makes the centre unstable in my view and does nothing to improve the project,' he added.

Shopping areas which offer a wide and varied range of retail outlets to shoppers are likely to be the most successful. In order to get the best retail mix that will attract the greatest number of shoppers and the greatest combined retail turnover, it may well be far sighted management policy to lease some outlets to some retailers whose retail turnover will only enable them to pay low rents, but whose presence in a centre will add greatly to its overall attractiveness to shoppers. The presence of such retailers in a centre may be essential to create a 'complete shopping environment', that is a centre which caters for all tastes and needs over a comprehensive range of goods. The returns to centre owners from such enlightened management policies are likely to be enhanced rentals paid by other retailers whose retail turnovers will benefit from the greater success of the centre in its entirety.

In circumstances in which property owners implement such policies it is important for retail occupiers to accept that in the interests of the overall success of a centre, some retailers may occupy retail outlets at rents considerably lower than those paid by others. In the same way that it is desirable for centre owners to accept that not all retail trades will enable high rents to be paid, it is equally desirable for retailers to recognize the same facts of business life.

It is clear that the success of both landlords and tenants of business properties can best be assured by them working together to achieve a successful business environment, whilst legislation to control relationships between any parties should in general be a last resort solution. Prior to the enactment of the Retail Leases Act 1994 in New South Wales, the Hon Ray Chappell said in his second reading speech to the Retail Leases Bill that

> the New South Wales Government's objective in introducing the Retail Leases Act was to 'foster good leasing practices in the retail industry' The Minister said 'in an ideal world, this Bill would not be necessary … and any disputes would be dealt with through negotiation between the parties'.

Despite the fact that the best business arrangements are those agreed by negotiation between the parties, we live in a far from ideal world as many events in the first few years of the 21st century testify, and there are certainly circumstances in which the public interest and the interests of some minority groups can only be properly protected by statutory intervention.

A code of practice for commercial leases in England and Wales

In an effort to reduce the number of problem situations which can arise in the landlord and tenant situation, in the United Kingdom at the request of the Department for Transport, Local Government and the Regions 'A Code of Practice for Commercial Leases in England and Wales' was drawn up by a working group which comprised representatives of the Association of British Insurers, the Association of Property Bankers, the British Retail Consortium, the British Property Federation, the Confederation of British Industry, the Forum of Private Business, the Law Society, the National Association of Corporate Real Estate Executives (UK chapter), the Property Market Reform Group, the Royal Institution of Chartered Surveyors, and the Small Business Bureau.

For a group from as many diverse interest areas as the above to reach agreement in itself is probably a worthy and notable achievement, and the Code and the accompanying Explanatory Guide provide 23 recommendations for landlords and tenants who are involved in the negotiation of new leases of business premises and for dealings during the terms of leases. The objective of providing guidelines for both landlords and tenants is sensible, and hopefully their existence will lead to fewer difficulties in the agreement of lease terms and fewer problems during the term of a lease.

The Royal Institution of Chartered Surveyors on 3 May 2002 reported to its members that:

> The Code of Practice for Commercial Leases in England and Wales was launched by Sally Keeble MP, the parliamentary under-secretary of state for housing, planning and regeneration, on Monday 22 April 2002
> ....
> A cross industry group was set up in September 2000 to address these issues and revise the existing 1995 Code of Practice ...
>
> The government will monitor the effectiveness and use of the new Code ... If the government is dissatisfied it has said that it will consider legislative intervention ...
>
> The Code makes 23 recommendations that are considered best practice in both negotiating commercial leases and conduct in the duration of a commercial lease.
>
> Members operating in England and Wales are advised to draw the attention of clients to the Code ...

The RICS further reported on 8 April 2003 on the results of a November 2002 questionnaire '...to establish the use and impact of the new Commercial Leases Code of Practice in England and Wales.' Its summary of the survey results included the following statements:

> The impact of the Code on the prevalence of upward only rent reviews has, so far, been negligible ...
>
> Surveyors are in the majority of cases bringing the Code to the attention of prospective tenants and landlords. Less than half of surveyors reported they were bringing the Code to the attention of existing tenants however.
>
> Where tenants do seek greater flexibility surveyors report they are likely to achieve more flexible terms...
>
> Finally when asked if landlords had been willing to offer more flexible terms as a result of the Code a third of surveyors agreed...
>
> ... a member in the south west ... reported that 'The RICS should, however understand that the shift in bargaining strength of landlords and tenants had already resulted in increased flexibility and a reduction in lease length without the incorporation of reviews. In other words, the changes envisaged by publication of the code are happening anyway, as a direct result of market conditions.' However, the same member inserted one important caveat: 'The only exception to this rule would be highly sought after premises such as prime retail'.

The 23 recommendations are contained in Appendix B, and those recommendations and the above observations highlight areas which have given rise to problems between landlords and tenants in the commercial property sector in England and Wales to the extent that it is considered they have to be addressed. It should be noted that the recommendations only apply to the commercial sector, and it should not be forgotten that there are large rental sectors for other types of property also. The passage of time will reveal the effect of the Code in the market place, and it is interesting to note that the government has already indicated its willingness to intervene should it consider that perceived problems have not been mitigated by the existence of the Code.

Concluding observations

There is little doubt that the best lease arrangements are those which satisfy the needs of both landlords and tenants and which are fair to both parties, and that the ideal market situation is one in which neither party is at a disadvantage when negotiating lease terms. However, the existence of planning controls can in some circumstances restrict the supply of property and therefore weaken the hand of would-be lessees by restricting their choice in the market: the ownership of certain types of property by a few owners or one owner can give them extremely strong market positions with oligopolistic or monopolistic powers, to the disadvantage of potential tenants: other factors such as economic conditions can disrupt the operation of the property market at various times: whilst the length of time taken to create new properties generally results in a time lag between shortages in supply becoming evident and the creation of new properties to satisfy market demand.

Consequently, it is rarely the case that lease arrangements can be made in true open market conditions, and markets affected by factors such as the above have sometimes resulted in what has been perceived as the exploitation of tenants or would-be tenants. As a result in some countries statutory controls have been introduced to regulate relationships between landlords and tenants in an attempt to bring stability to the market, and to create a state of affairs which legislators believed would create a fairer market for rental properties. There are those who believe that there should be no legislative interference in the landlord and tenant situation and that the free market should be allowed to operate, but with the existence of planning control in many countries there can be no truly free market for the supply of property.

In any event there are many examples in various countries of a range of serious problems which have resulted in free property markets. Whilst many problems may have been caused by only a minority of landlords, there are numerous examples of governments having decided that it was essential for them to intervene, generally to protect tenants from exploitation. Whilst the ideal market would theoretically be a free one with landlords and tenants all acting reasonably to reach mutually beneficial agreements, not all people are reasonable. Moreover, in a given set of circumstances different people would make different judgements as to what was reasonable behaviour. Consequently, the existence of landlord and tenant legislation in some form is almost inevitable in most countries. However, the extent to which it is necessary could be very much reduced if in general landlords and tenants entered lease negotiations with the attitudes that both parties had to benefit from any eventual agreement, and that agreement is more likely if the benefits to both parties are roughly equal, with neither party seeking to unreasonably exploit the other.

Chapter 16

Report Writing

The Concise Oxford Dictionary, seventh edition, defined 'report' as

> account given or opinion formally expressed after investigation or consideration or collation of information.

A report is the means whereby a professional consultant relates to a client details of work undertaken on the client's behalf, and whereby the professional's considerations, conclusions and recommendations are conveyed to the client. Above all it should clearly convey to a client the information that the client needs.

The importance of a report

The need for good quality reports is stressed in the International Valuation Standards Committee (IVSC) Valuation Standards and those of TEGoVA, and the report is often the main means of communication between a professional consultant and a client. It is critical that it communicates what it is intended to communicate, otherwise it will be a waste of both the reporter's and the client's time and money, whilst if it fails to do so adequately it may also leave a professional open to criticism and possibly to claims for professional negligence. Additionally, a sub-standard or defective report will probably result in a reader losing confidence in the professional abilities of the writer.

It is therefore important to ensure a report is well-structured, easy to read, and easy to understand in order to ensure it is carefully read and fully understood. A good report will clearly transmit the required facts to the commissioner of the report and, perhaps just as importantly, to anyone who has the right to read it and who is likely to depend upon it as guidance towards decision making. It is frequently the only real means of communication between the professional and those for whose use it is intended, for jobs will often be commissioned by the secretary or another executive of a company or organization, with the resultant report actually being intended for consideration by others, such as a board of directors or a committee, some members of which may never actually meet the professional consultant.

As with the purchase of any goods or services, the client will expect the report writer to deliver the service which was ordered, and they will also expect a report to represent good value for money. Ultimately their assessment of a professional's abilities and performance may well be based on the quality of the report, particularly in the case of those whose only knowledge of the professional is through reading the report. A report can easily be put to one side by a bored reader, so it is important that there is a logical and easy to follow treatment of its contents. Achieving the correct structure requires very careful consideration, as do the decisions on what to include and what to exclude.

The objectives and the terms of reference

The precise objectives of a commission, and therefore of the report also, should be agreed right at the outset of a task, and they must be determined by the professional with great precision, for they will dictate what is done and how it is done, and also what work is irrelevant to the task. Agreement must be reached before any inspections or research are undertaken otherwise essential preparatory work might be overlooked or might be inadequately or inappropriately covered. Such agreement will also determine the structure and content of the eventual report. At the same time the date by which a report is required should also be agreed, for this will also determine the time frame within which necessary work has to be done.

It is also most important that the terms of reference for the job and the report should be confirmed in writing to avoid the possibility of any later misunderstanding. In addition it is important to agree the level of fees or the basis of charging together with responsibilities for any other costs and expenses, for from the professional's point of view this will determine the depth of investigation and the amount of work which can be provided. Agreement on these points is also important for the client, for not only should they know their likely financial commitment in advance, but they should not be misled into expecting a £10,000 job and report if the agreed fee is only £2,000.

If the actual preparation of the report is likely to prove expensive, for example if special photography and graphic work is needed, it should also be agreed in advance whether the costs of producing the written report are to be borne by the consultant out of his or her fees, or whether they are to be paid as an additional cost by the client. If the latter is the case, the consultant should agree with the client the type of report expected and the number of copies required, and should cost it and obtain the client's agreement to that cost.

The agreement of financial matters before work is commenced will help the consultant to know exactly what a client expects, and should also clarify what the consultant is prepared to deliver for the agreed sums, including precisely what level of reporting is agreed.

Whilst agreement of the objectives and the fees should clarify what a client has requested and what they are paying for, case law – and good professionalism also – suggests that there are occasions on which a professional should provide the client with information over and above that requested. The majority of those who commission work from professionals do so because of the professional's special knowledge and expertize in a particular area of work in which the client is likely to have only limited or even no knowledge and expertize. For this reason the client will not always be aware of what is really needed as opposed to what they have asked for, and the good professional will at least point out such need to the client, even though it could be argued that it is outside his or her brief.

For example, a valuer may be asked to provide a client with a market valuation at a specific date of a house the client is considering purchasing. If the valuation figure is assessed in the knowledge that a nearby property is soon to be redeveloped in a way that will adversely affect the subject property taking into account the client's proposed use of that property, this information should be conveyed to the client, even though technically they may only have asked for a valuation figure A client should likewise be advised if the professional thinks that further research or investigation of any matters is required, or if further reports from other consultants should be sought.

The title

It is important that a report should have an appropriate title which distinguishes it from other reports and which enables it to be easily identified. The title should be carefully chosen; it should preferably be brief and should clearly indicate what the report is about.

The reporting brief

The objectives of a report having been determined at the start of the commission, they should also be clearly stated in a prominent position in the report, preferably at or very near the beginning so that a reader will clearly understand the context in which subsequent observations have to be considered. For example, a report could start with a statement such as:

> Instructions: In accordance with your instructions dated 1 January 2003 we have inspected 27 High Street, Smithstown, in order to give our opinion of its current rental value if available for letting on the open market with vacant possession on full repairing and insuring lease terms.

In the case of an example such as the above, there should also be a very clear statement of exactly what 'full repairing and insuring lease terms' means for the avoidance of any misunderstanding on the part of a reader who may not be familiar with property terminology.

Clarification of the instructions given to the professional is very important, as a clear indication of the objectives of a report may restrict the number of purposes for which a report may be used, thus reducing, and hopefully eliminating, the possibility that a report (or any of the statements within it) may be misused or misinterpreted. This is necessary because a report prepared for one purpose, or a valuation made on one basis, may be quite inappropriate for use for another purpose, even though that purpose may relate to the same basic subject-matter. Statements taken out of context can often be very misleading, and the possibility of this occurring should also be reduced by a very clear statement of the objectives of the professional's work and the purposes for which a report has been prepared.

There should in addition also be a very clear and conspicuous indication in the report of any limitations placed on its use, which may include limitations both on the purposes for which it may be used and on the people or organizations allowed to use it. It is sensible for such a statement to be linked to the terms of reference or to the instructions statement to avoid the possibility of mis-understanding.

The summary of a report

It is desirable for a report to have a summary which will enable busy people to rapidly gain an understanding of the contents of the report, the investigations and considerations undertaken, the conclusions and recommendations reached, and the fundamental reasoning for them. Even with a long report it is preferable for a summary not to exceed one page in length otherwise the objective of briefly summarizing the contents may be defeated, and it should convey the key contents of the report to a reader.

The conclusions and recommendations

These are probably the most important part of any report. In all cases this is likely to be the part of a report which most interests a reader, and it is therefore good policy to make the conclusions and recommendations very prominent in the report. As indicated above, they may be referred to in a summary near the beginning, although their importance is likely to require their fuller coverage in a separate section of the report, whilst if they are lengthy it may be inappropriate to include them in full in the summary.

A conspicuous section devoted to conclusions and recommendations should be placed either right at the end or preferably right at the beginning of a report where it can be found easily. This section should be concise, precise and unambiguous, and a reader should be left in no doubt at all what the actual conclusions and recommendations are.

If, because of the nature or content of a particular report, it is difficult to present all the conclusions and recommendations prominently within it, it may be advisable to bring them additionally to the notice of the recipient of the report in a covering letter which accompanies it. If this is done a copy of the covering letter should also be bound in with the report at the beginning in order to avoid the possibility of the report ever being read without the letter also being seen.

Giving prominence to the conclusions and recommendations and expressing them with great clarity is always good policy, but it is particularly important when the recipient of a report is a busy person with little time to spare for anything other than the most important items. The advice given as summarized in the conclusions and recommendations is also particularly important to a client who lacks specialist knowledge of the subject-matter and who employs a professional consultant primarily because of their specialist knowledge.

In addition to making recommendations, a report should also advise of the likely implications of recommended actions. All decisions have consequences, and whilst these may not always be clearly predictable, it should be one of the duties of a professional adviser to inform a client of the anticipated outcome of any recommendations made in a report. In doing this the report should indicate not only the likely immediate results of recommendations, but also consequential implications 'further down the track'.

Other contents

Apart from the objectives of the report and the conclusions and recommendations, a report should contain other essential, supporting information. Non-essential information should always be excluded, although it will not always be easy to decide what is essential and what is not. Careful planning of a report is therefore needed before it is begun, and the reporter must decide what material must be included and the most logical order for the presentation of that material. As already observed, the brief (or instructions) and summary should be at the beginning, the conclusions and recommendations should either be at the end or near the beginning, and it is then a question of deciding the most appropriate order for the remaining essential material. The order chosen should result in the methodical treatment of the material and a clear, logical line of reasoning being followed throughout a report. The original terms of reference should in fact determine what items have to be covered in a job and therefore what has to be reported upon. It will be a matter of judgement on the part of the professional to determine these items, for they will vary from job to job depending upon the client's needs and the circumstances of any particular job.

Probably the easiest way of deciding whether information is essential is to ask whether it is necessary in order to make rational judgements and recommendations, and whether it adds to the quality of the report or assists in the understanding of parts of the report. If it does none of these it should probably be omitted. Material which should be included is likely to be factual, background information about the subject of the report, together with the analysis and reasoning which led to the conclusions reached and the recommendations made.

Where supposedly factual information is included every effort should be made to ensure its accuracy, and the use of hearsay evidence or information of dubious value should be avoided. Whenever possible any necessary factual information should be ascertained first hand, and if this is not possible it should be clearly stated in a report which purported facts have been obtained second hand together with the source of the information, whilst any unconfirmed facts or information should be drawn to the client's notice in the report.

It should also be clearly indicated in a report when contents are not factual but are the opinion of the writer.

A bulky and unduly long report is best avoided whenever possible, and if there is a lot of information which has to be included it is good policy to put much of it into appendices to keep the main body of the report more compact. As a general rule, if necessary material is ancillary to a report it is best placed in an appendix rather than in the report itself.

However, the body of the report should contain the reasons for reaching the conclusions arrived at and for making the recommendations made. It is important that the justification for these should be clear to a reader, as the person commissioning the report is unlikely to be satisfied with unsubstantiated opinions.

Additional aids to understanding

In some reports the use of such aids as photographs, plans, diagrams, tables, statistics and graphs may be desirable. A good rule to observe is that such items should only be used if they add to a report by making it easier to understand parts of the report, or if they present parts of it in a simpler or more condensed way. They should never be used for the sake of including them, and they should likewise never be used unless their inclusion improves the report.

Whenever such items are used they should be well prepared and carefully presented, whilst they should clearly and easily illustrate the points they are intended to make. Their quality should always be high. The use of inferior quality items, particularly poor photographs, should be avoided at all costs. Similarly, a poorly prepared or inadequate plan should not be used, but a clear, easily interpreted plan may be invaluable in assisting a reader to fully understand a report.

Items such as photographs and plans may often appear expensive, but if they achieve the objectives of improving the quality of a report and making it easier to understand they can be invaluable. In any event, in most cases their cost will be small in comparison to the fees earned by the professional specialist. undertaking the commission. However, because of their relative expense, they should only be used if their inclusion improves the comprehensiveness of the report or makes it easier to understand.

The preparation of a report

When a professional person is preparing a report it should never be forgotten why the person or group commissioning the work has not prepared the report themselves. Some of the most common reasons for commissioning reports are:

1. The person commissioning the work and the report is not a specialist in the area of work involved;
2. The person commissioning the work and the report cannot afford the time to do the work themselves; or
3. The circumstances are such that there is the need for a report by a third party who is clearly independent and who also has appropriate specialist knowledge and experience.

If the person who has commissioned a report is not a specialist or an expert in the subject-matter this ought to influence the way in which a report is prepared, for the resultant report ought to be easily understandable by someone with limited knowledge of the subject-matter. It is probably best to assume that at least some who need to read any report will have no specialist knowledge of the subject-matter, and accordingly the use of specialist terms and jargon should be avoided wherever possible, or they should be clearly explained when their use is necessary or unavoidable. Similarly, the use of abbreviations and acronyms should also be avoided, even though they may be regularly used by specialists. If they are used it is best that on first usage the relevant expression or title should be used in full with the abbreviated form in parentheses afterwards, subsequent use of the abbreviation or acronym then being acceptable. If a report includes a large number of abbreviations, acronyms, and specialist terms used regularly it may also be advisable to include a glossary (or glossaries) as an appendix to the report.

   In the quest for high quality reporting, once a report has been drafted it is good policy for it to be put to one side for a while and then to be reconsidered later, preferably at the very least a day later and preferably when the mind is fresh. Worthwhile amendments and useful clarification, including additional information which ought to be provided, often become more apparent at such later reading, whilst they might otherwise be completely overlooked. It is also possible that with the benefit of more time for consideration a reporter may take a slightly different view of some matters previously covered in the draft, including the correct way of explaining some points and the precision of grammar used. If this is not possible because a report is needed rapidly, it is sensible, and in reality essential, for a report to be reviewed and edited as necessary by a third party. Such a person reading it as it were in lieu of the client is likely to notice shortcomings or ambiguities which may easily be overlooked by the person who has actually prepared the report. In any event it is good standard practice to seek the views of others before submitting a report to a client, particularly the views of others who may have been involved with the subject which is being reported upon.

Careful proof reading is essential, for there are few things more likely to give a poor impression of a professional person than a report which is badly prepared or which contains mistakes. If a non-expert is to be the recipient of a report or if non-experts are likely to have to refer to it at some time, it would be sensible policy to have a draft report proof read by another non-expert who should be well able to identify those parts which might be difficult to understand for any other than specialists in the subject-matter. They are also more likely to identify possible ambiguities or misinterpretations than the person who has prepared a report who will know what is meant by various parts of it. Proof reading by another specialist, whilst essential at some stage of preparation, may not necessarily detect such shortcomings as their knowledge may result in them correctly interpreting parts which others might find ambiguous or difficult to understand. This will not eliminate the need for very careful proof reading by the specialist who has prepared the report, for they are ultimately responsible for its contents and must take great care to ensure precision and accuracy in everything they say.

Despite the importance of very careful editing, it is advisable for the person responsible for preparing a report to pay great attention at the outset to its structure and content, and to make a plan and notes regarding the same. Preparation of this type should help to reduce the need for extensive editing of the initial draft, and should also reduce the number of drafts needed. Although some later changes will be inevitable in the quest for improvement, it is wise policy to try to make the first draft as accurate as possible and as near to the final report as possible, both in the interests of economy and accuracy. Too many stages of editing and too many editorial changes can often result in a final report being drastically different from the original draft, and in such circumstances the final product may not necessarily be what was originally determined as being necessary.

Even if a professional person's instructions are received from another who is a specialist in the subject-matter, it is still advisable to prepare a report so that it will be easy for a non-specialist to understand it. A property developer may instruct a valuer to do a valuation of a development prospect, but the board of directors which will consider the report may include specialists in other fields whose knowledge of property and valuation matters may be limited, and it is therefore advisable to make a report easily intelligible to as wide an audience as possible.

Style of presentation and use of English

As suggested earlier, reports are often commissioned by people who do not have time to make their own investigations, and this fact should be remembered when they are prepared. Time is always important whilst it also costs money, so a reader's time should not be wasted; what has to be said must be stated clearly and unambiguously, whilst the inclusion of superfluous material should be avoided.

The essential content of a report should be conveyed as concisely as possible, and maximum meaning should be achieved with economy of words. Repetition, the use of unnecessary words, and the use of unnecessarily long words should all be avoided, as should little used and unfamiliar words. For example one should use 'end' rather than 'terminate', 'go' rather than 'proceed', 'measurable' rather than 'mensurable', and 'unchangeable' rather than 'immutable'.

It is wise to use the same technical word or expression to describe an item once chosen; for example, once the word 'house' has been used do not change to the use of 'dwelling' or 'home'. However, in some circumstances undue repetition of the same word or phrase can become tedious and should therefore be avoided. Thus 'start', 'commence', and 'begin' may all be used to avoid tediousness and to give variety.

At all times the use of colloquialisms, local expressions, and clichés should be avoided. It is therefore preferable to use an expression such as 'refuse-heap' rather than 'midden'; 'now' or 'at present' rather than 'at this point in time'; 'at present', 'currently' or 'today' rather than 'in this day and age'.

Short sentences, or shorter sentences, are usually more easily understood than longer and perhaps unwieldy sentences, and the latter should be avoided as much as possible to avoid the need for re-reading caused by a reader having difficulty in properly understanding what has been written. The need for re-reading is wasteful of time, and will not endear the writer to the reader. Although a report should read fluently and should be made as interesting as possible, it is not being written for literary reasons but to enable a reader to easily understand the subject-matter. Even though short sentences are preferable, it is important to avoid a jerky presentation which lacks fluency, and the sparing use of longer sentences is acceptable for such purposes.

Great attention should be paid to the careful use of punctuation, for meanings can be altered by a misplaced punctuation mark. Punctuation should always be carefully used to make a report easier to read and easier to understand. Punctuation used should never cause ambiguity or give rise to uncertainty, and it is better omitted, as in legal documents, if ambiguity or lack of clarity might arise from its use.

The need for too much punctuation may indicate that sentences are too long, in which case a writer is probably well advised to break a long sentence down into two or even more separate sentences. Many readers find difficulty in following long sentences, and some authorities recommend that no sentence in a report should exceed 20 to 25 words in length if a report is to be carefully read and easily understood by readers. In the interests of clarity and easy comprehension it is also important that the structure of each separate sentence is carefully considered.

The structure and content of paragraphs should also be carefully thought out, for many readers also find it difficult to concentrate on long paragraphs, whilst the objective of using paragraphs is to make a report easier to read and easier to understand. As with the length of sentences, there are commentators who suggest that paragraphs should preferably not exceed about 100 words in length, with an absolute maximum length of about 150 words. Consequently, the contents of a report should preferably be separated into reasonably short paragraphs which communicate one point together with elaboration and explanation of that point. It is also important to ensure that the topic of the paragraph is adequately emphasized and that, wherever possible, the end of one paragraph leads the reader's mind neatly to the point to be covered in the following paragraph.

It is critical that spelling should be carefully checked for the use of one wrong letter can completely change the meaning of a sentence, or indeed a report. There is a world of difference between a statement that 'This should **now** be done' and 'This should **not** be done', whilst words like 'complimentary' and 'complementary', and 'affluent' and 'effluent' have significant differences in meaning. Tedious though it may be, the choice of the correct word and ensuring that it is correctly spelt is a most important task with any report, or for that matter with writing of any sort.

General presentation

The general presentation of a report and its quality of presentation are both very important as a good quality report both impresses and assists a reader.

Careful layout aids comprehension; cramped typescript, small typescript, and closely packed paragraphs are not visually attractive nor are they easy to read, whereas generous spacing between lines and paragraphs and easy to read typescript make comprehension easier. The use of upper case letters where appropriate, bold type, italics, and underlining can be invaluable in assisting under-standing and in emphasizing points which need emphasis.

The numbering of sections or paragraphs can greatly assist readers, the use of decimal numbering for sections and paragraphs often being particularly helpful as it assists note taking and subsequent reference to specific parts of a report. The inclusion of cross-references when different parts of a report relate to each other is also a great help, just as its omission can be extremely annoying.

The appropriate sub-titling of sections of a report or the use of margin notes which indicate the various topics covered are other devices which assist readers to refer to particular parts of a report as necessary. Sub-titles, when used, should be easily under-standable and should clearly indicate the contents of the following section.

The use of margins sufficiently wide to allow a reader space for note making is also helpful, for readers who are particularly interested in a report will frequently wish to make their own comments on various points and also to highlight matters of particular interest.

If a report becomes lengthy it is also very helpful to include a contents page, whilst with particularly long reports it may occasionally be advisable to include an index. The need for an index is likely to be the exception rather than the rule, and when included it must be carefully prepared; to include an inadequate index is possibly worse than omitting an index.

Summary

A good report should contain all the information a reader needs and should be well presented and written in an attractive style which assists reading and understanding. It should clearly state its purpose, the considerations and investigations covered, and its conclusions and recommendations. It should contain no irrelevant material, but it should contain the essential supporting information together with the reasons for the conclusions reached and the recommendations made. The likely consequences of implementing the recommendations should also be indicated. A report should convey the essential information clearly, objectively and accurately in the shortest possible way.

A good report should be informative, concise, precise and lucid.

Chapter 17

Service and Improvement

A prime objective of professional people should be to provide high quality specialist service to those who need and require it, fees for services being the rewards for so doing. It is not always clear that those who purport to be professional people see the order of things as being first the provision of a service, with payment for services second, and it is worth remembering the quote in chapter one of Paul Volcker which contained the statement

> …The basic responsibility of the firm was corrupted by a business model that emphasised revenue and consulting services to clients over faithful allegiance to the interests of the investing public …

It is a regretful observation that there are probably members of the general public whose impression of many professional advisers is that their main objective is to get their fees as quickly and as easily as possible, with many who would classify themselves as professionals giving inadequate consideration to the quality of service provided.

There has in recent years been a trend in the property professions which possibly may have operated against the concept of service to the client as being a leading objective, that being the listing of many firms in some countries as public companies. When companies are listed, those who work for them theoretically have a duty to place a high priority on pursuing the interests of shareholders which may sometimes conflict with the duty owed to clients. Additionally, listed organizations are also subjected to external competitive forces which make the maintenance of a high share price extremely important not only to attract investors but also to ward off takeover bids, this high share price in turn generally being dependent upon the achievement of good profit levels. Moreover, there seems in the modern world to be an expectation of improved profit levels and improved returns to shareholders being achieved on an annual basis, with problems awaiting firms which are not thought by analysts and investors to be performing to an acceptable level.

There may therefore be extreme pressure on professional firms which are listed companies not only to maintain profit levels, but to increase them as often and as much as possible. Profits can be enhanced by producing a better product or service than competitors, thereby increasing business done as a result of offering purchasers better value for money. However, in the short term in particular, profits can often be fairly rapidly enhanced by offering less product or poorer service for the same money, or by economising on inputs to reduce total expenditure. Such moves to boost immediate profitability may be tactically attractive to an organization in pursuit of improved profits or a good stock exchange rating, particularly if there has been criticism of past performance or if a company may possibly become subject to takeover activity in the market. However, it is arguable that such tactics are not acceptable in a professional environment as true professional people should always be driven first and foremost by a desire to provide the highest possible level of service, a professional person's and a professional organization's first duty being to the client rather than to the organization or its shareholders. It is arguable that in the circumstances outlined above there is sometimes likely to be an inevitable and unavoidable conflict of interests situation.

Another trend which may well result in opportunistic short term policies being implemented to the detriment of sound long term management is the modern emphasis on the reward of staff through performance related bonuses. Where key property professionals can substantially increase their personal incomes through improving short term profits, there will, not unnaturally, be the likelihood that short term profitability will sometimes be more important to them than long term profitability, for in the long term they may be working elsewhere, retired, or dead! This is a problem which is not restricted to the property professions, and many commercial and industrial companies face the same danger that over emphasis on short term success may result in a reduction in professional standards within an organization. This may in turn result in the self destruction of an organization in the slightly longer term when the market turns against it because quality control is deficient. It will be interesting to see if the conflict of interests between the short term personal objectives of executives and the long term objectives of organizations can be satisfactorily resolved in the property professions – and other professions also – in which the quality of service provided should be all important.

It should in fact be a prime responsibility for professional organizations to ensure that their members observe the need to provide high quality service, and in an effort to do so they will also need to encourage members to incorporate change as an essential part of their daily operations. Change is essential in a true professional person, for no person or service is perfect.

A basic objective of a true professional should be to constantly seek to provide an improved level of service. Moreover, the environment in which professionals work is constantly changing so necessitating change in work practices. Those involved in manufacturing who are successful recognize that to remain successful they have to be constantly changing to offer improved products in order to survive in a competitive market place, improvement only being possible as a result of changing to adopt improved techniques, materials, designs, or philosophies. It is not always apparent that such a need is recognized by some who practice in the professions, and an objective in the various chapters in this book has been to encourage consideration of how clients might perceive the way professionals operate and how they might assess the quality of the services offered by them.

There are many who say one should not look back, but those who refuse to do so are perhaps reluctant to look back on their own mistakes, or even to admit to ever having made mistakes. The analysis of past performance is, however, a valuable process in the quest for improvement. To analyse performance one has to look back, and those who deny the merits of considering the past deny themselves the opportunity of learning both from past mistakes and past successes. In doing so they commit themselves to a more difficult future learning process than is necessary, that is assuming they wish to continue learning and improving.

The topics considered in these chapters are a few of the considerations which should receive regular attention from professional people and professional organizations. The world changes regularly and rapidly and practices have to change and conventions have to be adapted to respond to external change. If the contents have encouraged further consideration of these and other topics, if they have caused discussion and debate of professional considerations, and even if they have caused an element of controversy which concentrates the mind, they will have served useful purposes.

In any activity one of the most dangerous conditions is complacency, and constant introspection and assessment of the quality of service provided have to be essential qualities of a true professional person and a truly professional organization. There should be a continuing assessment of performance and a continuing quest to provide higher levels of performance and service.

Appendix A

The Carsberg Report

On 17 January 2002 the Royal Institution of Chartered Surveyors introduced the Carsberg Report with the following statement.

> The report of a working party chaired by Sir Bryan Carsberg was commissioned by RICS last year to investigate issues relating to valuations for the commercial property investment market in the UK. It makes 18 recommendations to RICS on how the valuation process should be tightened up. This will minimise the risks of valuers' objectivity being compromised and ensure that public confidence in the system is maintained.

Recommendations of the Carsberg Report

1   The RICS should enter discussions with Investment Property Databank with a view to agreeing a means by which their data could be used to produce ongoing annual reports on the correlations between valuations and achieved prices as observed by IPD, and consider with the wider academic community how the data can be additionally analysed to provide better information on the currency of valuations. The RICS should also encourage research into the valuation process and behavioural issues and ensure that the knowledge gained is fully integrated into the educational system.

2   The RICS should approach IPD to identify what further information about the composition and performance of valuers contributing to its Indices could be published.

3   The definitions of 'Internal', 'External', and 'Independent' valuer should be clarified to avoid ambiguities and misunderstanding by clients and users, and amplified in each case to make it clear that all valuers are required to have independence, integrity and objectivity in the performance of their task, whichever role they fulfil.

4   The RICS should publish more extensive guidance in the Red Book on how to identify and deal with threats to objectivity, drawing on the concepts developed by the Institutes of Chartered Accountants.

5   The RICS should introduce a requirement for disclosure by valuers producing 'valuations for third party use' of their firm's total fee earning relationship with the instructing client, to be expressed in a formalised manner. This disclosure must appear in their valuation report and any published reference thereto.

6   The RICS should require valuers to declare their firm's fee earning relationship with any party directly interested in the outcome of a valuation if asked by any party to whom they have a fiduciary duty.

7   Valuers producing 'valuations for third party use' should be required to state within their valuation report and any published reference thereto, the length of time that they have been carrying out valuation instructions for the client.

8   The RICS should publish guidance on good practice in rotating personnel producing 'valuations for third party use'.

9   The Red Book should contain specific guidance on the recording of occasions when a valuer discusses the outcome of the valuation with the client or any other interested party.

10   The RICS should set out, in the Red Book, standards of best practice and minimum requirements for the conduct and recording of draft valuation meetings designed to show what information was produced by the client which might influence the value derived, and how that information was used to influence, or otherwise, the final valuation figure. Rules for the disclosure of the record during monitoring should also be established.

11   The RICS should undertake an examination of the influences and pressures on valuers who are instructed to undertake valuations for secured lending, and of those parts of the valuation process particular to this context, with a view to establishing Practice Statements designed to ensure public confidence in the valuation process in this area.

12   The RICS should prepare and publish a guide to the Red Book which sets out the valuation process and its regulation from the client's viewpoint.

13   RICS should publish an interim information paper, pending the outcome of the ESRC funded Reading research, covering valuations based on limited information, giving examples of different situations in which such valuations are requested and best practice on how they should be approached. The topic should also be addressed in CPD seminars.

14 The exemption from the Red Book for valuations given in the course of estate agency should be reviewed to ensure that the exemption is restricted to the proper circumstances.

15 RICS should commission work to establish an acceptable method by which uncertainty could be expressed in a manner which will be helpful and will not confuse users of the valuation. RICS should also seek to agree with appropriate representative bodies of those commissioning and using third party valuations the circumstances and format in which the valuer would convey uncertainty.

16 The RICS should review the current Practice Statements in the Red Book and introduce such amendments as necessary to ensure that a valuer is prohibited from producing a 'valuation for third party use' of a property on which his firm has received an introductory fee unless another firm has produced a full, formal valuation for the client between the date the transaction was agreed and the date of the third party valuation. Such a prohibition should last for at least one year.

17 The RICS should create a Valuation Monitoring Committee to create and manage a Review and Monitoring System in accordance with the principles set out, and make amendments to the Red Book to enforce the System.

18 The RICS should explain and clarify with the Financial Services Authority and other appropriate regulatory authorities the role that it will fulfil in monitoring the processes of valuation. This should occur at the same time as the Valuation Monitoring Committee is created so that any reasonable requirements of the regulatory authorities can be included in the Monitoring System.

Appendix B

A Code of Practice for Commercial Leases in England and Wales

Introduction

This updated Code contains recommendations for landlords and tenants when they negotiate new leases of business premises and where they deal with each other during the term of a lease. The Code consists of twenty-three recommendations which an industry-wide working party, including landlord and tenant representatives, consider reflect current 'best practice' for landlords and tenants negotiating a business tenancy.

Explanatory guidance notes ... provide the background to each of the recommendations.

Landlords and tenants should have regard to the recommendations of this Code when they negotiate lease renewals. Under current legislation if a court has to fix terms for a new lease it may decide not to change the terms from those in the existing lease.

Negotiating a business tenancy (lease)

Recommendation 1; Renting premises: Both landlords and tenants should negotiate the terms of a lease openly, constructively and considering each other's views.

Recommendation 2; Obtaining professional advice: Parties intending to enter into leases should seek early advice from property professionals or lawyers.

Recommendation 3; Financial matters: Landlords should provide estimates of any service charges and other outgoings in addition to the rent. Parties should be open about their financial standing to each other, on the understanding that information provided will be kept confidential unless already publicly available or there is proper need for disclosure. The terms on which any cash deposit is to be held should be agreed and documented.

Recommendation 4; Duration of lease: Landlords should consider offering tenants a choice of length of term, including break clauses where appropriate and with or without the protection of the Landlord and Tenant Act 1954. Those funding property should make every effort to avoid imposing restrictions on the length of lease that landlords, developers and/or investors may offer.

Recommendation 5; Rent and value added tax: Where alternative lease terms are offered, different rents should be appropriately priced for each set of terms. The landlord should disclose the VAT status of the property and the tenant should take professional advice as to whether any VAT charged on rent and other charges is recoverable.

Recommendation 6; Rent Review: Rent reviews should generally be to open market rent. Wherever possible, landlords should offer alternatives which are priced on a risk-adjusted basis, including alternatives to upwards only rent reviews; these might include up/down reviews to open market rent with a minimum of the initial rent, or another basis such as annual indexation. Those funding property should make every effort to avoid imposing restrictions on the type of rent review that landlords, developers and/or investors may offer.

Recommendation 7; Repairs and services: The tenant's repairing obligations, and any repair costs included in service charges, should be appropriate to the length of the term and the condition and age of the property at the start of the lease. Where appropriate the landlord should consider appropriately priced alternatives to full repairing terms.

Recommendation 8; Insurance: Where the landlord is responsible for insuring the property, the policy terms should be competitive. The tenant of an entire building should, in appropriate cases, be given the opportunity to influence the choice of insurer. If the premises are so damaged by an uninsured risk as to prevent occupation, the tenant should be allowed to terminate the lease unless the landlord agrees to rebuild at his own cost.

Recommendation 9; Assigning and subletting: Unless the particular circumstances of the letting justify greater control, the only restriction on assignment of the whole premises should be obtaining the landlord's consent which is not to be unreasonably withheld. Landlords are urged to consider requiring Authorised Guarantee Agreements only where the assignee is of lower financial standing than the assignor at the date of the assignment.

Recommendation 10; Alterations and changes of use: Landlord's control over alterations and changes of use should not be more restrictive than is necessary to protect the value of the premises and any adjoining or neighbouring premises of the landlord. At the end of the lease the tenant should not be required to remove and make good permitted alterations unless this is reasonably required.

Conduct During a Lease

Recommendation 11; Ongoing relationship: Landlords and tenants should deal with each other constructively, courteously, openly and honestly throughout the term of the lease and carry out their respective obligations fully and on time. If either party faces a difficulty in carrying out any obligations under the lease, the other should be told without undue delay so that the possibility of agreement on how to deal with the problem may be explored. When either party proposes to take action which is likely to have significant consequences for the other, the party proposing the action, when it becomes appropriate to do so, should notify the other without undue delay.

Recommendation 12; Request for consents: When seeking a consent from the landlord, the tenant should supply full information about his/her proposal. The landlord should respond without undue delay and should where practicable give the tenant an estimate of the costs that the tenant will have to pay. The landlord should ensure that the request is passed promptly to any superior landlord or mortgagee whose agreement is needed and should give details to the tenant so that any problems can be speedily resolved.

Recommendation 13; Rent review negotiation: Landlords and tenants should ensure that they understand the basis upon which rent may be reviewed and the procedure to be followed, including the existence of any strict time limits which could create pitfalls. They should obtain professional advice on these matters well before the review date and also immediately upon receiving (and before responding to) any notice or correspondence on the matter from the other party or his/her agent.

Recommendation 14; Insurance: Where the landlord has arranged insurance, the terms should be made known to the tenant and any interest of the tenant covered by the policy. Any material change in the insurance should be notified to the tenant. Tenants should consider taking out their own insurance against loss or damage to contents and their business (loss of profits etc.) and any other risks not covered by the landlord's policy.

Recommendation 15; Varying the lease – effect on guarantors: Landlords and tenants should seek the agreement of any guarantors to proposed material changes to the terms of the lease, or even minor changes which could increase the guarantor's liability.

Recommendation 16; Holding former tenants and their guarantors liable: When previous tenants or their guarantors are liable to a landlord for defaults by the current tenant, landlords should notify them before the current tenant accumulates excessive liabilities. All defaults should be handled with speed and landlords should seek to assist the tenant and guarantor in minimising losses. An assignor who wishes to remain informed of the outcome of rent reviews should keep in touch with the landlord and the landlord should provide the information. Assignors should take professional advice on what methods are open to them to minimise their losses caused by defaults by the current occupier.

Recommendation 17; Release of landlord on sale of property: Landlords who sell their interest in premises should take legal advice about ending their ongoing liability under the relevant leases.

Recommendation 18; Repairs: Tenants should take the advice of a property professional about their repairing obligations near the end of the term of the lease and also immediately upon receiving a notice to repair or a schedule of dilapidations.

Recommendation 19; Business Rates: Tenants or other ratepayers should consider if their business rates assessment is correct or whether they need to make an appeal. They should refer to the DTLR Business Rates – a Guide or obtain advice from a rating specialist. The RICS provides a free rating help line service (see below) and advice is available also from the Institute of Revenues Rating and Valuation (IRRV).

Recommendation 20; Service charges: Landlords should observe the Guide to Good Practice on Service Charges in Commercial Properties. Tenants should familiarise themselves with that Guide and should take profesional advice if they think they are being asked to pay excessive service charges.

Recommendation 21; Dispute resolution: When disputes arise, the parties should make prompt and reasonable efforts to settle them by agreement. Where disputes cannot be settled by agreement, both sides should always consider speed and economy when selecting a method of dispute resolution. Mediation may be appropriate before embarking on more formal procedures.

Recommendation 22; Repossession by the landlord: Tenants threatened with repossession or whose property has been repossessed will need professional advice if they wish to try to keep or regain possession. Similarly, landlords should be clear about their rights before attempting to operate a forfeiture clause and may need professional advice.

Recommendation 23; Renewals under the Landlord and Tenant Act 1954: The parties should take professional advice on the Landlord and Tenant Act 1954 and the PACT (Professional Arbitration on Court Terms) scheme at least six months before the end of the term of the lease and also immediately upon receiving any notice under the Act from the other party or their agent. Guidance on the Act can be found in the Department for Transport, Local Government and the Region's 'Guide to the Landlord and Tenant Act 1954'.

It should be noted that the above recommendations are accompanied by extensive notes which enlarge upon and explain various aspects of the recommendations.

Index

S